CAN I BE HONEST WITH YOU?

An Edgy and Empowering
Romantic Comedy Dating Memoir

AMY PALATNICK

Copyright

Copyright © 2021 by Amy Palatnick

First Edition

Published by Jungle Beach Press

Eugene, Oregon 97405

All rights reserved. No part of this book may be reproduced in any form, by electronic or mechanical means, including information storage and retrieval systems, without permission in writing from the publisher, except by a reviewer who may quote brief passages in a review.

Requests for permission to reproduce any content of this publication should be addressed to junglebeachpress@gmail.com

Editor: Sara Zolbrod, Reach Editing and Writing: www.zolbrod.com

ReachEditingAndWriting@gmail.com

Cover Illustration and Design by Kozakura www.fiverr.com/kozakura

ISBN 978-1-954930-00-1 *(paperback)*

ISBN 978-1-954930-01-8 *(e-book)*

ISBN 978-1-954930-02-5 *(IngramSpark)*

Library of Congress number: 2021905477

Printed in the United States of America

The events and conversations in this book have been set down to the best of the author's ability, although most names and details have been changed to protect the privacy of individuals.

Dedication

This book is dedicated to my beloved grandfather and favorite human, Robert L. Shiner. Grandpa was the only adult I knew who spoke matter-of-factly about sex. Starting when I was in my teens, he offered this sage advice nearly every time we spoke:

**"A woman has to tell a man exactly what she wants.
Men do not understand a single thing about women's bodies."**

With wizardly intuition, my Grandpa knew exactly what I needed to hear.

Contents

Introduction ... xi

Part I
Okay, Cupid!

1. **STEPPING OUT AND FALLING DOWN** ... 3
   - Date #1: Not Such Perfect Strangers *April 2015* ... 3
   - Date #2: Learning to Pay Attention to My Inner "No" *May 2015* ... 5
   - Date #3: More of What I Want and Less of What I Don't *June 2015* ... 8
   - Date #4: German Tim and His Knives *June 2015* ... 11
   - Date #5: The "Hawt" Millennial *(Told from both perspectives) June 2015* ... 14
   - Date #6: Actionless Jackson and the Toilet Bowl Alibi *June 2015* ... 18

2. **HONESTY MUSCLES** ... 21
   - Date #7: The Pushy, Lushy Lawyer *June 2015* ... 21
   - Date #8: So Close and Yet So Tall *June 2015* ... 22
   - Date #9: Leave Me Cologne *June 2015* ... 25
   - Date #10: Just the Three of Us? *June 2015* ... 26
   - Date #11: Struggling to Admit I'm Björed *(Told from both perspectives) July 2015* ... 28
   - Date #12: A Picture Tells a Thousand Lies *July 2015* ... 32

3. **PAIN AND DELIGHT** ... 34
   - Date #13: The Cutest Masochist *(Told from both perspectives) July 2015* ... 34
   - Date #14: Midnight Coffee? *July 2015* ... 37
   - Date #15: Consent Lament *August 2015* ... 39
   - Up-*Dating* My OkCupid Profile ... 42
   - Date #16: His Train, My Tunnel *August 2015* ... 43
   - Date #17: Up in Smoke *August 2015* ... 46
   - Date #18: The Best Kiss of My Life? *August 2015* ... 48

4. LONG DAYS OF LONGING	52
Dates #19 & #20: Too Bad You're Not Jonah *September 2015*	52
Date #21: Mental Shaving *September 2015*	54
Date #22: Too Much is Not Enough *September 2015*	55
Date #23: Rawr *October 2015*	57
Date #24: Pleather Together *October 2015*	58
Date #25: Shooting Stars *October 2015*	60
Date #26: A Short Reign from Spain *October 2015*	62
Date #27: Potter Seeking Potter *(Told from both perspectives) October 2015*	64
Date #28: Sexy Professor! *October 2015*	66

Part II
Archetypal Encounters

5. A TASTE OF CONSCIOUS SEXUALITY	73
Date #29: Karezza Boy *October 2015*	73
Date #30: Karezza Man *October 2015*	74
Date #31: Captain Clitoris! *October 2015*	76
Date #32: Between a Gemstone and a Soft Place *October 2015*	78
Date #33: Finding Bliss with an Australian Nonmonaut *(Told from both perspectives) October 2015*	79
Date #34: Embracing My Inner Chill *November 2015*	84
6. WIZARDS AND OTHER MYTHICAL CREATURES	87
Date #35: I Break for Wizards *December 2015*	87
Date #36: Armpits, Whips, and Spanks *January 2016*	90
Date #37: Cardboard Chemistry *January 2016*	91
Date #38: A Leprechaun Carrying STI Results *January 2016*	92
Date #39: He's Just Not That Into Me *January 2016*	93
Date #18, Jonah Continued: How to Love a Ghost *February 2016*	97
7. DOWNS AND UPS	99
Date #40: Something Off On Broadway *February 2016*	99
Date #41: Breaking the Mold *February 2016*	101
Date #42: My Muddy Valentine *February 2016*	102

Date #43: The Cute Guy from the Grocery Store *February 2016*	103
Date #44: Reservations *March 2016*	104
Date#45: The Effeminate Dom *March 2016*	107
Date #46: I Flew Through the Air with the Greatest of Ease *(Told from both perspectives) March 2016*	108
Date #47: The Pragmatic Poet *April 2016*	113
Date #48: Heartbreak, Wizard-Style *April 2016*	114
8. BURNED BY MAGICAL FLAMES	**126**
Date #49: Not Sleeping in Seattle *(Told from both perspectives) June 2016*	126
Date #50: Sex in a Temple *(Told from both perspectives) July 2016*	128
Date #18, Jonah Continued: You Can't Put Fog in a Jar *August 2016*	136
Date #51: Falling for a Tree *September 2016*	139
Date #52: The Shaman *October 2016*	141
Date #53: We Should Really Hang Out ... *November 2016*	143
Date #54: Too Many Frozen Sausages *January 2017*	144
Date #55: Plane Attraction *April 2017*	145
Date #56: Boxers Do Not a Proper Swimsuit Make *April 2017*	147

Part III

Erotic Evolution

9. SEXUAL CHRYSALIS AT SUMMER CAMP	**153**
Sexual Healing *July 2017*	153
Date #57: Easy on the No's *(Told from both perspectives) July 2017*	159
Date #58: The Snake Charmer *July 2017*	163
Date #59: The Wildest First Date *(Told from both perspectives) July 2017*	165
Date #60: Body Love at Summer Camp *(Told from both perspectives) July 2017*	169
10. WALKING THE WALK	**175**
Date #61: Amy the Ripper *October 2017*	175
Date #62: Going Beyond Walkward *October 2017*	176

Date #63: A Man With a Sloth *October 2017*	179
Date #64: Above the Belt *November 2017*	180
Date #65: Toastmaster Flash *November 2017*	183
Date #60, Warren Continued: A Rocky Fall *Autumn 2017*	185
11. ANGELS, GHOSTS, AND THE SCUM OF THE EARTH	**191**
Date #66: "Can I Be Honest With You?" *January 2018*	191
Date #67: The Tortoise and the Hawk *January 2018*	193
The Sexual Healers' Tribe: 2017–2018	198
Date #68: Tin-derrrrrr! *February 2018*	208
Date #69: An Angel at My Table *April 2018*	210
All the Beautiful Girls: 2017–2018	211
Date #18, Jonah Continued: A Ghost in the Flesh *May 2018*	212
12. LOVE IN A BOX	**215**
Date #60, Warren Continued: Heart in a Blender *Winter 2017–Spring 2018*	215
Date #70: Like a Virgin *May 2018*	220
Date #52, Raphael Continued: Return of the Shaman *May 2018*	223
Date #71: Sex Without Love *June 2018*	224
Date #72: What About That Raw Juice Diet? *June 2018*	225
Date #73: Undercover Husband *June 2018*	227

Part IV
Spiraling Towards Something Divine

13. ECSTASY AND AGONY	**233**
Date #74: Liquid Skin *July 2018*	233
Date #75: What Happens at Summer Camp Stays at Summer Camp *July 2018*	239
Date #76: Wrestling With a Champion *August 2018*	242
Date #77: Don't Go Partner Dancing on the First Date *(Told from both perspectives) Summer 2018*	248
Date #78: Just Don't Make Me Eye Gaze *July 2018*	258

14. FROM CHEMISTRY TO CUDDLINGUS — 261
Date #60, Warren Continued: Chemistry is Chemistry *Fall 2018* — 261
Date #79: Three Beautiful Pairs *September 2018* — 263
Date #80: Perfect Tens? *November 2018* — 268
Date #77, Amir Continued: The Boyfriend Proposal *Winter 2019* — 274
Date #81: From Baby to Babe *February 2019* — 276

15. THE EXQUISITE ORDER OF THE UNIVERSE — 288
Date #77, Amir Continued: Cuddlingus *Spring–Summer 2019* — 288
Date #82: A Tantric Dream *November 2019* — 291
Date #18, Jonah Continued: A Bird and a Leaf *2021 – Forever?* — 296
Date #60, Warren Continued: Making Love Eternal *2021 - Forever?* — 298
Date #77, Amir Continued: Persian Mensch *2021–Forever?* — 300

Acknowledgments — 307
About the Author — 311

Introduction

Newly single in my mid-forties, I was ready for action and adventure. My relationship life had been mostly a series of three-year commitments. At twenty-eight, I had a daughter, but never planned to stay permanently with her father, because I identified as a serial monogamist. I know this wasn't mainstream, but as a relationship style, it worked well for me.

That was the pattern until I met Samantha, my first female partner. She had two girls; they all moved in with me and my seven-year-old daughter. Supporting the family through pottery and dance classes was both a blessing and a burden. Towards the end of our ten-year relationship, I felt caught between a sense of responsibility to Samantha and her girls, and what I truly wanted: to move on, to grow and learn, like I always had. I longed for the freedom to rediscover myself through new connections instead of feeling stuck in a relationship with entrenched patterns.

My daughter had been increasingly uncomfortable living in our crowded house of five powerful females. At fifteen, suffering in the family, she moved away to live with her father. It was heartbreaking for me, and I felt an even stronger urge to shift my relationship. I too was unhappy.

Approaching middle age, a deep, aching, spiritual mandate pressed me to transform my over-accommodating nature and move towards being radically honest everywhere, all the time. So when I was 45, Samantha and I broke up and a few months later, I leapt into dating.

∼

Dreamy, idealistic, and vowing to prioritize myself, I felt open to the mysteries ahead. But when my first date—coffee with a handsome Mediterranean actor—was downright painful, I ran home to journal, to figure out why. The immediate catharsis and clarity that came from writing about my experience inspired me to blog. Heartfelt responses from blog readers motivated me to learn and grow, both for myself and others. Dating became my dojo, a place to work on my sacred goal of radical honesty.

I loved finding tricks to make dating easier, and eventually played freely on multiple dating apps; dating was both my life unfolding and a research project. Originally, to retain my freedom, I hoped to find a lover, not a partner. But I also knew that one day I would crave committed companionship again.

I went on more than a hundred dates over a five-year period and had an inordinate number of communications online. It was a huge opportunity to "work on myself," but some of my relationship patterns felt like molasses—dark, slow, and sticky. My dating life became a delicious blend of magical potential and personal challenge.

This period of my life was a blessing, with an abundance of fun and drama. My experiences ranged from disconcerting to healing to absolutely ecstatic. Several connections I made along the way overlapped, and I joked with my best friend Jess about my ever-evolving "harem"—even if they were mostly just flirtations, not swooning around, fanning me, and peeling me grapes.

Many of the people I met were interesting, brilliant, and truly beautiful. Several of my dates were willing to write their perspectives (before they read mine), and those are included in this book. I am deeply grateful for each connection I made—everything from light chatting on dating apps to the deepest soul-stirring transformations.

If you are on a quest for love, yearn for a new style of relationship, or want to shift something about yourself or your circumstances, you are not alone. This journey was about taking risks to be my raw, authentic self, which ultimately led to relationships where I could feel honest, loving, and free. It is an honor to share my story with you, and I hope this book will support you to go for whatever you want in life and in love!

Part I
OKAY, CUPID!

1

STEPPING OUT AND FALLING DOWN

Date #1: Not Such Perfect Strangers *April 2015*

When I stepped into Perugino coffee shop, I recognized the lone, handsome Mediterranean man instantly. Sergio looked exactly like his profile pictures. But as I approached him, I felt instantly overwhelmed by the expectation of romance with a total stranger. Needing space already, I said a brief, awkward hello and escaped to order coffee. I wondered, *why am I getting coffee? I don't really want any.* Something was already off; I was out of my element, doing what I thought I was supposed to do.

Just out of a decade-long relationship, I felt excited about my freedom. But I had never dated before. Every one of my previous relationships arose naturally out of established friendships or work. Clueless about dating apps, I started my adventures by cautiously dabbling in the Craigslist "personals." Communications there seemed like trying to buy garage sale-type items from people I maybe shouldn't trust.

When a friend told me that OkCupid was free and simple to use, I snapped a few selfies and crafted a profile. OkCupid was a huge upgrade. People posted a variety of pictures, and there was plenty of room for written descriptions. I clicked the "Like" button on a few people and felt encouraged when Sergio and I matched. He was an actor with professional photographs that highlighted his sensual appeal.

As I dressed up for the date, I smiled in the mirror. My adventure was beginning! I felt thrilled about the potential connections and experiences that lay ahead. Sergio and I had exchanged only a couple of messages, and POOF! I was on my first date.

I glanced over from the coffee counter. Sergio looked dreamy in the cozy nook; the cafe's red brick wall was a dramatic background to his dark skin and warm smile. I paid for the coffee, took a breath, and sat down with him. After some "nice to meet you" formalities, I defaulted to my social m.o. and started asking questions. "What do you do with your days?" "What type of acting?" "Where did you grow up?" "What was it like?"

Once I started, I couldn't figure out how to stop asking questions. Sergio was so open and expressive that the conversation quickly tipped way out of balance. He grew more dramatic, gesticulating as he enthusiastically re-experienced his childhood, his relationship with his parents, and even his parents' childhoods. This felt more like an interview than a date. Nodding and giving encouraging cues, I grew weary, silently assaulting my digestion with the acidic americano.

Why was I continuing to ask questions and give signals of interest when I didn't want to hear any more details? In the hour and a half we spent in that once-promising nook, Sergio never asked me a single question about myself. I didn't blame him. Both of us sat at that table, and extreme one-sidedness was the result. At the end of the date, as we hugged goodbye, he breathlessly said that he would love to get together again. "Let's be in touch," I squeaked out. Internally, I was cramping and contorting. Pangs in my jaw seemed to be screaming at me, *"Stop your weird smiling!"*

With sweaty armpits and an uncomfortably vibrating body, I was relieved to be back in my car. I shook on purpose, trying to get rid of the stress. Desperate to understand what the heck had just happened, I went home and straight to my computer journal. Typing feverishly, I realized something: *my need to be liked was an emotional straitjacket.*

At any point during the date, instead of continually generating questions and conveying interest, I could have simply been quiet and said nothing. I could have volunteered information about myself, finished my coffee—*or not!*—and said goodbye, or I could have spoken the truth: I felt uncomfortable that we were only talking about him. Instead, by feigning enthusiasm, I was basically lying.

Why was I so bound to accommodate others? The resentful passivity I felt on this date was reminiscent of my previous partnerships. Falling in love was invigorating, but my pattern was to sacrifice my freedom and independence for relationship security. I wasn't usually brave or mature enough to articulate my needs, and after a few years, preferred to follow my resentments out the door.

Looking in this mirror, I saw a version of me I didn't want to be anymore. In this new phase of dating, I needed to let go of some old habits and beliefs so I wouldn't waste hours, or years, accommodating (not such) perfect strangers.

I went back to OkCupid, resolved to use dating to practice radical authenticity. The journey ahead would require communicating in new ways, and I assumed I would stumble and fail repeatedly. But I was ready for whatever training was needed to get over my conditioned impulses and to find the courage to speak my truth.

Date #2: Learning to Pay Attention to My Inner "No" May 2015

Reid and I connected on OkCupid, and from the get-go we were messaging voraciously. Physically, he was plain, fair-featured, and younger-looking than his age (he was 35). I felt drawn mostly to his smile. From his pictures, I thought, *what a sweetheart.*

In our messaging, Reid was active and attentive, and I basked in the regularity of his cyber affection. I loved that he wasn't afraid to talk about sex and found him sensitive and not overwhelming. He let me know that he was very interested in pleasing women. Since I have always been a pleaser, receiving sounded divine to me.

But as our online flirtation continued, certain mannerisms started to make him less appealing. His writing had a formal, corny tone. He apologized often. Filing these traits away as idiosyncrasies, I stayed open and curious about this quirky character. After a week of racy messaging, I texted a short video and asked him to send one back. His wide cheeks and round eyes reminded me of a toddler. Something in me sank; I was really expecting someone very different. I recoiled when he nervously said, "I'm *way* into plants ... instead of people."

I had imagined an attractive Reid until I saw him move and heard him speak. Still, I was ready to get my dating party started! My hopes about Reid were rapidly declining, but I didn't want or need him to fill any specific role, so instead of abandoning ship, I drifted onward.

We planned to meet for dinner at Cornucopia on 17th Avenue. Riding my initial excitement, I quickly called him when I had what I thought was a great idea, and asked, "What if, when we first meet, you kiss me right away, before a word is spoken?"

I conveniently ignored the wobble in his voice when he said, "Uh, OK, sure." I giggled as I told my friends about the plan. I thought it was such a racy, fun, out-of-the-box idea.

But Reid showed up at the crowded outdoor courtyard awkward on his feet. Totally stoned, he launched into feverish chatting. *How could he forget?* When I leaned in and whispered loudly, "You're not supposed to talk," Reid stumbled towards me and kissed me strangely, messily, on the side of my mouth. *Such a disappointment.*

During dinner's flat conversation, the final remnants of my fantasy dissolved; there was no way Reid was going to be my next boyfriend. But there had been so much buildup that I optimistically clung to the potential and invited him home anyway. My hopes for this date were more powerful than our actual connection. I wasn't attracted to him but rationalized that maybe I could have a novel sexual experience. I hadn't been sexual with a man in almost a decade. After all that flirting, it seemed silly not to follow through with some action.

Back at my house, we went straight to my bedroom and quickly undressed. I wanted to become a new, more open and wilder version of myself. I hadn't seen a penis in a long time, and suddenly one was naked in my bed.

~

My high school boyfriend used to call me "fiercely independent." By my early twenties, I had already been through three major breakups. Afraid that I didn't know how to make a long-term connection work, I sought guidance from a trusted high school teacher and mentor. When she pragmatically reflected, "Amy, maybe you are a serial monogamist," I started to glow. *There were options besides marriage?* I joyfully and immediately adopted "serial monogamy" as my style.

I had wonderful partners who formed a long chain of three-year "love chapters." Then, in my thirties, I had a partnership with a woman that lasted a decade. There were many reasons for its longevity. Samantha and I were very good friends. She had two daughters and her financial dependence on me was challenging. The idea of breaking up our beautiful family was very different from my previous endings with single male partners.

However, I had never wanted "together forever," and ten years was extreme for me. My spirit always eventually busted me out of committed partnerships, needing to be free. When that long relationship ended, I made a promise to myself: I would no longer commit my sexuality exclusively to any one person. I needed a big change. The most honest and self-honoring path I could take was to no longer consider myself monogamous. I was determined to find a relationship configuration that fit me better.

~

As soon as Reid and I were skin-to-skin, everything felt unfamiliar. I was detached and disconnected. After a little of his "giving" (as advertised in our messaging) my mind went foggy. I couldn't feel my body as his penis entered me. He was floating confusingly above me, moving with a gruff vigor that made him seem lion-like. After a few re-positions, when I felt his testicles slapping into me from behind, I was finally able to find my voice and croak out, "I can't do this."

He stopped immediately and whispered, "We could just snuggle."

With my head buried in the pillow, I answered, "I'm sorry. I think I need to be alone." I could feel his disappointment as he put his clothes on and left. I had always had trouble speaking directly in sexual situations, especially about things I didn't like, and longed to feel more sexually present and connected to myself. In the past, even when I was having sex, I was performing, or just going through the motions, and didn't usually *feel* sexual.

With Reid, I didn't give enough attention to the messages along the way telling me something was off between us. There were so many ways that I wasn't attracted to him. I ignored my intuitions, observations, and body signals. I had my work cut out for me on the path towards radical honesty.

As much as I wanted to be free, this experience reminded me that I shouldn't try to separate my heart and my body.

Date #3: More of What I Want and Less of What I Don't
June 2015

Bruce's written OkCupid profile was scant, but his face was cute. We both had dogs; walking and talking while they played sounded like an efficient, no-pressure date, so I suggested meeting at my regular dog park. Also, I figured I might learn a lot about Bruce from the way he interacted with the other animals and owners.

We walked for an hour, talking about our dogs and our lives. He was sweet, but sad. When I asked about his demeanor, he spoke openly about his troubled feelings. My therapist side came out. I knew that I didn't want to date someone who had a lot of emotional or mental health needs, but I didn't know what to do other than ask questions and offer insights. My childhood "good girl" conditioning had matured into knee-jerk helpfulness.

Even though being of service came naturally and was becoming my new profession, feeling like a therapist on a date was about as sexy as picking up my dog's poop. I wanted to stop asking so many questions about people's emotional struggles. My conditioned response dragged out unwanted dates and exhausted me.

Most people, at least most dating people, seemed to be suffering in some way. *Is there anyone out there who is emotionally stable?* I wondered. *If not, staying single might be a better choice for me.*

~

I grew up in various suburbs of New York City, and my life seemed perfect until my parents divorced when I was ten. Any idyllic views I'd had about marriage were vanquished. Let down by my family, I resolved to raise myself. I was successful academically and socially, and planned to go to a good college, get a great job, and make lots of money. *Medical school it had to be.*

Despite this intention, my freshman year at Wesleyan University turned out to be academic misery. The following summer, however, a series of *fortunate* events changed my life's direction. On my first day home from college, a "Help Wanted" sign near my old high school in New Jersey mysteriously seduced me. I followed my nose into the Domino's Pizza, and within moments I was signing a form and walking out with a stack of pizzas. I had to laugh: *I was a delivery girl?*

That same night, I was mugged on the job at knifepoint. I was so scared that when the guy ran away with the pizza money, I called him back to give him the tips from my other pocket. At that moment, I was irrationally desperate to please the mugger, so he would like me and I would be safe. When I returned to Domino's, my manager punched a hole through the wall. But I decided to stay on. A week later, on another delivery, I saw lovers kissing on the sidewalk, and they were more interesting than my life. Staring at them instead of the road, I rear-ended an elderly couple. Completely shaken up, I decided to go back to campus for the summer instead.

There, I found a job that seemed safer: working in the library. I couldn't believe it when my new boss handed me a videotape called "Murder in the Stacks." *What was the world trying to tell me?* It turned out to be a training video about how to properly handle books, but that title went under my skin. On my early morning and late-night walks to and from work, I brandished a long stick and adopted a *don't fuck with me* gait. I asked to work at the well-lit information desk when possible, and did my best to avoid "the stacks," the library's vast, dim storage area, where I was certain I'd be killed.

It was a good job. I loved the rich mahogany trim and the huge Corinthian columns. Wisdom floated in the ether. One night, I grabbed a book to look through in the lovely solitude of the information desk: *The Power of Myth* by Joseph Campbell. When I opened it to a random page, these words jumped at me: "Follow your bliss."

I went into an altered state. Standing in the echo tunnel of my existence, the words reverberated like a mandate. *Follow my bliss? What would that mean?*

In an instant, I realized that I had been creating my *entire life* for other people. I didn't want to go to med school. *Maybe my love of science was really just a crush on my high school biology teacher.* In the silent foyer of that great, old library, I drew a picture of myself following "Bliss" down the path of life.

"Following My Bliss"

From that day on, in the daylight hours, I started dance-walking everywhere, listening to cassettes on my big yellow Walkman. Those three words instantly changed the course—and *style*—of my existence.

I switched my major to religious studies and started taking the classes I was drawn to: white water canoeing, South Indian drumming, ceramics, and Eastern and Caribbean religions. Many late-night college hours were spent spinning a pottery wheel in the 24-hour ceramics studio. After I graduated, I became a professional potter, later a pleasure-based movement teacher. And eventually, a somatic therapist.

When I received the "follow your bliss" memo from the Universe, my life became a fool's journey in the best sense: every subsequent major personal choice I made was based on intuition and passion. Whenever I was headed in a wrong direction, signs would appear to help me navigate.

∾

At the dog park, Bruce surprised me when he looked up and said, "Ideally with dating, both people get more of what they want and less of what they don't." Suddenly Bruce was a dating Buddha; his gem was a simple litmus test. I resolved to work toward more good dates and fewer bad ones.

Looking for words as we were saying goodbye, Bruce shrugged and said, "Maybe we'll get Chinese food." I responded, "Maybe." We agreed to get back in touch if it felt right. Walking away, I felt expanded, even giddy, relieved that I didn't show any false interest in going further. Chinese food with Bruce was not going to happen, and leaving with a dating gem and a smile—and without promises—was a thrill.

Date #4: German Tim and His Knives *June 2015*

Tim had a boyish, curly-dark-haired look I adored. His OkCupid photos were mostly of him biking and traveling. He worked at a popular local home and garden store. And he wasn't too tall (I'm under five feet and feel most comfortable with shorter men). We dove into emailing eagerly and vigorously. Tim's Monty Python-esque stories about his days sometimes made me burst out laughing. Excited and engaged, my heart fluttered.

I texted him a selfie and asked him to send one back. "I'm tired, but here you go," he messaged. I felt shocked when I saw it. He seemed much older, and worn, not at all the Tim I had been imagining.

"Wow, you looked very different in your profile pictures."

"Yeah," he replied, "those are mostly from ten years ago."

I felt disturbed—angry, even—and texted back, "Tim, you HAVE to use current pictures. People will get upset." This should have been a sign. But I forgave him and kept my eyes on the younger man I saw in the profile pictures. He did say that he was tired. *Bad lighting?*

Another strange red flag was the way he was obsessed with Germany. When he waxed romantically about his homeland, there was an odd, haunting feeling. In his emails, he referred to it so often and with such wistful longing that I oddly felt a part of him was *buried* there. My ancestors from the concentration camps seemed to be whispering in my ear.

I ignored the photo and the ominous feeling, favoring a romantic vision of me and the younger Tim as deeply compatible souls. After a week of messaging, we made a plan to meet at his house for dinner. He was really excited to share Germany with me, and proudly planned a multi-course meal. The morning of our date, he texted a long list of ingredients for me to buy. Feeling hopeful, I dressed up in a short, red, ruffled skirt and a tight black top. I picked up a heavy bag of strange-to-me, expensive groceries: wurst, spaetzle, curd cheese, wienerschnitzel, juniper berries, and marzipan. I brought roses from my garden.

Tim lived in a neighborhood of grey, boxy bungalows. As I parked my car in his driveway, he emerged from his house to greet me. Seeing him in person, I was filled with a creepy visceral feeling, which was all the information I needed about attraction. I imagined saying, "Sorry, I have to go!" but instead went into autopilot: my legs walked me inside, and a fake smile plastered itself on my face. I marginalized the part of myself that didn't want to be there. *For what?* The messaging buildup, the groceries—it felt like an irrevocable promise.

He gave me a brief tour; I felt numb looking at his barely furnished rooms. When he waved blithely towards his messy, unmade, motel-feeling bed, my skin crawled. The last stop was the kitchen, where we unpacked the groceries. I looked down, rolled up my sleeves, and mechanically took sous-chef orders. Conversation was strained. We were tasked with too many complex dishes to prepare in his cramped bachelor's kitchen. I regretted my choice to wear such a revealing outfit, in contrast with his sweatpants and T-shirt. I was confused, trying to understand my mistaken perceptions. *How could he have seemed so different through email?* A few short hours ago, we were hot-lovers-to-be. Standing next to him, I felt uncomfortable, and trapped.

Cooking dinner took two hours but felt like four, as we were making *nine dishes*. I faked my way through our choppy conversation. Mid-way through our prep, he spoke with cryptic reverence about his expensive knives. Inspecting one carefully, he told me with bent eyebrows, in a harsh tone, about an ex-girlfriend who would "stupidly" clean knives with the scrubby side of the sponge. He gritted his teeth as he spoke about her, gripping one of the freshly sharpened babies tightly. With a quickening heartbeat, I admitted that I too had always cleaned my knives with the scrubby part of the sponge. He peered at me through narrowed eyes and said, "You're not supposed to."

In the awkward silence that followed, I turned back to my cutting board and shifted down the crowded counter to put some space between us. This definitely wasn't one of those "better dates!"

Eventually, finally, all of the dishes were ready. We sat down to German food overwhelm: fatty wursts, oily potatoes, cooked fruits, and strange, pickled foods. I pushed the food around on my plate and ate what I could, but the combination was gastrointestinal hell. When it finally came time for the desserts, I had to say "No." I couldn't possibly eat anything else. His face turned sad.

When Tim optimistically asked if I'd like to play video games, which I absolutely did *not* want, I finally found the courage to be honest. I suggested that we speak openly about how we were feeling about the date. Sober and incredibly heavy, I looked directly at him and said, "I don't sense any romantic potential between us."

His smile disappeared, and his hands clutched the table. Anger and desperation rumbled in his voice, and he pleaded for more of a chance: "Meet me again, just for coffee. We could be friends." I shook my head; it was a definite *no*. "I'm not looking for new friends." There was not an ounce of chemistry between us.

We hastily cleaned the kitchen. Tension filled the room. I could sense the volcano rising and didn't want to turn my back to him. Sharp knives were everywhere. As soon as I felt that I had helped enough, I grabbed my stuff and rushed out in a streak, barely saying goodbye. Neither of us mentioned him helping to pay for the expensive German groceries.

My takeaways from this date:

1. Do not have a first date at a stranger's house.
2. Written messages do NOT give a clear picture of a person.
3. Old pictures are a red flag.
4. Tell the truth ASAP, and from a distance!
5. Beware of eating too much German food.

Date #5: The "Hawt" Millennial
(Told from both perspectives) June 2015

I was uncharacteristically awake at 2 a.m. at my friend Andrew's house in Portland. We had enjoyed some marijuana and were hanging out on the street under the summer stars. A bike streaked by and made a sudden U-turn. Recognizing Andrew, the rider swung back to say hi. His name was Joe, and he was strikingly cute and smart.

I was caught off guard. It felt synchronistically magical to meet such a beautiful stranger on a street corner in the wee hours. The next day, I asked Andrew for Joe's number and sent a text:

Amy: Hey, Joe! This is Amy, Andrew's friend. We met last night. I'm going to be forward. I was super drawn to you. I found you beautiful, brilliant, intriguing, and funny. I am looking for a lover. Not a relationship, but a soulful, sexy, vibrant, short-term connection.

I was in an altered state and froze when I met you. You are one of the first people I've met in a while who I've felt "wow" about. I live in Eugene but come to Portland one day a week for school. I'm probably much older than you. Let me know if you have any interest. Andrew can be my reference.

Joe: Hawt.

Yep. One word. *So millennial,* but good enough for me. We made plans to meet the next evening at "our intersection" to go for a walk. Just as we were hugging hello, a bloody, severely beaten-up guy stumbled out of the bushes and came straight at us, asking for help. It was a scene right out of a B-movie, or "Portlandia." Witnessing Joe's grounded warmth and presence with this questionable character, I liked him even more. At the same time, I wondered about this incident as a potential sign from the universe: would our connection wind up in high drama? Would someone get beaten up?

Joe was open and vulnerable, with big, pouty lips and huge puppy eyes. We walked the streets of Portland getting to know each other. I learned that he was a musician, a dancer, and an activist, and had a young daughter who he co-parented.

I needed him to explain many of his twisty-poetic phrases as he passionately expressed himself. We confirmed the age gap: 20 years. *Oof, that was a lot, much closer to my daughter's age than mine.* After a long, meandering walk (where he pointed out dumpsters where one could reliably find free pizza), we circled back to his house.

Inside, he picked me up and spun me around in the air. It was romantic. We made out. Joe's lips were perfect and his wise, young hands traced my body with sensitivity and curiosity. Soon, he asked shyly, "Would you maybe want to meditate together?" *Was meditation the next millennial "base" after kissing?* We sat side-by-side on the edge of his twin bed on the floor, closed our eyes and breathed together for twenty minutes. It was a beautiful experience. Then Joe walked me outside and we embraced on the sidewalk.

But as we were parting, he got spacey. I started to question things between us when he said, "I can't believe this is happening. Me and my buddy used to always talk about landing a hot older babely lady." I felt partly flattered—*babely?*—and partly objectified. *Was he "landing" me? Was I more a type than a person? Was he playing a role for me too?* I had to be careful with Joe; he had a familiar, hypnotic, boyish cuteness.

We met up again the next week. I dressed up in a revealing outfit. I could feel that his initial curiosity and enthusiasm had already waned. That night, my feelings crumpled a few times. He poked at my ignorance of millennial slang, brushed things off that I found important, and only seemed excited when he brought up the prospect of "scoring free pottery" from me. My hopes took a downturn.

On our third date, the following week, we moved into bed. Sitting naked next to his skinny, young body, I felt like I had thoughtlessly hooked up with an unknown boy from the county fair and didn't know what to do with him. Our sex was awkward; we were like molecules without the proper affinity to bond. My interest in him made me feel embarrassed and vulnerable.

Throughout the month or so that we were dating, we had several honest phone conversations about our feelings and concerns. We were from different worlds. Just out of college, he was canvassing for an environmental organization. Our generational differences resulted in choppy misunderstandings.

We agreed that it wasn't working but decided to have one final date. He lay a blanket out in his garden and invited me to sit in his lap. We embraced one last time under the almost-full moon, indulging in the part of our relationship that worked best: kissing. We had a sweet, painless goodbye and transitioned to social media friends. I asked Joe if he would write about his experience.

Joe's Perspective

When I first met you, my thought was, "what a sweet, progressive, vaguely woo but intelligent older lady; we had lots of those in Boulder!" You and Andrew were stoned on the street in the middle of the night, looking at stars, and it was funny and cute.

When you sent me a text message listing all of the positive attributes that many people allude to but rarely name outright, I was ... flattered? Grateful? Stunned? I was so excited about you being super into me, that it took me a pretty long time to ask myself if I was into you.

We went on a date, had deep conversation. It was cool. We walked and held hands and kissed in my kitchen. You're a good kisser! There was a funny generation gap where you were often taking me seriously, which any post-irony millennial can tell you is a waste of time. It felt either refreshing or tarpit-y depending on the moment.

We even had sex. The sex was hot, even! From the start, I felt like my attraction was a lot to your heart, your brain, your hands and your voice, and a little to your sex. But what guy says no when a foxy lady wants to do it with him?

I just assumed that if I ignored my lack of desire, and focused on your surfeit thereof, the boners would come. You sent me epic love sonnets and I responded with memes. Because I'm not a bullshitter, it became clear pretty fast that there was an imbalance.

This was perfectly crystallized by an experience that didn't seem to bother you very much, which is funny, because the main reason it bothered me was that I was worried that it bothered you! Anyway, the next week when you came to sleep over, I wasn't feeling the doink. And I felt awful—you were this super charming, sweet, sincere babely lady—and my engine wasn't revving, and I didn't wanna make you feel bad, so we were cuddling, and it was fine except for the unspoken sexual tension.

What the fuck of course would happen but my roommate decided to consummate her yearlong friendship with a Tantric master by triumphantly cumming over and over again in throaty tones that trumpeted through my bedroom wall, ringing in my ears as testaments to my own failed virility. I imagined that it was a frustrating and shameful experience for you but didn't ask. It was a very Woody Allen, neurotic anxiety comedy moment for me.

I think you're a really special person and I enjoyed our co-navigation through the sea of discomfort. I'm glad that my own deep legacy of Mennonite mortification hasn't interfered with our e-friendship, and I'd love to hang and giggle and talk when next you're in town, or the next time I go to Eugene. I'm a little bummed we didn't keep dating long enough for me to get some free pottery.

I laughed as I read it, but also felt sensitive hearing his side. Joe's obsession with free pottery made him a lot less "hawt" to me, but our valuable conversations made him a great sparring partner in the dojo of direct communication.

Date #6: Actionless Jackson and the Toilet Bowl Alibi *June 2015*

One day, I came across an OkCupid profile that floored me. I squirmed in my seat and started to sweat as I read Jackson's graphic vision of his ideal sexual relationship. The scenes he depicted were strangely close to the things I fantasized about doing but wasn't sure I actually wanted to do. I was so turned on and energetically activated by reading his profile that I felt compelled to reach out. Jackson responded instantly. My impression of him through messaging was that he was confident, warm, smart, and successful.

I had never sent revealing selfies to anyone before. With Jackson, I felt inspired. I had fun doing my best to strike pin-up girl poses and he appreciated them. He sent back some seriously up close, fetishy pictures of him with ropes in his hands and dildos up his ass. I would stare at the images, incredulous that I actually received them.

Things had really changed from the good old newspaper "Personals Section" days. In the early 2000s, I tried the newspaper "women seeking women" ads. Leaving and retrieving hollow, crackly-sounding voicemails through the newspaper's clunky system was uncomfortable. Meeting a stranger based solely on a 25-word ad, the one time I tried, resulted in instant regret. Before smartphones, first sight wasn't until first meeting. Now, this potential date was showing himself to me on a strangely intimate level.

We messaged feverishly, daily, for several weeks. It was intriguing and highly flirtatious—but I also felt out of my element. He said he liked having strong, active sex for hours on end. I imagined him geared up with small, muscle-bound, sexually athletic women, tossing them up against walls, over bathroom vanities, and across kitchen counters. *Could I be that woman?*

One day, Jackson divulged this recent discovery: if he masturbated with a vibrator up his ass, he would "come buckets." That phrase and image never left me. I wasn't sure that I wanted to get too close to those buckets.

I wondered, *should a real-life sexual experience actually happen between little me and big Jackson?* Our first date would have to be in public. Lesson learned. I decided it was tantalizing enough to continue on the Jackson trail. I reached out several times to see about getting together, but he was always busy, out of town, or unresponsive when it came time to connect. Eventually, I suggested that we video chat. He suddenly disappeared. A week later, he finally messaged: "I'm so sorry. I dropped my phone in the toilet."

Was Jackson the man he said he was? *Was he the man in the pictures? Was anything he told me real?* I had heard about fake profiles. He could be anyone sitting in their kitchen, anyone! Suspicious, I started to interrogate him and he got annoyed. I had the weirdest feeling and went to see Joanne. *Was I getting catfished?*

~

Joanne was a wonderful, playful, older woman who had been coming to my Nia (pleasure-based movement) classes for many years. When we first met, she told me she was an "energy intuitive" and asked if I would like to trade sessions for classes. Curious, I decided to try. We sat in her living room, in chairs. "Ask anything you'd like," she offered.

I decided to share, "I'm going to see my father soon, for the first time in many years, and I'm a bit nervous about it."

She took a moment and looked out the window. When she turned back to face me, her mouth was contorted, her lip pulled way down towards her shoulder. She showed me the world from his perspective. A week later, when I landed in Los Angeles and saw him for the first time in several years, I was shocked: his mouth was distorted *exactly* as she had shown me. I had forgotten that he had surgery on his tongue a while back; his mouth was still healing. After this experience, I knew that Joanne was the real deal and I continued to visit her regularly.

∽

I asked Joanne about Jackson. She repeated his name out loud, and then her whole body contracted and twisted intensely. She shook herself out of it. Full of conviction, she said, "Stay away from this guy! He is NOT who he says he is!"

"Jackson" continued to send OkCupid messages from time to time. I didn't see the point of messaging him back.

But who knows? Maybe he *did* drop his phone in the toilet!

2

HONESTY MUSCLES

Date #7: The Pushy, Lushy Lawyer *June 2015*

Davis pushed my "cute guy" button. He had big, heavily lashed eyes, and hair that framed his face in loose brown curls. A young, alternative, hippie lawyer, he seemed healthy and grounded. Because of the attractive traits listed in his impressive profile, when he suggested meeting for dinner, I didn't vet him further. We chose to meet at Tacovore, my favorite local restaurant. It's in the Whiteaker neighborhood (affectionately known as "the Whit") which reminds me of Brooklyn, with old colorful houses, lawns turned into art galleries, high-quality homegrown restaurants, and a rainbow of international food carts.

We arrived at the same time and openly checked each other out as we waited in line. My nipples were tingling, stimulated by the pheromonal, sensual feeling between us. But when we stepped up to the register, I was taken aback when he ordered two drinks for himself.

We found an empty picnic table in the bustling courtyard. Davis leaned in as he spoke. Our eye contact was compelling, and at first I felt adored and flattered; it seemed like he was trying to impress me. But when our conversation shifted to speaking about other people, Davis had a scowling, sour tone that revealed unmistakable misanthropy. His expert drinking and emerging negativity made me wary. I ignored the invitation that continually pressed from his eyes. The more he tried to seduce me through his body language, the more aloof I became.

After dinner, we walked to Blair Alley, a nearby retro arcade. Even though I wasn't interested in him, I liked being a "dater," out in the world doing novel things, and was willing to continue. On our walk, when Davis draped his arm heavily over my shoulders, it felt like he was trying to claim me, alpha-style. Not taking this date too seriously, I stayed emotionally detached and erected an energetic boundary against his tentacles.

At the arcade, Davis grabbed two more drinks for himself and we played a few games. For a short while, it felt good to receive the cocky lawyer's bold caresses as I flexed my video game muscles and kicked his ass at Ms. Pacman. When he finished his drinks and went back to the bar for more, the coffin of our date was sealed. He was already sloppy, and I felt done. As I gathered my things and said I was ready to leave, he quickly downed the drinks and said he'd walk me to my car.

Back on the street, Davis grabbed my shoulders, pulled me into him and kissed me hard. Adrenaline flooded my system. His entitlement enraged me. I don't mind public displays of affection, but *I do prefer to be asked to be kissed*. I broke away and said I had to go. Feeling unsafe with this pushy, drunk stranger, I marched off, using the "don't fuck with me" walk I had cultivated in college after I got mugged. Relieved to be back in my car, I got the heck out of there.

The next day, Davis sent a message to push a little more. "What I'm really looking for is someone to be sexual with, next to another couple. I would be willing to start off just the two of us. Why don't you come over today and we can practice?"

My hackles rose and I gave my final verdict on this date: "I'm not interested." Case dismissed.

Date #8: So Close and Yet So Tall *June 2015*

The dating pool in Portland had more fish than Eugene. James's smile in his profile pictures hooked me; it was as wide as Nebraska. At 6'4", he was way over my height limit. Since I'm barely 4'11", I tend to feel awkward simply standing next to, much less kissing, very tall people. When I mentioned the height difference, it didn't bother him, so we met up the next week when I was in Portland.

We met by a park near Portland State University. He locked his bike up and bent way down, laughing, to hug me. James had rich, ebony skin, and was legally blind; his eyes moved slowly in two different directions behind ultra-thick lenses. Because of his impaired vision, we connected straight from our hearts, and fell in easily, emotionally and intellectually. We grabbed take-out Thai nearby, and reclined lazily in the late afternoon sun. Relaxing together in the soft grass felt oddly familiar. Like old friends, we reached our chopsticks into each other's to-go containers. Lying down neutralized the height discrepancy and amplified our heart-to-heart connection. We were both from the East Coast, and a magical moment happened when we realized that we both went to Wesleyan University in overlapping years! *That was the familiarity!*

As we parted, James handed me a mixed CD, and I popped it in for my drive home. My heart expanded like James's smile, hearing the artists I had first learned about from friends in college. The sounds of that time poured in and carried me back: Norah Jones, Dave Brubeck, Anthony Braxton, Miles Davis, and others. *What a sweet, thoughtful gift.* I didn't feel a strong sexual attraction, but we definitely had a friend vibe, a really *good* friend vibe, and I hoped to stay in touch.

∽

When I left Wesleyan, Religious Studies diploma in hand, I jumped into my car with Princess, my dog/soulmate, and Gorgeous George, the sexiest black cat ever there was. We all moved to McQueeney, Texas for a year-long, hard-core pottery apprenticeship.

There, I fell in love with Thanh Binh, a beautiful, wise, and huge-hearted Vietnamese master potter. Somehow, I always knew I was heading to the Pacific Northwest, and when my apprenticeship was done, Thanh Binh and I decided to relocate to some cute little misty Northwest town. We packed up our stuff and went to get our U-Haul. When the man at the counter asked where we were heading, I brightly exclaimed "the Pacific Northwest!" That wasn't a good enough location for him. Laughing at us, he said they needed to be able to track their truck. I asked, "Do you have a map?" Honing in, we chose Eugene, which looked like the midpoint between Northern California and Seattle, and planned to explore from that central location to find our perfect little PNW town.

We made the pilgrimage to our new region with two dogs, a cat, and Thanh Binh's boa constrictor, "Teapot." The day we arrived, Eugene welcomed us with a huge double rainbow. A few days later, we visited the Saturday Market, a bustling outdoor weekly crafts venue. The artist vendors were all so welcoming; we could easily picture having a pottery booth there. A casual and charming woman selling ingenious magnesium fire starters told us about Club Mud, a well-equipped potters' co-op nearby. Rainbows appeared in the sky every day that week, and it was clear Eugene was our new home. We settled down, started a business, our relationship lasted three beautiful years, and I became "Amy the Potter."

∽

James wanted to continue exploring our connection, but it didn't feel romantically compelling for me. Soon after our date, I had an intuition that James and Isla, a beautiful Australian friend, might like each other. The three of us met at the same soft-grass park in Portland. Blushing, Isla's eyes sparkled when James beamed his big smile. I felt privileged to witness their ultra-sensory exchange. We all shared a quick lunch, and then I left the two of them to spend the afternoon together. He was an extraordinarily sincere person, and matchmaking was an ideal solution.

Isla and James wound up dating for a few months, then transitioned into close friends. Actual resonance between people can't be faked or forced, and I believe that each relationship eventually finds its own perfect equilibrium. When Isla was moving away, James and I were both invited to her small going away party. It felt warm and wonderful to all be together. I have always hoped that James finds someone special. He has a huge, golden heart. Get in touch if you think it might be you. Last I heard, he was still single!

Date #9: Leave Me Cologne *June 2015*

Boyishly attractive, Jeremy lived in Portland and was a professional photographer, which explained the high quality and great lighting in his photos. He suggested meeting at the Radio Room, a restaurant on Alberta Street, a hip part of the city. The menu online looked great—parmesan crusted brussels sprouts, salads and grilled sandwiches, and happy hour mac and cheese. I felt excited. We made a plan to have dinner when I was there for school the following week.

Approaching each other, I knew from a distance that we already had a problem: cologne. Physically, he was conventionally attractive, like a JCPenney model, with short brown hair and a toothpaste commercial smile. I thought, *I need to say something in my profile about my strong aversion to cologne.* Sitting down in a corner booth, I tried subtly leaning away, but there was no escape.

As Jeremy spoke, the end of each of his sentences was punctuated with an apologetic shrug. Each time his shoulders rose, he looked at me with "oh well" eyes. *What was he shrugging and apologizing for? The cologne?*

Other than the smell issue, I was able to be direct with Jeremy. I told him that I thought he was cute, but that his shrugging made me feel uncomfortable. Still, I found him attractive enough to suggest a kiss. We tried it right there in the restaurant booth. Holding my breath, I scooted towards him. Just like the Brussels sprouts I had ordered, the kiss was dry. As I shifted away, he asked how I liked it.

"Well ... " I said. It was now my turn to shrug.

Still with a shred of hope, I suggested we try it again on the way out. That kiss was no improvement, plus I wound up drenched in his chemical cloud. When he asked about a second date, needing an immediate out, I urged, "Let's walk away and see if there is a pull to meet again."

Phew. That line was a lifesaver. There was no pull. Jeremy's scent lingered on me for the whole two-hour car ride home. I squirmed, opened the windows, and held a rag to my nose to filter the air. I couldn't wait to get home and wash the date off me.

Too often, the menu gave a more promising impression than the meal.

Date #10: Just the Three of Us? *June 2015*

OkCupid thought Craig and I were a 97% match. He was in a relationship with a woman named Ev, and they sometimes dated together. I wondered, *could I date a couple?* In his profile pictures, he seemed like a hippie but she looked more corporate. Craig messaged enthusiastically, and although dating a couple hadn't been on my radar, I felt open to meeting them and checking it out.

I had no experience with alternatives to monogamy, and jealousy had plagued me in the past. Being welcomed into a couple seemed like a soft landing; I probably wouldn't be jealous because I would be the novel one. *But what were the chances I would be interested in both of them?* My track record so far in clicking with even one person was abysmal.

The three of us met at Cornucopia, a small, popular neighborhood pub not far from my house. I was running late and didn't change out of my tattered pottery studio clothes. I hopped off my bike feeling uber-casual, like I was meeting old friends. They saw me come in and seemed bright-spirited and excited as they waved me to their table.

Ev was a public defender, thin and sharply dressed, with short, spiky hair, angular features, and piercing eyes. She was like a dark-featured Jamie Lee Curtis, and seemed like someone who was constantly on the go. Craig, by contrast, was soft and relaxed, with round, fair features and loose, blond curls. A field biologist, he seemed earthy and natural. Wearing a T-shirt and torn jeans, he was dressed kind of like me.

I thought, *they must be authentic people, to be with someone so different.* I wondered what they had in common. We shared fries and inspired conversation. They were smart and passionate, but also attentive and gentle.

After sharing a bit about our lives, Ev advertised Craig's unique romantic capabilities. He sat shyly, smiling beneath the curls that partially covered his face. Ev explained that because of her career and independent nature, she wasn't as available as he was. Shaking her head, her eyes got bigger as she said that he had "a *lot* of love to give." *Was she pleading with me to share some of her burden?* A funny fantasy flashed through my mind of Craig running back and forth between her house and mine, fixing things, starting gardens, cleaning, giving us massages, and who knows what else that might spring from his generosity toolbox.

I was impressed by their interesting relationship. They appeared to have excellent communication, high integrity, and even "compersion"—joy in a partner's additional romances, the opposite of jealousy. Craig stole quick glances at me, while Ev acted like his personal dating manager, conducting an interview. I didn't sense any romantic intentions on her side. It seemed like Ev's role was to make me feel comfortable as a potential recipient of Craig's excess love. I felt no sparks with either of them.

Craig sent an OkCupid message later that evening: "You are way sexier in real life than your profile pictures let on." I was surprised that my uber-casual could be seen as "way sexy." He said that he was interested in dating me and that Ev was supportive. I responded, letting him know that I didn't feel romantic potential between us, but that I really enjoyed meeting them both, and that I appreciated his thoughtful, artistic email. His language was anachronistic—he used words like "behoove" and "betwixt." Craig was rugged, built like a tree, but I sensed that underneath, he was deeply emotional. Between us, there would have been too much mush.

Ev and I became Facebook friends and messaged for a while, with the intention for the three of us to become neighbor-friends. They suggested we share dinners, play board games, and snuggle, but the one time they reached out, I declined.

Was I finally becoming more radically honest?

When Craig and I crossed paths a few times in the following months, the moment he recognized me, his eyes turned sad. His shoulders slumped and his entire being seemed to get heavy. What I interpreted as him feeling rejected made me feel awkward, and this motivated me to understand the underlying nature of the dynamic.

I wondered, *what exactly is romantic chemistry?* All of my past relationships were founded on an undeniable mutual attraction that could never have been forced. Sexual and personality compatibilities were both necessary for romance. "Chemistry" implies something factual and scientific, which made me feel suspicious of Craig's, or any, one-sided attraction.

It's common to hear, "I had chemistry with so-and-so, but they didn't have chemistry with me," but this sounds illogical to me. When attraction is out of balance, it must be a psychological bias. Either it's a projection—a fantasy triggered by beauty or specific desirable traits—or a willful block against chemistry, like being monogamous and not open to outside attractions.

I rested into using this simple model of humans bonding like molecules—either strongly, weakly, or not at all, but always mutually and matter-of-factly. This newly-forming "Chemistry is Chemistry" theory, inspired by the Craig situation, helped me move forward more confidently. If romantic chemistry was objective, we could all relax and stop worrying about hurting people's feelings.

For me, dating was more than a quest for romance; it was also a place to grow my communication skills and come up with dating theories that would lead to better experiences.

The sad look in Craig's eyes helped me articulate this concept. He seemed to be focused in fantasy. But in fact, we did not have the palpable, mutual bond of true romantic chemistry.

Date #11: Struggling to Admit I'm Björed
(Told from both perspectives) July 2015

Björn was a successful, bona-fide inventor. He was older, distinguished-looking, and seemed charming. His claim to fame was that he designed an eco-friendly mechanical component for a high-end sports car. That impressed me. In his write-up, he disclosed that his photos were old. Appreciating his honesty, I felt curious and drawn to this kooky inventor. I sent a message. No reply. Then I sent another, and he responded warmly, appreciating my persistence.

We exchanged links to our YouTube videos—mine were laid-back pottery tutorials, and his were technical engineering videos. Unfortunately, when I saw him move and heard him speak, I didn't feel any attraction. I could have stopped there but rationalized that my apathy could be from the subject matter. We planned a video date. I had used video chatting with potential dates who lived far away, but none of those calls had amounted to anything. My intention was to keep these chats very short.

Wishful thinking!

With Björn, the combination of my being terrible at ending conversations and his being great at asking questions resulted in a *two-hour* date, during which I obsessively dug my fingernails between my toes and peeled the skin. By the end of the call, I was emotionally exhausted and my feet were bleeding. Björn was intelligent, but I didn't feel romantically drawn.

Why did I stay on the video call so long? Why did I say yes to an in-person date? Partly, I was just bored, and wanted to be getting a lot of action. When I looked up our astrological compatibility, it wasn't promising. We decided to meet up anyway. I could sense his sincerity and was curious about him as an inventor.

Björn had to drive an hour to see me. In person, it was verified: no chemistry. He had the clean-cut attractiveness of a weatherman, not a soulful, earthy vibration. I felt obliged to spend time with him because he had traveled to meet me. *Ugh*, I thought, as he opened the back door of his matte-grey, primed-but-not-painted, sports car for me.

Inside the vehicle, I perked up. It was a super cool inventor-modified sports car, and I had to ride in the back because the front passenger seat had been removed. Devices were mounted everywhere, and there was no internal plastic. Dashboard guts spilled out in a brilliant array, like loose brain parts, from their normally hidden places. It was the most interesting car I had ever been in, and it was the highlight of the date for me.

We went to Tacovore. Over chips and guacamole, Björn accelerated into a frenzied state, speaking quickly with dart-like hand motions and wide, alert eyes. Meanwhile, I was shutting down, fighting persistent yawns. I was probably falling asleep to escape the pain of not speaking my truth.

∽

In college, I spent a few days in silent meditation. After the retreat, I had clarity about the power of words, and attuned my speech to truth. Fearlessly, for about a week, I spoke my truth to everyone, everywhere. This spontaneous period of complete transparency resulted in a spiritual high. Soon, I reverted to a place in between, sometimes able to speak clearly and directly about my feelings, but often oppressed by my fear of hurting or losing others. I realized I was caught between hiding my truth to secure and retain relationships, and being honest, which felt so enlivening but could offend people and leave me solo.

After chips and pescado tacos, Björn suggested a walk, but I was too tired, and he drove me home. When he asked to meet again, I croaked out, "Let's walk away and see how we feel." He liked that idea. A few days later, I emailed him to say that I wasn't interested in continuing. I was grateful that he was open to sharing his side of the experience.

Björn's Perspective

I don't date much. I'd rather continue my free and content single life than complicate it with a partner, if it means anything less than an amazing relationship. I'm fortunate to have experienced a few beautiful soul connections in my life, which made me picky. Those rare bonds seem to show up in their own time and way, with a feeling of life's behind-the-scenes creativity and disregard for human plans. I prefer serendipitous meeting over checkbox-matching dating sites.

I do want to experience a special relationship again someday. Maybe a history of fairy tales has influenced my belief that finding a partner is out of my control; she will arrive when the time is right, not when I desire. When Amy persisted against my silence with a second message, I figured it was worth stepping out of my comfort zone to explore. After a few messages, we had a good video chat connection. I wished we could be together that evening, not isolated by screens. I felt curious and hopeful.

Upon meeting, I loved the unusual color and style of her house. Her artistic presence made me comfortable, and she was cute—no fake photos here. We shared a short hug (I hope in retrospect that I asked consent properly) and there came my first concern. I sensed that she might have been less than comfortable with the hug, especially for someone who had made it clear in her profile that she was interested in an intimate lover. It was my impression that she wasn't into it. Had her possible attraction suddenly dissipated upon meeting? Anyway, off we went to lunch. We shared some interesting ideas but our discussion lacked passion.

I wrote in my journal, "Amy and I connect OK, but we don't seem like kindred spirits. I feel she lives in a different universe; mine feels more rooted. My time in Eugene felt foreign in an uncomfortably overloaded way."

I felt tired on the drive home, which I've since confirmed as a not-so-great-connection sign.

As usual, when hopes are built up and let down, I felt a bit depressed. But before long, I returned to smiling at real, live strangers, which could work for dating, or for just having a happy life.

I still don't date much. One or two a year seems to be enough effort for now. Meanwhile, Amy's adventures in dating are fun to read about and I hope that she finds all she is seeking.

It was a relief to hear that we were on the same page. I was intrigued to realize that his high energy didn't signify romantic interest, and his asking for a second date didn't mean he actually wanted one. When I heard about his post-date exhaustion, I wished we had just laid it all out on the taco table. We chose to suppress our truth, instead of enriching our time with nutritious honesty.

When people had to travel to meet up, I felt pressured to have a long date. I decided to be more discerning with out-of-towners.

Bjorn and I stayed in touch through Facebook. I'm glad we met. He supported my dating experiment through enthusiastic contributions on my social media posts. We didn't drive off into the sunset together, but positive sprouts still arose from the connection.

Date #12: A Picture Tells a Thousand Lies *July 2015*

Mack's OkCupid profile photos conveyed a wild, adventurous spirit. Unfortunately, when we got together at Falling Sky Brewery, he didn't seem anything like his pictures. I had hoped to meet the guy screaming down a snowy slope in his underwear, or the one in makeup and women's clothing dancing provocatively in the streets. His features were the same, but this Mack seemed very ... normal. The discrepancy bothered me, and I wondered: *do I look like my pictures?* Of course, people use their best photos, but when the image is far from reality, I feel disappointed.

Often, at the end of a series of model-esque pictures, I would notice a single, more recent, far less attractive photo. *Grrr.* I sometimes stepped in as a vigilante dating coach and message these people: "Why don't you just post a current picture of yourself? Won't using older photos sabotage your dates?" Authenticity is way sexier than false advertising.

The discrepancy between Mack's exciting-seeming profile and in-person presence meant that after a quick cider, I was ready to go. I didn't blame Mack; this was another case of my own hopes and projections. I seemed to have great chemistry with people's *profiles*, but in the flesh, not so much. Sensing for any flicker of attraction as I walked away from Mack, there was a flatline in my wake.

I loved using the "Walk Away." It gave me physical and energetic space to feel for attraction. It was a friendly, mutually respectful way to end any date, good or bad. Even when I knew there wasn't chemistry, walking away would allow me to center myself and communicate from a distance. The Walk Away went into my back pocket as a tool for regular use.

Messaging with people online was often dissatisfying; many conversations and flirtations went nowhere. When I discovered an even mildly intriguing profile, my hopefulness engaged. But I didn't like the feeling of being in person on a date with someone I felt no attraction to. I needed a better front-end filter system and decided to request video chats more often before meeting in person.

3

PAIN AND DELIGHT

Date #13: The Cutest Masochist
(Told from both perspectives) July 2015

I felt instantly drawn to Jake when I saw him on OkCupid. Goodness emanated from his pictures and I reached out right away. He lived in Portland and seemed like a baseball and apple pie kind of guy, with thick blond hair brushed to the side, rosy cheeks, and round, childlike, blue eyes. In his profile, he shared that he had a stable career. His body looked muscular under professional, tailored suits. Through messaging, he seemed Midwestern-sweet, almost saccharine. We texted excitedly, and our well-matched communication felt oddly close and natural. But then he wrote this:

> **Jake:** There is one thing almost nobody knows about me, but I feel I need to tell you. I like to be beaten. I see a domme.

> **Amy:** Oh, cool! I have nothing against BDSM. I think it's healthy and important for people to follow and explore sexual fantasies and I'm intrigued by it myself. Plus, I'm working on developing my inner dominatrix, trying to be more direct! How often do you see her?

Jake: You are sweet. I usually go once a week. But I'm kind of extreme in this area. I like to be beaten to a *pulp*.

Amy: That sounds intense. I would love to hear more about it sometime if you want to share.

Jake: It's a big deal to even tell you. We can talk more about it if you want.

Being a therapist, I am open to people's kinks and non-mainstream behaviors, but when it came to considering Jake as a potential lover, this information worried me. *Why would someone so sweet desire such harsh treatment?* I wondered if his psychosexual world might be too extreme for me but quieted my concerns and stayed open.

On a personality level, Jake and I clicked and authentically liked each other. We had a few video dinner dates, each of us at home in our separate towns. After a couple of weeks, we decided to meet up for coffee at Ken's Artisan Bakery in northwest Portland, near my school, Process Work Institute. As we relaxed into our seats, I imagined his trillions of cells all smiling at me. Our eyes danced and lingered over each other's bodies, and our fingers touched easily as we sipped our lattes. Eventually, we licked the sweet, decadent breakfast crumbs from our fingers, cleaned up, and headed out. He extended an inviting hand which I enthusiastically grabbed. Strolling off into the cool morning mist, the world felt new as we walked hand in hand through clouds that hugged the city streets. We ducked into a vintage shop and I tried on a flowy, lacy, off-white dress; he loved it, and I bought it.

Our final stop was at a city park nearby. Straddling a damp bench, we faced each other and let the Oregon mist fall slowly upon us. We were like lovers in a snow globe. Individual droplets clung like jewels to his lashes, which made him seem soft and feminine. I asked him to kiss. Our lips found each other perfectly and we moved closer. *Oh, to kiss!* It felt delicious. When I looked down at his crotch, his strong erection was pressing through tight jeans. A wave of scintillation flushed through my core. I placed my hand on his cock and spent a moment of eye contact soaking him in.

The date in the cloud was sexy and romantic, and we agreed to meet again. I was really attracted to him and felt excited about our potential.

I always asked Joanne, my trusted psychic, about any promising dates, so the next time I went to see her, we talked about Jake. I felt deflated when she firmly shook her head and said that he had serious psychological processing to do. Trying to bargain, I asked about us having a therapeutic sexual relationship. Joanne said that I was *not* supposed to be the one to support him, that he needed a therapist, and I needed a lover, and I shouldn't try to be both.

After that session, I was conflicted. She was so insistent, and I trusted her. I felt guilty for switching gears and abandoning Jake when we had both been excited about what could be between us. *What to do?* I called him to cancel and explained how Joanne said the only way our connection could work was if he stopped seeing his domme and started psychotherapy. Requesting such a huge personal transition seemed like way too much to ask after just one date.

Jake said he understood, and that he was going to consider whether he wanted to let go of his masochistic relationship. Mutually, regretfully, we decided to back off and let the connection fade.

Jake's Perspective

At the time I met Amy, I was in the process of ending a 16-year marriage and my life was very unsettled. I was unhappy with my job and battling depression. I wasn't in a good position to date and had lots of reservations. Despite all that, I was in need of connection and decided to give dating a try.

Amy was the first, and only, person I met on OkCupid. She was very friendly, and I was enchanted with her smile and her enthusiasm for life. I really enjoyed our first date at a coffee shop. Amy was so open and approachable, and I felt completely comfortable. Afterwards, we walked to a nearby park and sat on a bench, where she asked me if I wanted to kiss. I was surprised by her invitation, not because I didn't want to, but it's just not something I would have initiated myself on a first date. As we kissed, I felt a strong connection to her. When we parted ways, I was hopeful that we would go out again.

We kept in contact through video and text messaging. I felt our relationship deepening. We exchanged a few racy pictures, and I was looking forward to seeing her again. Shortly before our second date, however, Amy told me that her psychic had said that I was not a good match for her because of the instability in my life. I was hurt and disappointed, but also knew that my life was messy. While my heart ached, my head told me she was making the best decision. As it turned out, my life spiraled downhill over the next year and I would not have been able to be the partner Amy deserved.

Oh yeah—the domme: I think I shared too much with Amy too soon, but she was so easy to talk to and I didn't want to mislead her about my situation. The truth was that I wanted out of the domme relationship but was afraid to let go if that meant being alone. Anyway, more than two years and a ton of therapy later, things are going well for me. No more domme, and I'm dating again, seeking healthier relationships.

My only regret is that I wasn't in a position to get that second date. If I get another chance, you can bet I'll take it.

Date #14: Midnight Coffee? *July 2015*

Sometimes the people Facebook suggests I might know are stunningly attractive! That was the case with Dan the Riverman. In his main profile picture, he was on a boat, shirtless and burningly sexy, beaming a supremely life-loving grin. He reminded me of Aragorn from *Lord of the Rings*. When I saw that we had a lot of friends in common, I sent a friend request and message right away.

I started by asking about his rafting business, but soon came clean:

> **Amy:** I have a confession. When FB suggested you as my friend, I thought "God, he is gorgeous! I should go out on the river with him." I mean, I *do* want to go for a float, but ....
>
> **Dan:** Sounds like we're going to have lots of fun 😊
>
> **Amy:** Great! First, I should let you know what I'm looking for. I'm hoping to find a lover for a soulful, romantic, sexual connection without commitment or expectations. I'm so ready for excitement, fun, and passion. I'm even open to falling in love as long as it doesn't lead to sexual exclusivity. I spent my last decade in a monogamous relationship and I'm ready for a change!

Over the next three months, we messaged on and off. Casting my line for Dan the Riverman, I invited him to go out a few times, but he was always busy. One day, he spontaneously invited me to coffee at midnight. I was tempted, but chose not to go, prioritizing self-care because I had to wake up early the next day.

After a period of not hearing from him, preferring closure to letting our communications fade awkwardly away, I sent him a message saying I felt we should let it go. He responded right away to explain that he had recently become serious with someone. We "peaced out" warmly. The next year, when I was politically involved in the 2016 primaries, Dan and I reconnected. He messaged me with lots of election-based questions, and always commented on my enthusiastic Facebook posts.

One day, I was stranded with a dead car and pleaded to the world for help, via Facebook. Dan generously offered a ride, but by the time he responded, I no longer needed it.

In 2018, I finally went for that float with Dan. I organized a small group of friends; we planned to meet at the river, but since my house was on his way, Dan offered to pick me up. It felt exciting and a little mythic to jump into his truck in the wee hours for our first in-person meeting. I couldn't help feeling romantic, driving with this attractive man through the early morning Willamette Valley mist. As we wound along the McKenzie River, I learned that when we were first flirting, the woman he was seeing got pregnant immediately. They married, and he had a vasectomy. Smiling, Dan passed his phone over to show me the *action shots* of the medical procedure! I appreciated his freedom to share such vulnerable pictures—which, of course, included his penis. I loved his open nature.

On the river, Dan was in his element. Joyful and luminescent, he seemed larger than life, and I felt enamored. I considered asking how monogamous his marriage was, but though I longed to connect with him, I knew I wouldn't be able to enjoy partying with him while his wife was home caring for their toddler.

I took midnight coffee off the table but regretted missing that boat. We had the chemistry I sought, and I couldn't help wondering what would have happened if I had said yes to him years ago. I trusted that there would be more coffee, and more rivers.

Date #15: Consent Lament *August 2015*

Once Ivan and I matched online, he kept texting me, pushing to meet. He emanated extreme confidence. With a large, shaved head and the attractive, strong bone structure of an athlete, he reminded me of a younger Mr. Clean. Feeling pressured, I told him I needed a video chat before meeting in person. Even for scheduling a video date, I kept moving my availability back. After I postponed a few times, he sent an ultimatum, "Meet me soon on video, or lose me." Amused, I decided to give him a chance.

On the call, I was happily surprised to feel attracted. Ivan had a football player body but the refinement of someone raised in royalty. He oozed charisma, with impressive forwardness—I too strived to be more direct—but it also intimidated me. When he invited me to his house the next day, I hesitantly said yes. He lived in a familiar neighborhood, right around the corner from my best friend's house. Jess knew everything about my life, especially my dating schedule. The idea of being close to her gave me comfort: a nearby escape, if needed. Preferring to envision a positive experience, I repressed those thoughts.

In person, at first, I felt relaxed with him. It was a hot summer afternoon, and we sat on his back porch like old friends, drinking chilled pinot gris. Once our glasses were emptied, he invited me inside. He led me down a narrow staircase to a small, crowded storage area to show me his bicycles. That seemed odd. I have no special interest in bikes and wasn't sure what I was supposed to be looking at. Wobbly from the alcohol, claustrophobic, and uncertain as to why we were down there, I wondered, *am I safe?* Caution about my well-being returned.

I led the way back up and felt Ivan close on my heels. When we arrived on the landing, he stepped up to me and started touching my face and arms. I did not want to have sex with him, and knew I had to set some boundaries. But when he came even closer and started kissing my neck and ears, I felt weak. I said, "I'm not going to have sex with you." But he was busy with his intricate approach to my sensitive jugular area and didn't respond. I realized I was giving him mixed signals, saying I didn't want to have sex as I squirmed and laughed and moaned from his expert affection. It reminded me of being tickled as a child; I didn't like it, but my response made it seem like I did. I never learned to set boundaries or even speak up about touch I didn't like, and instead suffered silently through whatever happened to my body. Ivan selectively listened to the part of me that was responding to his touch more than the part that was saying "No."

Everything was moving too fast. I was getting turned on but was unsure and felt rushed and overwhelmed. The combination of pinot gris and hormones completely scrambled my frontal lobe. Ivan was whispering "come on," and we both ignored my inner conflict as he picked me up and carried me to his bedroom. In an instant, my clothes were off. Confused, I felt the wine move through my vulnerable breasts. Tingling with desire, they gave in, reaching towards his hungry mouth.

Somewhere in the middle of all this, he said, "I had a vasectomy; you're not going to get pregnant. Also, I have herpes type 2, but I take so much medicine for it that there is no way you'd ever catch it from me." His body was heavy with muscles and the next thing I knew, he was going down on me. I moaned loudly as jolts of confusion mixed with incredible sensation had me writhing around his king-size bed. Then suddenly, his incredibly large, condomless penis was inside me. I was twisted up inside. It didn't feel right and yet I was going for it, climbing all over him, and matching his primal energy. I felt like someone else, with a shiny, sweaty, acrobatic sex body. Not knowing exactly what I wanted, I succumbed to the part of me that craved sexual abandon. The silent and marginalized part of me cowered inside—a scared little girl who wasn't ready for Ivan's huge cock, his supposedly innocuous sexually transmitted infection, and his missing feedback loop.

I don't remember how it ended, but walking down his driveway, out into the night, I felt like a person who had been riding horseback too long. Shaking, I was lost in emotional and physical pain. Feeling deep shame as I hobbled off, I wondered who I was, and why I had just done what I did.

Afterwards, I couldn't stop turning the experience over in my mind. *Was it rape? Why did I trust him about the herpes? Why didn't I at least require a condom? And, most of all, when I said out loud that I didn't want to have sex with him, why didn't either of us listen?*

Perhaps the worst part was the gnawing feeling that I was complicit. I couldn't blame it all on him, although I do believe he raped me. But at any point, I could have spoken up or walked out to prevent the experience, and I didn't. I felt angry with both of us. The day after our date, I called Ivan to let him know how I experienced our time together.

"Hey, I just wanted to talk about last night."

"Great," he said, "what's up?"

"I'm upset that you pushed the experience forward even when I said clearly that I didn't want to have sex."

"I never heard you say that. When did you say that?"

"When you started kissing my neck."

"Oh, wow. I'm deaf in one ear. I guess I just missed it. I thought we had a great time. I was hoping you were reaching out to plan our next date."

On the phone, I felt strangely at ease with him, and drawn to him. Against my better judgment, I softened and decided that we should give it one more try, but this time we would do it *my way*.

(I hope you, like a horror movie watcher, are screaming "Don't do it, Amy! Don't go down those dark stairs!")

My rationale was that being with him again would allow me an opportunity to use stronger communication, and fearlessly state my clear "No." Obviously, my direct honesty muscles needed way more practice. We made a plan to meet at the local cafe the next day. But when the time came, I didn't want to go. I messaged him to say that I was feeling ambivalent. He said he felt the same, and we let it go.

But my vagina did *not* let it go. Pain and burning continued for a long week. Kneeling at the altar of my symptom, I tuned in to the sensation. Bodies have an amazing ability to guide us to grow. My pain poked me sharply. I visualized the pain and imagined a larger-than-life tough love angel telling me to honor my self-protective signals above everything else. Above charisma and my response to it, above neck kissing, above external and internal pressures, and above the sexually free self-image that I preferred.

The moral of this date was completely clear: in the future, *all* parts of me had to consent if I was going to have intercourse. I couldn't afford to ignore hesitation—my physical and psychological health depended on it.

I wished men in general were more sensitive about their impact. Moving forward, I wanted to steer myself towards soulful, connected, conscious sex.

Up-*Dating* My OkCupid Profile

I needed to start calling in what I really wanted. Dating lightly was landing me in situations that weren't fun. Sexually sporty was just not me. I tweaked parts of my OkCupid profile:

About Me:
I'm a professional potter, a dancer, a writer, a coach, a therapist. I'm interested in personal evolution and seek connections that will help me grow.

I often don't respond to messages when I don't sense potential. If you would prefer a response either way, please say so.

If you have a backlog of psychological issues that need processing, and you aren't actively working on that, it probably won't work out between us.

You should message me if:
You are a deep soul, intelligent, and wise. You have a huge heart and you are passionate.

I am looking for truly amazing human beings for spectacularly deep connections with strong chemistry, mutual respect, and excellent communication. I am interested in spiritually-based connections with pristine awareness, and long for freedom to explore the depth and magic of sexual, romantic intimacy.

I believe every relationship, with the right balance of respect, trust, and freedom, simply and organically finds its natural equilibrium.

Date #16: His Train, My Tunnel *August 2015*

One summer evening, looking through Facebook's "suggested friends," I was struck by Cyrus's picture. I thought he was the most handsome man I had ever seen. He had a trimmed beard, contemplative eyes, and shoulder-length, wavy brown hair. Cyrus looked different in every one of his breathtaking pictures—sometimes deep and mysterious, sometimes light and goofy. I messaged him, pretending he looked familiar, and struck up a "do we know each other?" conversation. He actually recognized me from my Holiday Market pottery booth, where he had once bought a mug. Sheepishly, I admitted that I was reaching out to him because I thought he was gorgeous.

After I typed the "I'm attracted to you" bomb, his messaging silence seemed to last forever. Finally, minutes later, he replied, "Wow, thanks." Suddenly shy, I sent a blushing smile emoji, and closed my laptop. I felt embarrassed about boldly revealing my attraction, but it also felt good to speak so openly. Our message thread stayed silent for the next few weeks.

I mentioned him the next time I visited Joanne. She is so expressive and funny when she does psychic readings. Addressing Cyrus's higher self to see if he was available, her eyes grew big and buggy. She pointed a huge finger right at my heart and, moving her head like a Muppet, said, "For YOU, I am!" This emboldened me with optimism, so I sent him another message:

Amy: This might sound strange, but I feel drawn to connect with you. If you ever want to grab a coffee or go for a walk, I would love to do that. If not, no worries!

Cyrus: Yes, we could do that! I'll likely have some time in the next few weeks. Whatever we do will be perfect.

He said yes! The next time I saw Joanne, I swooned, "Maybe I'll fall in love with Cyrus." We messaged sporadically for a few months, and my image of him as a hunky, soap opera-esque, dreamboat solidified. Because he lived outside of Eugene and traveled a lot, meeting up wasn't simple. In November, after four months, our stars finally aligned and we made a dinner plan.

Cyrus picked me up in an old clunky station wagon and we went to Tacovore, in the Whit neighborhood. In person, he looked cutely nerdy, not drop-dead gorgeous. He was skinny and dressed in plaid. As we waited in line to order, he wiggled around and was jumpy and chatty. I had imagined an earthy, deep, slow-moving soul. But like a pot that comes out of the kiln different than I'd hoped, on second glance, he had his own special charm.

We sat down at a table that hadn't been bussed, and he immediately and unapologetically dove into the chips and guac left by the people who had warmed our seats. I felt drawn to his quirky freedom. I loved that he yawned hugely. As we ate and talked, our feet touched under the table, having their own private conversation. After we devoured the fish tacos, he pushed our plates aside and extended his hands, inviting mine. This intimate gesture surprised me. By the time we were ready to leave, I was enchanted.

We walked out of the restaurant and our hands slipped naturally into each other's. Adventuring through the dark neighborhood, we inspected piles of construction materials haphazardly leaning against buildings. Then we found and jumped on a thick metal gas station ramp that vibrated through to our bones. The Whit was our funhouse. Cyrus's spirit was so bright and young. Wrapping a lanky arm around my shoulder, he casually reeled me in as we wandered down to the tracks. When a train passed, he explained what the different types of cars carried, and which ones were appropriate for train hopping. Leaning into him and talking about trains in the cool evening on a first date felt romantic. We imagined hopping on one together, right there and then.

It was almost midnight when we arrived back at my house. He parked the old station wagon, turned off the ignition, and looked at me, grinning. I asked if he wanted to kiss. Our lips softened into each other and we made sweet "mmm" sounds, giggling as we made out. Soon, his hand wrapped around my ribs, stimulating a gyrating, dynamic, kiss-dance. Cyrus cradled the back of my head and moaned. I undulated with desire. He was ramping up, and I felt conflicted. It was already late. I was leaving town early the next morning but yearned to play with him in my bed. Needing help, I decided to consult the I Ching on my phone. It's best to use yes or no questions; I spoke each word out loud as I typed, "Should Cyrus come inside?" We considered the results: hexagram 60, "Limitation." My interpretation: it was unwise to rush a first sexual experience; better to set a limit or boundary.

Saying no, even when I felt Cyrus's eagerness, felt like a success. Though I felt bad that he had a long drive home, I chose what was right for myself instead of being accommodating. *Progress!*

I texted him the next day to say I'd had a good time and hoped to see him again after my trip. When I returned, we texted:

Amy: Cyrus, I hear the trains! I'm thinking of you.

Cyrus: I was just thinking about putting my train in your tunnel! Now, I'm the one out of town.

Amy: Take care of your beautiful self and let me know when you're back!

He was gone for two months. We texted emojis a few times, but no substantial messages. When he was headed back to town, he reached out. I happened to be driving north to Portland while he was driving south to Eugene. Knowing that we would pass at some point on the I-5 highway, we were competitively calculating the moment. The feeling was pressured and momentous as we approached each other, like the intensity of subway cars passing. Cyrus thought he saw me whirr by. I searched for him in my rear-view mirror, but that train was gone.

We weren't really a match. I fantasized about falling in love with the romantic, earthy boy I saw in the Facebook pictures, but in person he was more quirky and intellectual. He wound up moving away from Eugene, so we never did have that second date. But when I hear the trains, I still think of Cyrus.

Date #17: Up in Smoke *August 2015*

Mikey had fleck-filled, striking royal blue eyes, and black hair pushed off to the side. In most of his profile pictures, he was reclining in "come get me" poses. I felt immediately engaged. He looked like a college lover of mine who had a dreaminess that disarmed me.

When we matched, we got right to it. I voice texted him from my car at a red light, letting him know how wet I was getting (!) from chatting with him, and he told me how hard he was (!). That was our communication style in a nutshell. Like my connection with phone-in-the-toilet-bowl Jackson, it was all about sex. In the following weeks, I sent Mikey more and more risqué pictures. He, in return, sent pictures of himself sprawled out naked in the morning sun and even *videos* of him *masturbating*. Having grown up in the eighties, I had no experience navigating this. Watching his personalized pornography, I felt a combination of embarrassment and awe as he exposed his most primal self.

Apparently, Mikey smoked pot all day, every day. On our video chats, the striking blue eyes from his profile pictures were instead slitty and red. He steadily nursed on joints, and said he used it to medicate low self-esteem. Because of the excessive nature of his addiction, my boundaries were up to maintain emotional distance, and to prevent myself from falling into the role of his therapist. He wanted to meet in person, but I needed distance between us and wasn't interested in a real-time connection. Also, Mikey's speech idiosyncrasies were eerily identical to a close, platonic male friend of mine from college. While we were being video-sexual, I would sometimes hit "mute" because hearing my old stoner friend's voice killed the sexy vibe.

I loved the perks of video sex: being as sexual and as promiscuous as you want with no worries about STIs (sexually transmitted infections), pregnancy, condoms, or other people's smells, hygiene, or body fluids. It was clean and simple.

Mikey liked to text me his sexual fantasies. I loved to receive them, and sent my own back. *I was actually "sexting!" And liking it!* Sexting filtered out some of the parts that didn't work, especially his voice. It was a creative way for us to channel our desires and felt just right with Mikey. Our flirty friendship continued for about two months ... until suddenly one day, Mikey disappeared.

I never found out what happened. *Did he feel like I was using him, taking what worked for me but blocking more connection?* We were in regular touch, daily, and then nothing. I sent a few unanswered messages wondering where he went.

Up in a puff of smoke, I guess.

Date #18: The Best Kiss of My Life? *August 2015*

Jonah's first profile picture stared straight into my soul. He was twelve years younger than me, with a shaved head, a five o'clock shadow, and full, pursed lips. Without a smile in any of his photos, he seemed deep and complex. I drank in every lyrical word in his self-description: artist, musician, meditator, wanderer, healer. He concluded his love quest description with a quote from Pablo Neruda, "I want to do with you what spring does with the cherry trees." Something deep inside me leaned towards Jonah.

He lived an hour away from me. Since I drove through Salem each week on my commute to Portland, I thought it would be easy to meet. In his profile, he apologized in advance for having very little free time. As we began to communicate sporadically, his soft-edged notes slipped straight into my heart.

When I asked Joanne about him, her crystal blue eyes expanded with childlike excitement. She said, emphatically, that Jonah was a match for me intellectually, psychologically, and physically, and that we could have a gratifying, deep connection. She was certain that he had the most potential of anyone I had come across thus far.

Because of her confident assessment, I didn't write Jonah off when he didn't text or call. Even though I hadn't seen him on video, I had a strong feeling about him. After a month of sparse texting, we finally had our first date at Teote, a brightly-colored, popular Venezuelan restaurant in southeast Portland. I was on edge, feeling like this could be a fated connection, and flushed with joy when I saw him in an adorable tweed cap. His smile was shy as he greeted me with soft, vulnerable eyes. We hugged hello, his strong arms wrapped around me for the first time. I felt thrilled when he suggested that we share entrees. We chose food together easily at the walk-up counter. Jonah offered to pay and I gratefully accepted.

After ordering, we scrambled up a narrow, winding staircase through the bustling restaurant, found a spot amidst the sea of Portland hipsters, and perched across from each other at a small table. Jonah's voice was tender and he spoke slowly. His boyish innocence combined with piercing acuity was intoxicating. Volumes were communicated with each sentence. Jonah explained that he had trained his body and mind, through years of discipline and attention, to remain blank and open. His spine seemed to float vertically, unhindered by gravity. Since I am chameleon-like by nature, being near him was like being him, which was highly energizing. He made my mind and spirit jump and buzz. At times, Jonah giggled sweetly, his laugh trailing off and revealing a sad undertone. I love men's arms and couldn't stop looking at his resting on the table. They were thick and sinewy, with the finest sprouts of curly, golden hair.

Our big bowl of deliciousness arrived: spicy, rich Venezuelan black bean stew loaded with rice, plantains, queso fresco, and topped with avocado, cilantro, and sour cream. Digging our spoons in, we hungrily leaned towards the food and each other. He spoke sensitively about his love for his five-year-old son. I felt enchanted with his monk-like, responsive, and alert nature.

Pushing our empty bowls aside, I asked if I could touch his arms. He nodded. Resting my hands on them, I felt his muscles vibrating with an ancient aliveness.

When I opened my eyes, he sweetly asked if I'd like to go for a walk, and off we went. We held hands and strolled through the evening, buoyant. My legs felt like they were kicking around freely below me. Eventually, I looked up and said, "I'm ready to kiss whenever you are." Jonah paused, smiled, and brought his lips to mine. Standing in the middle of the sidewalk in some Portland neighborhood, we kissed and kissed in an ever-changing, expressive poem that spiraled through every emotion. Jonah was playful, then serious, then animalistic, then sensitive and romantic. We kept breaking away and going back into it. Each time, I felt like I was surfacing from an underwater fantasy world, unsure what would happen the next time we submerged. My whole being was beaming, uncontained, as he walked me to my car. After a final, sweet embrace, I dropped into my seat. In a dreamy, ecstatic state, I watched him float away. It was absolutely magical, the very best kiss of my life.

When I messaged Jonah the next day and in the weeks after, he was mostly unresponsive. I made up stories in my head, *he must have fallen in love with someone, or maybe he thinks I'm annoying and needy.*

After a month passed with only a few curt responses, I felt I had nothing to lose by communicating from my heart and emailed him the blog entry about our date and a poem I'd written about our first kiss. I was thrilled when he wrote back right away:

> "The things you notice tell me much more about who you are and make me appreciate you in all the little ways. It was a lovely and magical time we shared and your quality of presence is profound and intimate. You are my favorite kind of strange and beautiful.
>
> My emotional lack of availability has been coming from a place of deep hurt, perhaps a result of intense inward examination, more than any significant external factors. Simply put, I'm going through something. As for resurfacing: it is inevitable. But for the moment, I'm unreliable."

I emailed him back, saying that I could be patient for a thousand years, and that I was so happy to hear from him that I was crying. Jonah said he wanted to connect but was headed off for ten days of Zen meditation. I teased him about the contrast between our ideas of a good time. My proposal was traveling together to Maui for late night stargazing and skinny-dipping, eating mangoes and fresh fish, and rolling around, kissing on a beach. That seemed much better than his choice of (literally) sitting in a cold room with no socks or jacket, eating watery gruel and getting hit with a stick. When he didn't get in touch when the ten days were over, I sent this message:

> "Jonah, I have strong feelings for you, but in reality, not much has happened between us. I don't want to put pressure on you, or me, but I want you to know that you are my first choice, my favorite, of all the people I've been dating."

After a few excruciating days, he responded, sweetly apologetic. We chatted a bit, and then he disappeared again. This became an ongoing pattern. I did my best to stay optimistic about our connection, but it wasn't easy. Although his sporadic messages were always warm, they were painfully rare, and almost always dropped off without a goodbye. I spent a lot of mental and emotional energy trying to figure out how to get his attention without scaring him away. Nothing seemed to be working, but I was enamored, determined, *hooked* ....

... to be continued ...

4

LONG DAYS OF LONGING

Dates #19 & #20: Too Bad You're Not Jonah *September 2015*

When Jonah showed up, deep harmonic strings inside me resonated. Light dating was fun and helped with my communication skills, but ultimately I wanted to find heart and soul connections and transformational sexual relationships that would usher me into other dimensions.

Jonah's elusiveness was disturbingly, addictively, gnawing. I strategized when and how I should reach out to him. My longing for Jonah left me uninspired about others, but it felt important to keep dating so I wasn't just waiting around for him. I decided to return to the online pool with higher standards. I wanted more good dates, and fewer tedious ones.

∽

Christopher emanated a deer-like quality. Soft, round edges and tear-shaped eyes made him seem harmless. We texted like old friends. I felt certain that we would get along.

We met at Tacovore (yes, dating for me meant a whole lotta tacos!) and were comfortable with each other from the start. He was the perfect height for me, with curvy muscles covered in tattoos of sacred geometry. As we began getting to know each other, his rich, heavily lashed brown eyes were mesmerizing. I felt compelled to flirt out loud, "You're so nice to look at. You have incredibly beautiful eyes." He mirrored my compliment, and we indulged in extended moments of eye contact.

The loaded pescado tacos were divine, and a margarita loosened me up, but our conversation lacked passion and flow. Also, he had two young children, which gave me pause. I know what it takes to parent.

When we finished our dinner, I said, "At the end of a date, I like to do something I call 'The Walk Away.' We separate, and then see if we feel drawn to get together again." Christopher thought it sounded great. I added, "Also, if you want, I'm open to kissing to feel for the chemistry."

"Sure!" Christopher responded as he grabbed the check, adding with a wink, "You can pay for our *next* date." His assumption of a second date irritated me, especially after I'd just suggested the Walk Away. I didn't say anything, felt low inside, and the date lost steam. In the parking lot, I noticed the cigarettes in his back pocket, and my attraction meter plummeted further. There was an industrial rubber smell in the air, and we had an OK kiss on the dirty sidewalk. Numbness filled me as I drove away; there wouldn't be a second date with Christopher. *Was my bar set impossibly high? Would anyone compare to Jonah?*

∼

A few days later, I met "Jeff-in-a-Box" (his profile username) in the sunny outdoor courtyard at Hideaway Bakery, the best breakfast, lunch, and coffee spot in South Eugene. Jeff was attractive in his pictures, but just a regular dude in person. In the first five seconds, I knew that I had no interest in being intimate with him. My inflated assumptions about people continually surprised me. I was almost always wrong and wound up having to immediately reconcile the discrepancy between my projection and reality. As Jeff and I sat down, I wished I could wind myself up and pop out of the box. I didn't want to be there, although sitting outside at my favorite bakery wasn't as bad as suffocating with German Tim.

What should I do when I'm on a date and not interested? In my ideal world, I would come right out with the boldness of my friend Stacy, and say something like, "I don't feel as attracted to you as I had hoped." She had recently tried to coach me, "Schedule ten-minute dates. If you like them, go have sex. If not, say thanks but no thanks." It seemed so raw and unlike me. *Could I be so blunt?*

The part of me that was done with the date crouched in the box, as I fished for things to talk about. I asked myself, *could I be attracted somehow?* I didn't think so. Jeff had no trouble pulling answers out of his box. On dates, the longer I lingered without speaking my truth, the more awkward and painful the time was. At the end of the hour, when Jeff asked if I wanted to get together again, I came through, and said, "It's been nice to meet you, but I don't think we're a match." My voice was definitely shaking, and my eyes were probably apologizing, but I said it, without even offering my handy "Walk Away."

As I left, I wondered, *why did I have an overly long coffee date with Mr. I'm-In-A-Box, when I'm really longing to smell the cherry blossoms with Mr. Where-Are-You?*

Where am I? was a better question.

A bit lost was the honest answer.

Date #21: Mental Shaving *September 2015*

Eric didn't live in Eugene, so we started with a video date. As soon as I saw him, I felt overwhelmed. His huge beard had only appeared in some of his profile pictures, and I was hoping it was an older look, but instead it had grown larger, big enough to occupy a large portion of his face and the screen.

Hipster beards are widespread in the Pacific Northwest, but not attractive to me, especially the huge ones that are the size of an extra head. I can't stop staring at them, looking for things. They remind me of nests, but on faces. When I imagine kissing someone with a big, fluffy beard, I feel squirmy imagining all the food and body fluids that must be lurking. *Where would it touch me? On my neck, my chest?* Like my cologne aversion, I feel embarrassed to say anything, not wanting to be critical, because it feels personal.

There was a sweet demeanor beneath all that fuzz. Eric lived in a woodsy area south of Portland. A person's home says a lot to me about who they are, and I was drawn to Eric's abode. His beautiful kitchen was in the background of the video; it looked earthy and herby, with rustic wooden cabinets and ceiling-high rows of mason jars filled with dried and preserved foods. I had some video dates where the chaotic dorm-room style ambiance was enough for me to lose interest. Eric obviously took good care of his space, and himself.

He was a self-employed jeweler with a thriving business. His questions about my passions were sensitive and thoughtful. With composure, he paused and closed his eyes to carefully consider his responses to my questions. Eric was like hot fudge, with a sexy baritone voice and eyes that stared steadily through the computer screen ... though mine wouldn't stop jumping around. I enjoyed so much about him but kept compulsively shaving the hairy mass in my mind. *Yes, much better without the beard!*

During our call, I was tearing at my feet, pulling off chunks of skin, like I did on my video date with Björn. This time, I dug so deeply that I could barely walk by the end of the call. As we were saying goodbye, Eric invited me to visit him in Portland. I gave him my spiel about chemistry, how I like to walk away and feel if there's a pull to reconnect. Looking down at my mangled feet, I was pretty sure my answer would be no.

That night, I dreamed that Eric was a fun, martial arts, hippie superhero-cop, and I was his buddy. We were sprinting around, bustin' the baddest guys in the Whit. I woke up and thought, *maybe Eric is hot, after all!* But when he reached out again, I just couldn't. I know it was shallow, but in the end, I felt like I dodged a beard.

Date #22: Too Much is Not Enough *September 2015*

Ethan's opening line had gusto: "I am *definitely* attracted to you." Even though he lived in New Mexico, the attention felt good, and I was flattered enough to write back. I thought he was sort of attractive in his pictures, but surprisingly handsome on video. He had thick, curly, silver hair and a distinguished, strong face. With his head held high, he spoke with bold confidence. Talking was easy; he was familiar and charismatic. I felt like I could say anything to him. But as the video date progressed, he became more and more forward, leaning into the screen with wide, hungry eyes and increasingly overt sexual questions. My profile said that I was seeking powerful sexual connections, and many cursory readers interpreted that to mean that I wanted to be sexual with just about anyone.

He spoke as though there was a private joke between us. His booming voice and big face seemed like they were constantly amplifying, pressing towards me like an impatient erection. His overly active, flirtatious eyebrows twitched wildly when he asked what I liked, and how often. He professed to be fluid and open but was steering the conversation towards the topic of sex from the get-go and ignored the fact that I wasn't enjoying it. I felt confronted by his presumptuousness and spoke intensely to him. I challenged the things he said, and the way he was speaking. "You are moving way faster than me. I feel pressured by you." These were unusual things for me to say so openly. Then he started gushing about his ubersexual, multi-orgasmic ex-girlfriend, and I shut down.

I had recently lost stoner Mikey as a video sex buddy and was hoping to find a new video sex friend. If Ethan wasn't so pushy, he might have been a candidate for sexting or video sex. But we were like repelling magnets—when he pushed, I could only push back. Also, like me, Ethan was Jewish, and I had never dated a Jewish man. I generally experienced Jewish men more like brothers or cousins than lovers, and it felt incestuous to imagine being intimate with them. I wondered, *was I was able to be assertive with him because he was Jewish, and felt like family?* Or was it just because he was so over the top?

When Ethan leaned the side of his enormous face towards the camera, winked a huge eye, and said, "How about we drop our pants and get to it," I took a deep breath and looked straight at him. "Ethan, I'm shutting down because of your pushing. I'm not ready for video sex with you." This call was a workout for my honesty muscles. Like a good day at the gym, I felt invigorated from being direct.

Undeterred, his eyebrows rose to the top of his forehead as he said, "How about a little sexting instead?" I was ready to be away from his big video-face, and said I was open to trying it. We ended the call and he quickly initiated sexting like a teenage boy with testosterone overload. I imagined him breathlessly yanking hard at his cock on the other end. He texted, "Do you like to be fucked HARD?" *What should I say to that?* I replied "LOL ... Sometimes?" Feeling done, I ended the messaging, saying I was tired and needed to go to sleep. His style was aggro, and not sexy to me. When I woke up the next morning, I texted him:

> **Amy:** I don't think this connection is right for me. Your style of fantasy doesn't feel like mine. I'm sure there are plenty of people out there who would be happy to do that with you. But not me.
>
> **Ethan:** Thanks for letting me know.

This was a dating dojo test, and I felt both exasperated from being forced to set boundaries and energized from speaking directly. My desire for more intimacy in sexuality grew stronger; I longed for sensitivity and authenticity.

Date #23: Rawr *October 2015*

Leo lived an hour away. His OkCupid profile hooked me: soft, black, curly hair framed his smiling face. In one picture, a bunch of kids were climbing all over him. In the next, he was dressed up at Burning Man (a wild, artistic community event held annually in Nevada). He was a doctor, *swoon*. I e-fell for this exotic, god-like fish I had found in the wide, dark sea of online dating.

Our initial messages brought me part way down to earth. Between his busy career, our extreme height difference (he was over six feet), and his marriage that was just ending, he became slightly less perfect. Leo was still living with his three young children and soon-to-be-ex and admitted that he had reservations about dating so soon because he was sensitive about hurting his wife. I appreciated that and corralled my pursuit.

Fantasies about a colorful future with Leo continued to marinate, and my heart softened when his sweet messages arrived, weekly, in our OkCupid thread. Because he was warm in our infrequent interactions, I stuck around, followed his snail's pace, and hoped that by going slowly, I might be able to reel this rare creature in.

After a few months, he messaged, ready to get together. We made a plan to meet up, but strangely, I felt overwhelmed. Tall, beautiful people feel like a different species, and when I'm near them, I feel nervous. *How to conduct myself on a date with a god?* A few days later, Leo canceled, which left me feeling both relief and disappointment. Maybe we both just needed more time.

He accepted my Facebook friend request, but he wasn't very active there. I sent a few unanswered messages and then let it go. Almost a year later, Leo surprised me when he showed up at my pottery booth with a tall, blonde new girlfriend. I broke into a sweat while we all made small talk and felt relieved when they walked away. He came back, alone, a little later, to say hello. Hugging the lower half of his sweater was, as predicted, immensely awkward. He was way too tall for me.

Facebook was as close as I was going to get to that fear-inspiring lion! On social media, we're all the same size.

Date #24: Pleather Together *October 2015*

Claud was married, polyamorous, and lived in Portland. My vision was to eventually find both an occasional, probably weekly, lover and also a more stable, committed partner. Logistically, I imagined either local or single people to fit these roles. Because Claud was neither, I hadn't given our upcoming video date much thought. I was semi-attracted to him in his pictures, but by this point I knew not to count on that.

I decided to work in my pottery studio while we talked, as I had often felt stuck wasting time on video chats. My first impression of Claud was that he was unassuming. I felt at ease with him. He had a friendly, expressive face. My enjoyment increased steadily throughout our conversation. It was touching to see him squint and lean in towards the camera, fascinated with my studio life. Questions poured forth: where did I get my clay, why did I choose that particular clay, how long did it take me to make a mug? He was charming.

After fifteen minutes, he respectfully suggested ending the call, heeding my desire to keep the video date short. I thanked him, shared that my feelings were on the "high end of neutral," and suggested we walk away from the date to test our magnetism. Speaking so directly made me feel expanded. *Was there something about Claud that made it easy for me to be open, or was I getting better at radical honesty?* I closed my computer and was smiling, bubbly inside. Our video chat was my most enjoyable one yet. I soon messaged to say that I did want to continue exploring with him. He felt the same. This was an instance where walking away resulted in my feeling intrigued and pulled back for more.

We communicated mostly through text, with an easy, flirty vibe. Claud had a complicated home scene, with a gaggle of kids—some his, some not. Understanding the challenges of parenting, I appreciated that he carved out time to communicate with me. In an early text, he said, "I feel really warm when I think of you, like we're cuddled up together in a fluffy blanket in the astral plane."

One afternoon, I was in bed touching myself and sending audio recordings to him. He was with all the kids, multitasking—sending sexy messages while monitoring jelly messes and sibling squabbles. Claud's effort to make me feel special, even when he was busy with his impressive parenting, felt extremely nurturing. My intense arousal lingered for hours after we hung up. I felt sparkly and swollen between my legs late into the evening.

About a week later, Claud and I made a plan to have video sex, but when the time came, the kids were nearby, so we wound up sexting instead. We sent pictures. In our play-by-play, we explained how we were feeling and what we were doing. Humorous misspelled texts abounded, as the voice translation function doesn't always work well. In the heat of the moment with hands occupied, there wasn't a lot of liberty to correct typos. Our orgasms rose and culminated at the same time, and then we texted sweetly for another hour.

We finally met in person the next week at a Portland coffee shop. When I saw him across the room, my insides sank. We only had the one video chat, during which I had mostly been attending to my pottery. Through our sexting, and the few photos we'd sent, the Claud I'd imagined was different than Claud in the flesh. We had a friendly time sipping our drinks and talking on a pleather couch, but I was disappointed to not feel more into him. Wondering if our hotter messaging chemistry could be revived, I suggested kissing. Recoiling slightly, he asked if we could find a more private place. A short walk led us to an uncomfortable flight of concrete steps where we sat down to kiss. It was ... OK.

Later that day, we texted to debrief our experiences. He said, "To be honest, I felt confronted by your suggestion to kiss at the coffee shop." As a woman, inviting kissing feels generous. Most men I know seem to be terrified of being labeled as a creepy guy. I presume they need all of the assistance they can get and feel happy to initiate. His sensitivity about public displays of affection was a shock; after all of our racy texting, I wouldn't have predicted the invitation would offend him.

If we wanted to get sexy, our only options were the streets and his child-filled home. Our lack of strong chemistry ushered this relationship straight into the land of dates gone by. We bid each other farewell through text, in friendly agreement that there was no future between us.

Date #25: Shooting Stars *October 2015*

Months before, through the grapevine, I had heard about Jorge's relationship status change. He and his wife had been distant acquaintances for about twenty years, and I'd always had a special feeling about him. He was not too tall, with longish hair, and had a "bad boy meets sweet hippie" vibe. When I heard that she had left him, my first guilty thought was, *well, that means he's available!*

There seemed to be three categories of potential people to date: strangers I found online, people I met or was introduced to in person, and those I already knew. This last category was the edgiest and most vulnerable for me, because a friendship—or my ego—could wind up compromised by my attempt to shift it.

I let some time pass before I got Jorge's number from a mutual friend in October, and left a voicemail boldly asking him out. A long day passed. The next day, he left me a message saying he was flattered and yes, he did want to get together.

In a delighted voicemail, I sang YAY! into the phone so much that my voice hit a high pitch and actually stopped the recording. The voicemail gave me the option to continue, so I did, and went back to saying "yay" a bunch. When I was sure I had celebrated too much, I hung up, feeling flustered. *Oops, the voicemail instruction had said, "Press 2 when you are finished leaving your message," but I didn't.*

A whole week passed with no response. *I never pressed 2. Did my message get delivered? Worse, did my enthusiasm scare him off?* I hoped he was on an outdoor adventure, out of range. In case my message hadn't gone through, I texted again to say that I would love to make a plan. He responded right away.

Amy: I hope I didn't scare you off with my near-psychopathic enthusiasm!

Jorge: No way! I'll call tomorrow to make a plan.

When he called, I squirmed in my seat as we spoke. I started sweating and felt like a hormonal twelve-year-old. After our call, I texted him because I couldn't remember what we had just planned:

Amy: Wait ... I went into an altered state! Did we say Monday?

Jorge: Yes, Monday!

Amy: Great. I feel strangely awkward with you. On the call, I got nervous and hung up too fast. I am excited to explore our connection.

Jorge: You're fun.

Amy: I'm looking forward to being fun with you :)

But when Monday arrived, Jorge postponed for two weeks. He

was heading out on a river-rafting trip and had too many last minute things to take care of. A few days later, he texted me from his campsite:

> **Jorge:** I saw a shooting star tonight. Tomorrow the river. I wonder what we might do when we meet.
>
> **Amy:** Maybe we'll see a shooting star.
>
> **Jorge:** And make wishes!
>
> **Amy:** Thanks for writing and telling me about the star. I'm smiling as I go to sleep.

When he returned from his trip, we finally met at Morning Glory, the best breakfast cafe in town. It was a sunny autumn day, so we chose to eat outside on the crowded sidewalk. My excitement had been building, remembering a Jorge from twenty years ago. I recognized him instantly, though something fundamental had changed. Sadness had carved itself into his eyes, in tragic contrast with his big-toothed, too-wide grin. The youthful bad boy hippie I remembered had changed: the bad had turned to sad.

In person, my attraction level was neutral, like with Claud. Our time together was sweet, but his melancholy betrayed Jorge's lack of emotional availability. He was getting ready to leave town for a few months, and there wasn't a draw for either of us to maintain contact. My Jorge hope balloon deflated.

Date #26: A Short Reign from Spain *October 2015*

Handsome, distinguished, wealthy, polyamorous, fetishy Hans, a Dutch entrepreneur living in Spain, reached out to me online. Our messages flowed easily. In our first communications, he leaned in with care and sweetness. Hans had a gentle nature and enjoyed my directness. Instead of pushing a personal agenda, he invited me to share my fantasies: "Could that be your next late-night fun, to tell me about the things you like or don't like?" I invited him to share first.

He responded right away, "I am into tenderness and lots of kissing and caressing. More recently, I have discovered that what arouses me most is anal—because of the tightness—and sex in public. Sharing that with you puts a smile on my face. Your turn, whenever you feel like it."

Hans spoke about sex in an inviting way, not at all pushy or overwhelming. *But, did anal sex or sex in public make any sense between us?* I laughed, imagining myself out in the world, running from bush to bush, holding my phone or computer while sticking things up my ass. That would have been something new. Although his delivery was velvety smooth, I felt cautious about how to interact with his fantasies.

We had a video date. Confident but not cocky, he was sexy: older, accomplished, and deeply kind. As we spoke, my body softened and relaxed towards the computer screen. The call was so lovely that I didn't want to hang up. We became Facebook friends and he immediately went through and liked every one of my profile pictures. Thoughts of him swirled through me for the rest of that day, and he sent this message later that evening: "It was great to see how delightful and natural you are. You are a rare, authentically happy person!"

The next day, Hans woke me up when he called to video chat. I was a morning mess but he didn't seem to care. I masturbated while he watched me from his desk at work, with his employees close by. His melodic voice and smooth accent provided a lovely soundtrack while I touched myself. He wanted to see my breasts, and showing them, imagining having them fantasized about, turned me on. This experience felt sexually nurturing. *What would it be like when Hans had privacy and was able to touch himself?* I looked forward to mutual sexual engagement.

He told me that he video-flirted with three or four women around the world this way. Our connection felt fun and sexy. Hans was at ease with himself, and comfortable in this video sex world. One day, he shared a link to a porn video he liked and we watched it, and each other, together. I enjoyed his choice; European pornography seems sexier and less violent. A naturally beautiful woman seemed to be truly enjoying herself as a man was joyfully working a glass dildo inside her ass while another man played gently and lovingly with her other holes. During the video, he sent me a message with his favorite Dutch phrase, "Whatever the heart is full of, spills over through the mouth."

Our video sex fling only lasted a few weeks. His "don't ask, don't tell" marriage meant he wasn't free to connect when his wife was home. He worked long hours most days, and because of the time difference, our schedules didn't line up easily. Although we liked each other, after a few novel experiences, video sex with Hans wasn't compelling or easy enough for us to continue.

Our connection transformed into a heartfelt friendship. I still feel his love and support, and whenever he likes or comments on my Facebook posts, my heart smiles. Occasionally, he checks in and sends a message when he senses that his experience and wisdom might be helpful.

Date #27: Potter Seeking Potter
(Told from both perspectives) October 2015

For a short while, I became a little famous among a Facebook group of fourteen thousand potters by posting lots of how-to videos. Each one received thousands of views overnight. It was fun!

Liam, an Australian potter, started messaging with me and we soon had our pants down on a video call. It was kinky and fun to suddenly be so exposed. But when we talked a bit afterwards, I didn't have romantic feelings towards him. He said, "My daughter saw your videos. She thinks we are soul mates. I'm considering a trip to the States and would love to come visit."

I froze and said "wow" a lot. When we got off the call, I knew that I didn't want to continue flirting. I explained; he graciously understood.

Then Sam, an East Coast potter, friended me on Facebook. One day, I received a bazillion notifications that he was "liking" and posting gushing responses on all of my profile pictures. I messaged him:

Amy: Sam, you are liking all of my pictures!

Sam: Yes, Amy, I am. Do you know the movie, *The Last of the Mohicans*?

Amy: No. Why?

Sam: It's a romantic movie set in the Hudson Valley. You might enjoy it.

Amy: What made you think of that? Do you have a crush on me, Sam?

Sam: Yes, of course I do.

Amy: What a great response!

Sam: Madeleine Stowe plays Cora and Daniel Day Lewis plays Hawkeye. In a quiet but strong scene, Cora raises her eyes to meet Hawkeye's. She asks firmly but with strength, not anger, "What are you looking at, sir?" He returns her glance and you can see his admiration for her when he says, "I'm looking at you, miss."

Amy: Ah, "You're liking all my pictures."

Sam: You got it!

After we messaged a bit, I said that although I was flattered, our connection didn't feel romantic. I appreciated the opportunity to keep working my radical honesty muscles. It was easy with Sam, and we stayed in touch. One time, when he was struggling with a body symptom, I offered to do a Processwork session with him on the phone (the therapy modality I earned my master's degree in). We both enjoyed the experience. The directness of our ongoing communication felt refreshing, respectful, and empowering.

Sam's Perspective

I'm flipping through YouTube how-to videos for making tumblers or bottles and I stumble upon a gem: Amy the Potter. I want you to imagine more energy, intelligence, spirit, strength, determination, wisdom, softness, and hilarity than you've ever encountered before. You've almost got my infatuation with Amy in your grasp. And I've never met her. There she is imparting how to best glaze mugs or carve a bottle into a candle holder, laughing all the while, and moving about, and completely enjoying herself. I was hooked!

I sent out a Facebook friend request, and I did what everyone probably does but many deny: I looked at Amy's profile pictures and ended up "liking" nearly all of them. Amy noticed. And being Amy, she sent me a note asking if I had a crush on her. I matter-of-factly said yes, and she thanked me for being direct with her. When we talked, she helped me understand a little more about myself. She has a rare insight and knowledge of our spirit and our bodies that few people have. I am forever thankful for our connection. And I'm always looking forward to seeing her captivating smile in her next new pottery video or profile picture!

Date #28: Sexy Professor! *October 2015*

Johann, a local professor, reached out to me on OkCupid. Just ending a marriage, he was incognito. Normally, I steered clear of picture-less profiles, but his initial message grabbed me:

> "Since you're so lovely and we're 99% matched, I must send a message. We seem so profoundly matched in so many areas that I think we should try to find some time in the real world to chat. Let me know if that's compelling to you."

His profile was sensitively and intelligently written. I asked him to send a picture, and he was—swoon—gorgeous. Then, I checked his reviews online and discovered that all of his students had crushes on him. We made a plan to meet for coffee later that same day and I was beside myself—*verklempt*—about it. Johann seemed sexy, artistic, and eloquent ... a catch!

The moment I stepped into the cafe, I spotted Johann leaning up against the counter, charming the baristas. I felt strongly attracted. He was older, with silvery hair, and interestingly triangular, friendly features. We sat down in an intimate corner booth and gazed at each other through smiling eyes. Both of us admitted to feeling shy and excited, and laughed about choosing to pour mid-day, high-octane caffeine on top of our nervous jitters. Earlier, I watched one of his YouTube lectures, and it bulged with esoteric vocabulary. I felt slightly anxious about feeling intellectually inferior, but Johann fortunately spoke like a normal person, and conversation flowed freely between us. He was just ending a marriage; I was his first date. At times, our feet or pinkies touched, lightly flirting, testing the waters. When I took a break to run to the bathroom, I was highly stimulated and breathlessly hurried back to my privileged spot next to the distinguished professor.

When our cups were empty, I suggested that it might be nice to kiss. Johann said that he would rather be out of the public eye and asked if I would like to see his new place, just a few blocks away. We walked over. Life-sized sculptures and Renaissance art imbued the urban apartment with elegance, and ceiling-high, fully-stocked bookshelves lined the walls. We stood unusually close to each other in that refined, tasteful space. Our eyes locked. He pulled me into a kiss.

Unfortunately, his lips were flimsy, and his tongue was ... *flaccid*. I wished he had kissed me harder, with more presence, so I could *feel* him. The tentativeness made me feel squirmy. A friend of mine calls that kind of kiss "shrimpy." *Maybe he was just hesitant because of his recent divorce?* I thought a momentary flash in his eyes betrayed a desire to go beyond kissing and was relieved that he didn't push a sexual agenda in his new bachelor pad.

Part of me wanted more, but not yet, and not all of me. We walked lazily back to my car and had a PG-rated hug goodbye. As I drove away, I was tingling. Everything except the kiss was exciting, and I was hopeful that communication could fix that. I wrote to let him know how excited I was to meet him. He said that he was still turned on from our time together, and we decided to masturbate together. During our phone sex, I told him that if someone were to come to my front door, they would be able to see me through the window. He liked that. For the next few days, I couldn't help looking at that window, hoping that *he* was going to be there. In our messages, I started affectionately calling him "S.P." for "Sexy Professor." When we were checking in via email the day after our date, he said:

> "The kissing and the post-date experience were delicious and delirious. I feel a bit foggy and blurry today. I loved it all, and I love the possibilities, especially the notion you described in your profile of 'pristine sexual awareness.' I hope I can move towards that. I might take some time to process our amazing afternoon; and then I'd love to meet for a glass of wine!"

The following day, I didn't hear from him. Before I went to bed, I texted to ask him if he'd changed his mind about getting together again, and he replied immediately:

> "I loved our date. I loved talking to you, walking with you, kissing you, and getting off with you on the phone! And it also feels like I've gone from zero to 100 very fast, from zero intimacy to suddenly sharing so much of myself. I think I need some time to reflect on it and get my feet on the ground, since they've been happily in the air since I met you."

I knew that some of these promising connections wound up being flashes in the pan, but I wished for a second date with Johann, to explore our potential, and for (hopefully) better kissing.

We both identified as writers, and in our racy messaging over the next few weeks, we shared some erotica. Mine were about random meetings, and encounters on best-case-scenario dates; his were about newbie orgy experiences at sex parties. Writing about fantasy sex was our new mutual thrill. The flirty messaging continued for weeks, but Johann never did initiate a second meeting for that glass of wine, and I stopped asking after a few times.

At the grocery store several months later, S.P. slipped past the corner of my eye and quickly disappeared down an aisle. *Was he avoiding me?* A short email exchange later that evening confirmed that it was him. He told me a few stories about his recent group sex escapades (quite similar to his written fantasies). S.P. was having a sexual rebirth!

Thinking back to my earliest dates, I remembered my desire to be open and free, to not get serious with some new person right away, and wondered if he avoided continuing with me for that reason. We all have our unique paths with sex and relationships. I would have gone further with S.P. but accepted that our paths diverged. The awkward kiss hinted that we were most likely incompatible. Good luck out there, Sexy Professor!

Part II
ARCHETYPAL ENCOUNTERS

5

A TASTE OF CONSCIOUS SEXUALITY

Date #29: Karezza Boy *October 2015*

Chad was a youthful Polynesian foodie from Portland who initiated contact on OkCupid. He practiced karezza, which—he explained in our first chat—is lovemaking without the goal of orgasm. "Karezza" means "caress" in Italian. It sounded tantric and mature. He suggested we meet at the Red Robe for Chinese food and ceremonial tea. Our messages were sweet, but I felt neutral about meeting.

The hole-in-the-wall restaurant in Chinatown turned out to be über-authentic. Just by stepping inside, I felt transported to a different place and time where the world was red and gold and magical. Chad knew what to order, and we shared mouth-watering, tender braised beef shank, and a complex-tasting noodle soup. He was a boisterous boy in a big body, with rich, dark skin and a very large face—attractive, but not in a way that clicked with me. He worked for a nonprofit and was in an open marriage with five kids. In his spare time he studied Chinese arts and tea.

Chad's long-fingered, soft-looking hands were adept at the ritualistic, refined handling of our tea. The cups were small and refilled many times. He became animated, a huge-eyed raconteur. The entertainment continued throughout the meal, as he stood up and danced and moved about, wildly gesticulating while narrating esoteric tales of tea. At times, he slowed to concentrate and perfectly execute the meticulous process. To be honest, I felt trapped. The entire evening was a theatrical presentation, but I was never engaged. I was just a woman writing a dating blog.

I did appreciate learning to tune into the subtleties of tea drinking. I even teared up a few times from the way he spoke about the lore and ceremony of tea. After he left for the bathroom, I noticed this poem that hung on the restaurant's wall. It captured the essence of the evening's stories, and I took a picture to remember it.

"Seven Cups of Tea"

The first cup moistens my throat.
The second breaks my solitude.
The third goes deep into my soul, to search the 5000 scrolls.
The fourth makes life's injustices vaporize through my pores.
The fifth lessens the weight of my flesh and bone.
The sixth brings me to encounter the immortals.
I'd better not take the seventh, the wind blows through my wings.

Chad was personable and attractive, but there was no juice between us—only tea. He explained that some teas had magical properties and told me about a local alchemist who had intimate knowledge of sacred plants and energy medicine. This wizard had an apothecary nearby, and Chad strongly encouraged me to find him. He even gave me directions to the shop, and for months, I stalked it, slowing whenever I drove past the intersection he'd named. I could never find the place. Many moons later, I unknowingly connected with its elusive proprietor on OkCupid (*more on this later*).

Date #30: Karezza Man *October 2015*

Scott messaged me on OkCupid. In his profile, he mentioned karezza, which grabbed my attention. It was only days earlier that I had first heard the word karezza from Chad. Scott's main profile picture was grainy and old, maybe taken in the 1970s. In it, he had big, poofy, light brown hair, and seemed joyful. *Why would he post such an archaic picture?* Plus, he lived halfway across the country. Aside from these cons, I was open to checking it out, and in our early messages, I sensed that Scott had impressive emotional depth.

During my two-hour commute to Portland, we had a long phone conversation. A hawk flew overhead. Then an eagle. And finally, a great blue heron swooped low, just feet above my car. I wondered if these glorious birds were hinting that Scott had the potential to accompany me in moving towards heightened sexual ecstasy. He said he had an unusual capacity for intimacy and would be honored to be a guide on my sexual journey. Scott was trying to seduce me into his karezza world. *Could I trust him?* I imagined my sexuality as a flower slowly blooming.

Once I became more receptive, his advances grew more assertive. He wanted to drive out to Oregon, from Iowa! *What if I didn't like him?* He tried to entice me with free-flowing visions of the sex parties we could go to together, and that he could even "move to Eugene"! A block went up inside of me against giving him any power. Scott was too hungry for me to be his student.

I told him on the phone that I was feeling hesitant. The tone of his voice shifted, betraying underlying desperation. Ramping up, panicking as I pulled away, he begged, "If I could just come visit, so you could meet me? I wouldn't have to stay at your house, if you'd just give me a chance!" He pressed, and as in a dojo, I sidestepped. When someone comes on strongly, if it is mutual, the experience can be exhilarating and flattering, but if I'm not interested, the same actions feel out of step and inappropriate. I appreciated the practice of setting a firm, clear boundary.

In our final conversation, Scott admitted to having a history of extreme jealousy in his relationships. That was what I felt underneath: possessive emotionality. He also revealed his preference for supermodel bodies, which mine is definitely not. I'm short and happy with my curves. Any residual interest plummeted and I ended our communication. I felt relieved when, after two weeks of intensity, the dramatic connection with Karezza Man was finally over.

My first response to his profile was resistance to his picture. Looks and style reveal information about a person, and I don't judge myself or others as shallow when we have responses to whatever we find attractive or off-putting.

Date #31: Captain Clitoris! *October 2015*

Isaac and I were a 99% match on OkCupid. In his first profile picture, he was wearing a homemade "Captain Clitoris" superhero t-shirt. Based only on that picture, I "liked" and messaged him right away. We texted sweetly for a few days, then video chatted. Isaac had short, curly brown hair and big, puppy-dog, tear-shaped eyes with long lashes. His face was shy and boyish, with a smile that filled the screen. Over video, we spoke openly about our shared desire for conscious sexual experiences. *Intriguing.* He was the third man in a row who was interested in higher-consciousness sexuality. It seemed the universe was finally sending my medicine. The only catch was that he lived in Bend, three hours away through the winding mountain roads.

Isaac was refreshingly confident and spoke about sex with both reverence and playfulness. The feeling between us was flirty and open. During an early video call, he asked what kinds of sex toys I liked, and then dashed off excitedly to fetch a huge box of his own! Before then, I didn't know they even *made* sex toys for men. It turns out there are many: devices that are used on the penis, sheaths the penis goes inside, cock rings, anal plugs, prostate toys, and all kinds of vibrating things!

On our next video chat, I invited Isaac to be sexual. He asked what that would look like, and we decided to drop into a sexual space and see what happened. Feeling open and drawn to explore something new, I put my finger inside myself. It was cathartic; I had never wanted fingers inside me and had only done it myself for tampon insertion. Old emotional and physical injuries were triggered; I had a somatic memory of some junior high boy's bony finger entering me too roughly. My own finger was gentle inside; the walls of my vagina relaxed and I started to cry. On the strangely intimate computer screen, Isaac's eyes softened. I felt vulnerable and safe. Isaac supported me like a sexual healer. *He would definitely be a special lover.*

He had never been sexual on video before—that first call was more like therapy than mutual sexual engagement. The next time we had a video chat, we tried masturbating together, but just a few minutes in, he asked to stop, saying it felt too impersonal. I realized men probably feel the same pressure to perform and follow through once a sexual experience is in process. Isaac modeled the courage to speak up and shift what was happening in the middle.

I had experimented a few times with sex-only video connections with men I didn't plan to meet in real life. Those dates varied, but were mostly awkward, which didn't bother me when I had no interest in knowing them personally. Because of Isaac's assessment, I started to question how great video sex could be in a more intimate relationship. So far, I wasn't finding fulfilling experiences through a screen. I wondered if my video sex ship had sailed.

We continued talking and messaging, and Isaac sent me a dildo and water-based seaweed lubricant in the mail. I learned that although water-based lube gets tacky after a bit, it can be reactivated with saliva or water. Sex toys usually seem awkward, lifeless, and cumbersome. The seaweed lube came in handy, but the dildo predictably wound up in a dusty pile with a few abandoned others.

Over the next few weeks, it became clear that the distance between us wasn't only in miles. Isaac was depressed. Struggles with his family, money, work, and past relationships were slowly revealed. We all have our struggles, but I didn't feel as drawn to romance with him as these traits surfaced. After a long history of having partners who struggled with money, I was ready for partners who were financially stable. Also, Isaac talked a lot about using psychedelics during sex. I wasn't sure I wanted that.

There was also the geographical distance. The earliest time we could possibly meet in person was in three months. *Could a relationship work when we had to plan a date months out? Was it worth the effort?* He had abandonment sensitivities, and due to the distance, we would constantly be leaving each other.

We let go of our hopes for love, but our affinity endured and we continued to message from time to time. I hoped he would find someone spectacular. Months later, he started dating a special friend of mine. When they first met on OkCupid, she reached out to ask me about him; I had a good feeling about them and gave him a strong recommendation. They began a serious relationship, which inspired him to move to Eugene.

Go, Captain Clitoris! Welcome to town. Whenever we run into each other, we smile knowingly. It wouldn't have worked between us, but I felt so grateful for the sexual healing, and glad when he joined my community.

Date #32: Between a Gemstone and a Soft Place *October 2015*

Cole's profile pictures and poetic self-description were deeply appealing. I followed a link to his website and his aesthetic moved me: he painted ethereal, melancholic worlds, blending rich tones to portray complex, abstract dimensions. The colors were like liquified gemstones poured onto canvas.

Like Karezza Man Scott, Cole had a 1970s vibe, but his version was more like a throwback heartthrob. He had shoulder length, straight, dirty blond hair, and round, emotional, emerald eyes that mostly looked sad.

We texted. I liked him. We talked on the phone; I still liked him. We had a video date and I liked him even more. With a refreshing blend of warm heart and cool detachment, he was available but not desperate, communicative but not pushy. Our exchanges touched me from the beginning. We shared openly about our families, emotional lives, and dreams.

As we were setting up a time to meet, he nervously revealed that he had herpes type 2. I appreciated his honesty; there is a lot of stigma around STIs. It's such a personal issue and must be difficult to navigate when to disclose that information with a new potential partner. I was still curious about him, even though I had a lot of dates in October. Cole was a lot more available and communicative than ghosty Jonah.

But on the morning of our date, Cole canceled, saying that it probably wouldn't work out between us because he had a hard time maintaining erections, and that he didn't like to use condoms. This was a deal-breaker because of his herpes. I felt let down. But no condoms? I had learned my lesson with Ivan: *No way.*

Date #33: Finding Bliss with an Australian Nonmonaut
(Told from both perspectives) October 2015

Everything in me started vibrating when I realized that a gorgeous, dynamic Australian man had viewed my OkCupid profile. Oliver was my age, and according to the algorithms, we were a 99% match. In his artistic pictures, he looked like a hip, cosmopolitan designer, with stylish hair, full lips, and a bright smile. He dressed in fashionable pastels. I devoured his profile, where he called himself a "nonmonaut," a word he made up to describe his experience of polyamory. I imagined him ascending in a space suit out of monogamy into the beautiful and unfamiliar world of nonmonogamy. *Like me!* Bug-eyed and drooling over his pictures, a flood of feelings transported me into an altered state. My fingers tripped over each other as I messaged him.

Oliver responded instantly. In our first texts, we had an inspired flow. Huge waves of "Yes!" rippled through every cell in my body. Even without having done my usual video date test, I knew I wanted to meet him. We talked openly about feeling attracted to each other based on our profiles. He was getting ready for a big trip to the U.S. and had some unscheduled time to fill. A visit wasn't out of the question!

When I started dating in 2015, my astrologer told me that until 2017, I should look for connections that wouldn't last. She literally said, "Someone from out of the country, who you'll never see again, would be ideal." Her prescription was for brief, colorful love affairs. *Could that be Oliver?* When he arrived in the U.S. for a week-long conference, we messaged a bit:

> **Amy:** Welcome to the States! Have you come up with a good reason to come to the Northwest? I would love to meet you!
>
> **Oliver:** Ah, I doubt I can make it up there this time.
>
> **Amy:** That is such a shame! I think the combination of me and you could have been tectonic!

Oliver: Believe me, I am tempted. I'm in Denver for the conference, then San Francisco. How far are you from SF?

Amy: It's an eight-hour drive or just over an hour by plane. I'm crazy busy, but we could have a short, steamy romance!

Oliver: I'll look into it! Thank you for being so open and lovely.

We sent just a few short texts during the week, as he was preoccupied with the conference. When the week was over, I got back in touch to ask about his plans.

Oliver: I am exhausted and elated. The conference was incredible. I came up with a third reason to come to Eugene today ;)

Amy: That is still a possibility? A love affair with you sounds delicious! My heart is beating fast. My whole body is electrified. What are your three reasons?

Oliver:
1. You
2. Shooting 360 video in the woods
3. Legal marijuana

Amy: Yes to all of that! Come! Let's have a video chat tomorrow. Sweet dreams, lover.

Our hearts burst open on video the next day. His boyish, shy face and thick, styled silvery hair made him seem ageless, and feminine. When he called me "darling," I melted. His accent poured over me and his warm nature soaked into my pores. Our eyes twinkled and our faces stretched into wide, drunken, moony grins.

By the next morning, he had bought his ticket and that same evening, I stood in the airport, ready to greet him. Surfing a cloud of anticipation, I waited for this familiar stranger to descend out of the sky and into my world, a unique soul in a crowd of travelers. We recognized each other instantly, both of us shy and excited. He stepped up to me, placed his bags down, and took my hands. We looked deep into each other's eyes, hovering in the timelessness. Our faces came close, as close as breath, and we stood together in a cone of silence amid bustling travelers. Then—before ever speaking a word—we kissed, softly, sweetly, easily, lips finding lips. *This beautiful man actually came to visit me.* Once home in my kitchen, he pulled me into his lap where we indulged in more exquisite, perfect kissing. We floated upstairs and made love. Just like that, just like water.

We slept cuddled together like lion cubs. By morning, we felt—and looked—like a couple who had been together for years. At breakfast, he screeched adorably when he saw a squirrel on the fence outside my window, pointing it out to me as though it was a mythological creature. Apparently, they don't have squirrels in Australia! When he came with me to Nia (the joy and pleasure-based movement class that I teach), he danced his heart out.

For four glorious days, he stayed and we played. He was the most sex-positive person I'd ever met. I opened up; my body and heart unfolded. Laughter, tears, and lovemaking flowed between us regularly and freely. Adventures took us to local hiking trails, to Portland, and around Eugene. Oliver's GoPro rig was his quirky, alien-ish, nonmonaut gear: a huge camera-covered lollipop that he carried everywhere.

On Spencer's Butte, we found a place just off the beaten path to be intimate. Looking in his eyes, I lowered onto my knees as I pulled his pants down. In a bubble of the world, cradled by the sun-bathed, pungent Douglas fir forest, I kissed and stroked him, full of love. Otherworldly beauty was all around and within us. I looked up and imagined the world through Oliver's eyes as he smiled, looking at everything, feeling everything. It felt like we were in the very center of the universe, the very center of our lives.

Our sexual experiences were playful and vulnerable. With effortless communication, we explored new territory. Oliver had a longtime curiosity, but also fear, of having anyone touch his anus, yet I felt very open to it. He let me use my mouth; it was deeply healing for him to explore his trepidation and fixation. His emotional beauty was thrilling. We kept deepening. Each time he had an orgasm with me, he cried. Spinning around the kitchen preparing a meal and stealing kisses, I said that we were "having a little forever together." I had no expectations of it continuing. Every moment was precious. We took care of each other, giving and giving until nothing was lacking and everything was fulfilled.

On our last morning together, I shared a secret wish with him. I dream of producing artistic lovemaking videos but had usually felt shy to ask past lovers to film our sexual experiences. With Oliver leaving so soon, I longed to preserve the spirit of our connection. My desire to capture our intimacy rose and exploded. To my great relief, he was enthusiastic about it. Oliver was a filmmaker with an interest in feminist, high quality erotica, so it wasn't a surprise that he was open to the suggestion. The bigger success was my asking for what I wanted, especially sexually. Crossing sexual edges together was blissful.

We filmed ourselves with his GoPro in a sweet, luscious lovemaking extravaganza. We became love itself. He expertly adjusted the camera, recording from many different angles. Our bodies wound through an array of positions, slithering in communion and transformation. He entered me over and over and we laughed and cried. Our mouths explored every part of each other, savoring our final experience. Capturing our love on film created a cherished gift.

Time pressed upon us. After we made love, there were only a few hours left before a plane would carry him away. I tried to imprint every moment, feeling, and word we shared. Our last hours were quietly precious. At the airport, I wanted the moment to be suspended in time. Oliver's emotional expressiveness surprised me; as we broke out of our final kiss, he made a loud barking sound that was followed by a stream of painful tears. His last words to me were, "Promise me we'll be in each other's lives forever." I promised. My cheeks were wet, and I felt confused in time as I drove away, the depth of our union swirling through and around me, trying to land in me. I had celebrated the limitations of our fantasy chapter, but in separating, resented the harsh reality and wished our joyful, temporary connection could last. *What in the world just happened? What would our future be?*

For several months, we spoke on video daily, dreaming together. We maintained our romantic, sexual feeling for some time. Oliver was an inspired spokesperson for polyamory, and his resolve to retain sexual sovereignty gave me peace, knowing he would never block me out of his life and heart. He called being in love, "loving with," which meant loving freely, open to loving others, without chains or limitations. Once he was back to sleeping with his lovers in Australia, I had some jealousy, but also experienced compersion for the first time. In spite of my fears and feeling left out, I authentically *wanted* him to be with other people. Because he was such a unique and sensitive lover, I thought the world would be a better place if more people experienced sex with him.

But keeping in touch was challenging in our disparate time zones. He was always going to sleep as I was waking up, which left us with a very small window of potential contact. I went into a phase of longing and introspection, studying our time together, wanting to preserve the special feeling between us as long as possible. My moods vacillated between soppily in love and depressed. Often, I combed through our pictures and videos to feel his soft eyes and brilliance again. Remembering my astute astrologer's advice, I knew I had to let the love be fleeting. *Would I find that openness and ecstasy with someone else?* I spent hours writing poetry and songs, being as close as I could to our love, lingering in the beautiful memories.

A few months after our visit, when Oliver found a new special lover, a gentle rift formed between us. At the same time, my heart was breaking because of Jonah's cancelations and disappearances. Oliver was always present, but I was tangled in my emotions and it broke my heart. I pulled away from him, unable to join in his excitement.

Our meeting felt fated. Oliver and I love each other, but our geographical reality eventually shifted our focus back to our present time and place. The other side of the planet was too far away to feel attached. Even though the in-love feeling between us shifted, our friendship is forever.

Oliver's Perspective

Our four days together were magical, as is our enduring friendship. In your arms, I found an acceptance of who I am that unfroze ancient aching viscera and opened my heart.

Your attention upon me was a warm afternoon sun, bucolic and calming. Your authentic generosity transformed my outlook. I felt like a pot forming under your strong, assured hands.

One of the greatest gifts I received was from you as a potter: the metaphor of the vessel, a place of self-forming, the primary form in which the protohuman mind imagined holding water, food, sustenance. Every day, I return to that metaphor to bring resilience to myself, to reassert my distinctness and understand my place in the world.

Ours was not a love that took the normative relationship escalator. When I left, the physical distance between us was harsh. We reflected love, care, and hope into each other's lives. I love, with you, forever.

Date #34: Embracing My Inner Chill *November 2015*

Amidst a sea of shoppers in the vast Holiday Market auditorium, a distinguished-looking man filed into my pottery booth. Lester was a "silver fox," about twenty-five years older than me. He was lean and healthy, with small, bright blue eyes. I felt attracted and was intrigued by the GoPro that was expertly strapped to his chest. As he started to walk away, I complimented his cool camera rig. He turned to thank me, looked into my eyes for the first time, and said, "If I were qualified, I would ask you to spend time together." His chivalrous poise charmed me. We exchanged numbers and planned to meet.

Because he was so much older, I wondered if he had any experience with polyamory, and decided to tell him upfront, "The one thing you need to know is that I am non-monogamous." His smile stiffened, and I felt a strange and sudden shot of intensity come out of him. My inner armor was triggered.

That would have been a good time to cancel.

I went home and found him on Facebook. I scrolled through his posts, reading the comments to get a sense of him through his interactions with friends, and to look for signs that he might be a serial killer. I found a recent video of him. Watching it gave me an eerie feeling: he had an over-the-top sales pitch twangy voice, and his tilted head seemed to be pecking into the camera. He acted like a cartoon. It scared me.

That would have been a good time to cancel.

Lester messaged and suggested that he could help me set up my pottery booth for the next weekend's sale. I knew that was a recipe for disaster. During the busy and demanding holiday season, I have my set-up down to a science, and prefer to do the job myself. Even with close friends, I get freakish in my booth. He seemed overly confident that he would be helpful. Despite it being the worst date concept I could think of, I foolishly said "yes."

On Friday afternoon, he showed up looking chipper. I gave him the simplest possible job. Within moments, I was sighing and rolling my eyes. The task of teaching him even a small part of my system frustrated and overwhelmed me. Even though I really needed to set up the booth, we abandoned my precious ship and went for tea. My recurring pathology returned: prioritizing a random person's wishes over my own.

At the cafe, I noticed that Lester resembled Oliver. His smaller, older, more angular version of my actual love confused me. I found myself comparing them, and had a hard time being present. His neediness became apparent when he turned a sales pitch on me, wanting to impress me with details about his diet and well-researched marketing strategies. I felt trapped. Whatever was lurking underneath his handsome exterior unnerved me.

After tea, when he asked if I wanted to go for a walk, I found my voice and declined. I had work to do, and this date felt like a burden. Hugging goodbye, he turned his face suddenly, pressing his lips firmly against mine. My body stiffened, my head moved back and my mouth went limp. His presumption made me angry. If I want to kiss someone for the first time, I always ask—unless it is one of those rare, romantic, cinematic moments when the mutual desire is crystal clear. I was done with Lester.

He sent a text after our date, saying that he was impatient for our next kiss. When I messaged him back and said that we weren't on the same page, he responded with a crying emoji. I had an intuition that he would come to my pottery booth the next day in a final attempt to woo me. I vowed that I would remain grounded and honest.

The next day, a sad-faced clown showed up at my booth. It was Lester. He just stood there with his painted face, holding balloons, frowning at me. Resisting a conditioned impulse to take care of him, I took a step back and just let him be the sad clown. He was obviously trying to manipulate my feelings, and I stayed detached. When he extended a balloon, I shook my head no. His face got even sadder as he walked away, dragging his big feet. Finally, I chose myself. What a relief.

An interesting, symbolic thing happened after this. Whereas I had always been sensitive to outside temperatures, needing to bundle up to protect against the cold, when I stepped out into the November air later that day, I felt immune to the chill. I didn't need my usual hat, scarf and jacket. I attributed the shift to my integration of the "coolness" of detachment. Ever since that day, I have had a completely different relationship to outside temperatures, understanding that my response to them is connected to my inner state.

All my life, I had been the good girl, a "warm" person. This date helped me find comfort with being cold.

6

WIZARDS AND OTHER MYTHICAL CREATURES

Date #35: I Break for Wizards *December 2015*

I fell for Giles years earlier when I met him at his alternative healing practice. In our first interaction, he burst into the therapy room and leaned his big, sunshiny smile surprisingly close to my face. Cocking his handsome head to the side, he looked into my eyes, and said, "Is there food in my teeth?"

As he prepared for our first session, he danced lithely around the massage table, his eyes spiraling mischievously around me. When he laughed, his face beamed total joy. Thick, greying hair was brushed casually to the side, giving him a compelling mixture of edgy, teenage boy appeal and deep, ancient wisdom. He was close to sixty, and quite tall, but jumped around like a puppy, and my spirit frolicked right along. But as the session began, he took on an otherworldly gentleness, and his large, healing hands became instruments of the divine. I felt uncommonly calm as we breathed together. He circled around me, tuning up my energy field from every angle. My crown chakra blew open and I felt extraordinarily activated on a spiritual level for over a week.

At the time we met, we were both in committed, monogamous relationships. Eugene is a small town, and we started running into each other, often with our partners. When he was nearby, I sweated and wobbled. My partner, Samantha, always teased me about it.

Once Samantha and I parted ways, I wondered about Giles' relationship status and sent him an email. I knew that he'd recently had a death in his family, so I broke the ice with condolences and asked if he'd like to get together sometime. His short thank you message ended with a promise to get in touch soon. Several months passed before he responded more thoroughly:

> **Giles:** I'm finally returning your kind, thoughtful, and warm sentiments at the time of my brother's catapult into the next dimension. Might you have time for a visit over the next few months? I hope so!

I was thrilled. We spent the next month sending "let's make a plan" messages, and eventually, one day in December, he sent this:

> **Giles:** I'm pretty sure that we didn't get together yet, unless it was so wonderful that I have no memory capacity for something so enjoyable! Let's schedule for next week?

> **Amy:** I love the idea of making the experience so enjoyable that it can't be remembered! A whole new paradigm of enjoyability!

Giles was as excited as I was. He invited me to join him for lunch at Cafe Soriah. Our eyes, minds and hearts danced as we dipped warm bread, sipped wine, savored garlicky tiger prawns, and shared a Caesar salad. As we ate and spoke passionately, a cosmic whirlwind was conjured. Each important topic that arose was overtaken by another, and another, in a passionate frenzy.

When he asked what was new with me, I said, "A lot! I left my relationship, and I'm dating, having wild adventures and lots of fun. I consider myself polyamorous now." With regret in his voice, Giles said he was still married. I'm sure my face showed disappointment. Through our nonstop talking, our eyes communicated unspeakable volumes about how we were organically, authentically drawn to each other. Our two hours together was too short. Eventually, when he needed to go, we shared a strong, long hug. I didn't want to let go.

We texted all the rest of that day. *My heart!* I knew I could love him easily without physical intimacy, *but was it OK for me to even have love feelings for him? Was our hug over the line? What was the boundary?*

A month later we met at Soriah again. I fessed up about my attraction. With shy giddiness, he admitted to feeling the same. Wondering about his marriage and boundaries, I said, "Wherever the line is, I want to walk right up to it and be as close to you as I possibly can." Our conversation danced around the many landmines regarding our mutual attraction. I wondered, *how would his wife feel if she could see or hear us?* From the way he spoke about their marriage, I gathered it wasn't very passionate. I felt jealous of her; it seemed like a waste of such a magical man. Yet, I asserted that I wouldn't ever cheat with him behind his wife's back, even if he were open to that. He wanted to take some time to ponder his boundaries.

We kept having lunch dates to dive into the space between us, but he never named a boundary; it developed on its own. We can love each other to the moon and back, but on the physical plane, we are friends. To me it is undeniably more than a friendship. It is a Love.

Our lunches have continued over the years, though their frequency has tapered. When we spend time together, we both get drunk off the connection. After indulging our hearts, a necessary period of separation follows: to let go, to not dream. Infrequent meetings seem OK, but more would be over his invisible line. Sometimes when we meet, especially if we share a glass of whiskey, Giles wistfully expresses his wish that his marriage were open. His eyes transmit that impossible desire every time we part. Sometimes I dream about having just one sweet afternoon to explore the love between us in every dimension.

I often wonder, *how did I wind up so close with this blessed man?* It is a true honor to be Giles's romantic friend. Our relationship thrives in dreamland, where we both feel at home. Even thinking of him creates an umbilical cord to the entire universe, where our eternal romance thrives in the cosmic beyond.

One spring day, as we were parting, he pressed his lips into my third eye for a long, delicious moment. When I tune in, I can still feel the permanent impression of that single kiss.

Date #36: Armpits, Whips, and Spanks *January 2016*

Zane, an actor, messaged me on OkCupid to say that he was attracted to me, "except for the armpit hair." Slightly offended, I wrote back and said, "We're not supposed to be attracted to everyone. Good luck out there!"

The next week, he reached out, horny. I thought it was strange—*if he wasn't interested in me, then why?*—but I played along. He sent me a series of nudes of his muscular, artistic, technicolor tattooed body; he was really a specimen! His jet-black hair, angular features and sapphire blue eyes drew me in. Zane looked even sharper wearing a police uniform in one of his staged headshots. However, he kept saying things that didn't land with me:

Zane: I would tease your lips with the tip. Then straddle you and slide my hard cock down your throat.

Amy: I guess I can pretend that I would like that ... but would *you* like a hard cock down *your* throat?

So he wasn't attracted to me because of my body hair, but he wanted to thrust his cock down my throat. And then:

Zane: You could straddle my face and grind your pussy on it.

Grind? That didn't sound pleasurable either.

Amy: In the picture where you are lying down, is that black thing next to you a whip?

Zane: Yes, just for fun—I'm not into pain at all.

And then:

Zane: Maybe you'd like a nice firm spanking?

I wasn't feeling drawn to Zane, with his throat-ramming cock, whip, and firm spankings. Later he texted:

Zane: Are you going to be in Portland on Thursday? Come fuck me.

Amy: We would have to communicate a bit more so I felt safe with you, Mr. "Pussy grinding, whips and spankings, swallow my cock, and by the way, I'm turned off by your body hair." Can you see how it might not be enticing from my end?

My point finally registered. It was one of those "no hard feelings but this just isn't right for me" situations.

Date #37: Cardboard Chemistry *January 2016*

Christian, an engineer with an impressive website, was my next online flirtation. He was bisexual, polyamorous, a stoner, a dog lover, and vegan (even his dog was vegan, *poor thing!*). He had short brown hair and seemed plain but attractive enough, and at only 5'4", he was someone I could kiss without being up on tiptoes. In our texting, he was active and engaged. As I often did with hopeful dates, I asked for his birth information (date, time, and place) and when I plugged it into my usually astute astrology app, Time Passages, we scored a whopping 10 in romantic attraction. That was rare, and the same score I had with Jonah. I perked up. We decided to meet for breakfast at Prasad, my favorite cafe in downtown Portland.

The moment I saw him, I shut down internally. He seemed mousy and plain in a way that bored the romantic in me. *How could my astrology program have been so wrong?* The depth I sensed in his messages and the beauty of his website didn't translate in person. He was nice, but I wasn't interested, and we had lots of awkward, dry pauses. I didn't fabricate questions or pretend to be enthusiastic.

I paid for myself. He walked me to my car, and as we were saying goodbye, I offered to kiss. Fancying myself a dating scientist, I wanted to study my chemistry theory: does the kiss always reflect the date?

This time, yes. The kiss was cardboard.

Christian surprised me when he texted again several months later wanting to meet up. He had said that he wanted to stay in touch but I had assumed it was a nicety. Our lack of chemistry seemed clear. *Different standards?* A date once gave me the graphic tip, "most men just want to get their dicks wet," but I didn't want any more cardboard, especially down there!

Date #38: A Leprechaun Carrying STI Results *January 2016*

My pet moniker for Kelly was "anachronistic alien leprechaun." He had the formality and writing style of someone from Celtic folklore. I imagined him as an XXL leprechaun doing a jig in a field of clover. He had incredibly wide-set eyes that seemed to be examining other worlds. My rule: when a mythical creature shows up, pay attention!

His OkCupid profile began with a glowing, detailed testimonial from a recent past lover. In our messaging flirtation, he was a hungry, all-day communicator. Kelly divulged that he fantasized heavily, usually staying up most of each night to work out at a gym to release excess sexual energy. His attention was flattering but overwhelming. This push-pull stayed constant.

Impatient to meet in person, Kelly successfully orchestrated our date. He chose the Duniway Portland boutique hotel, which had a fancy restaurant, thinking that we could potentially stay there overnight if our chemistry was strong. He promised to show me his recent STI papers to verify his health. I found all of this over the top, but entertaining.

Kelly was waiting for me at a table with two glasses of merlot. Beads of sweat covered his rectangular forehead. He had a large, blocky head, and a huge, square chest that pressed in every direction through a tight-fitting argyle sweater. Round, baby-blue eyes and pronounced, angular lips made him a very geometrical man! Despite his nerves, I felt at ease and comfortable in his presence; his sensitivity was endearing, and I trusted that his anxiety would subside. As we settled into talking, he relaxed into his sweet nature and sharp mind. He suggested the "Bateau," a large plate of oysters and clams, and we also shared a kale and hazelnut salad. The expensive dinner, which he made clear he would be paying for, was delicious. Kelly was full of curiosity about me and asked a myriad of questions. Partway through dinner, he hinted about the option to stay overnight. But even before arriving, I knew—and had told him—that regardless of chemistry, the chances of my having sex on a first date were close to zero.

In his profile, he had expounded in great detail about how kissing was a high priority for him. So, after the meal, we strolled into the cold evening, pausing at each intersection to kiss. *Meh.* We were both capable of better kissing, just not with each other.

The next day, we messaged to affirm that it wasn't right between us. We said our mutual thank yous, and in true Irish form, he wished me good luck.

Date #39: He's Just Not That Into Me *January 2016*

Finally, I felt a strong potential with someone local. Carlos had been a distant acquaintance for years. Pretty sure his marriage had ended, I wondered if I would see him on OkCupid, and one day, *voilà, there he was!* Carlos was on the short side, with a boyish demeanor and a light-up-the-room smile. I loved his curly black hair, long eyelashes, and mischievous nature. The casual business clothes he wore looked sharp on his small, strong frame. He was smart, successful, artistic, and passionate.

Part of what made him seem ideal was that although I felt drawn to him, I knew that I wouldn't fall in love with him. I hoped he might be my perfect once-a-week lover.

Carlos seemed excited when I reached out. We messaged enthusiastically and made a plan to meet at Highlands, a bar he liked. I felt hopeful about the date, which translated to more nervousness than usual. We grabbed hot toddies, shot pool, and played skee ball. I'm competitive, so games were a fun way to flirt, show off, and channel my nervous energy. Towards the end of our time together, we found some comfy chairs and sat close. He invited me to sit on his lap and wanted to look at my hands. Smiling, we found each other's eyes. Our lips moved slowly towards each other, meeting in an exquisitely sensitive kiss. Afterwards, he walked me to my car. I was wobbly. He asked about a second date, and because he had his kids the following week, we agreed on dinner at my house, in two weeks. *Was Carlos my weekly lover-to-be?*

We started flirting lightly through text. One day, he sent me a series of revealing selfies and I returned some from the bathtub. When the day of our second date finally came, I was blasting music, singing and dancing as I enthusiastically cleaned my house. The ingredients for our romantic dinner were on the counter.

In the middle of my preparation whirlwind, Carlos called to say that he needed time and wanted to postpone. So much for the special meal I'd planned, and my clean, fluffed-up bed, and the wine, and my excited, vulnerable heart!

Getting the message in the middle of cleaning was so awkward. *Should I stop sweeping, halfway down the stairs?*

Sulking, I finished the stupid stairs, turned the music off and started singing my woeful emotions out loud. Dramatically over-exaggerating, I belted out a song in a strange, new style. I howled freely about the astrologically-fated battle between restrictive Saturn (transiting in the sky) and my ultra-romantic natal Venus in Pisces. At the climax of the song, Venus orgasmed from Saturn's restriction. Satisfied, I felt like I squeezed lemonade out of a pile of shit.

Carlos's waffling crept under my skin. By the time our rescheduled date came around a week later, my eagerness had devolved to teenage-level awkwardness. We ate dinner, drank a lot of wine, and went up to my room to have sex. Our communication was choppy, and I felt racy and ungrounded. *Did I want this?* When he saw my matching purple bra and underwear, he noticed. "You really like purple." I smiled and nodded. He said, "I don't." *Ouch.* We smoked some marijuana and proceeded.

We got into bed and he reached down for me. In no time, his hand was moving hard and fast. I wasn't enjoying his aggressive touch, but wanted him to think I was, because I was still invested in him liking me. Pornographically, he asked, "Yeah, you like that? You like it like that?"

Falling back on my old people-pleasing habit, I lied, "I like it all." It felt awful to have to navigate through a porn-style scene with Carlos when I had wished to be more sensual.

∼

I was exposed to pornography way too young. My father liked to sneak my sister and me into R-rated drive-in movies. We'd hide under blankets until the coast was clear. It was a "cool dad" thing to do, but sometimes the movies had scenes we shouldn't have viewed. It was mortifying to see a woman get rammed aggressively from behind, especially sitting right next to my father, who seemed too curious about my response. At home, we had a big television with all the channels. I was often alone and would look for sex. *Would I act like these women one day? Was that pleasure?* Their screams didn't look or sound like pleasure; I had a lot to learn. At only seven, I decided that when I grew up, I wanted to be "good in bed."

∼

Carlos and I started to have intercourse. He was fucking me and I didn't like it. I pried away and decided to go down on him instead, to slow things down and feel more empowered and connected. After he came, he said, "You took me somewhere I have never been." A few quiet moments later, he got dressed and left. I offered to walk him out, but he said, "No, I'll find my way." I felt hollow. *He didn't show any interest in my pleasure.*

The next day, when he didn't call, I made up stories. *Did I hurt him?* I feared that in my unstable sexual state, I may have overwhelmed him by trying to match his vigor. I wished he would initiate contact and felt hesitant to reach out because of his previous request for space. After a few days, I sent a text, asking if he had a minute, and to his credit, Carlos called me on the phone right away.

When I asked about his silence, he said, "It seems like you're being overly analytical, overthinking it." That upset me. Checking in after having sex seemed normal to me. He continued, "You're an intense person. It will be a while before I would have the urge to meet up again." *Ouch. No wonder I didn't have an orgasm. He wasn't into me.* I told him that was fine; he could get in touch whenever. Feeling misunderstood, I reminded him that I imagined him as a lover, not a partner. Chuckling dismissively, Carlos said, "I've been there before. Women always say that, but in the end they want more." *Cocky bastard. How offensive, to put me—and all women—in that box.* I definitely didn't want to trap anyone or force anything. We ended the call. I felt even worse.

On our date, Carlos had brought a white chocolate bar over for dessert. He left it as a parting gift, and it sat on my kitchen counter for a year. I hate white chocolate. Finally, when I couldn't stand seeing it anymore, I threw it away. *Why did I stay hopeful? What was I hanging on to?*

Over the next three years, we ran into each other occasionally. Each time, a stale discomfort filled the space between us. If I spotted him first, I avoided contact. One day, Carlos started showing up at my Friday night salsa dancing. By that point, I had been Latin dancing for a while, and felt at home in the salsa community, and he was an insecure beginner. We had a role reversal—he became the awkward one. At first, I avoided him at the dance, feeling momentarily smug and superior. The rejection still stung. But then I noticed that he was too shy to join and was instead practicing the moves alone on the sidelines. Before the end of the evening, he made a point of complimenting me on my dancing, and I couldn't help softening. The next day, I sent him a text:

> **Amy:** Let's dance the next time you come to salsa! I noticed you mostly sitting out. Why didn't you join the lesson?

> **Carlos:** What a sweet message. Thanks for looking out for me. I'm a beginner and it's really tough to step in sometimes. I hope to get out on that dance floor soon.

At the next event, I invited him to dance. Our bodies fit well together; I love dancing with strong, short men. As I helped him learn the moves, he thanked me, apologetically, for being kind to him—implying "even when I acted like *el stúpido*."

The warmth I had always wanted to access with him was finally there. I let go of any lingering hard feelings, and we found a new groove as compatible dance partners. Our bodies were well matched. We might have made good lovers, if he had been more open or if I had been able to relax, to be more honest, more myself.

Carlos was a lesson in rejection; if I hadn't taken it personally, I wouldn't have suffered so much. Some people like white chocolate—or the color purple—and some don't. It doesn't have to be that big of a deal.

Date #18, Jonah Continued: How to Love a Ghost *February 2016*

We had only gotten together once, in August, but Jonah and I continued to message, and my hopefulness increased. Even though he would disappear, which my friends called "ghosting," I felt connected to him on a soul level and read his intermittent absences as self-protection. My longing for monkish Jonah felt romantic and creative. We made several plans to meet in person. Each time, I would put on my "lucky panties" (i.e. untattered) and get excited ... until his text would come, profusely apologizing, but irrevocably canceling. Last minute sickness, childcare, car problems, work, and other unforeseen obstacles were the norm. Jonah was always genuinely contrite. I struggled to retain my optimism.

I was willing to meet him whenever and wherever, even for a quick kiss at an I-5 highway rest stop. My ideal would have been to meet up every week, but weeks would pass without a word. I wondered, *why is it so hard to carve out a little bit of time? Does he need steadiness and patience in order to really trust me?* When I was accepting and open, the feeling between us was beautiful.

Waves of poems and songs swept through me, and I would send them to him, along with an abundance of heartfelt video messages. When we did talk, he swore that he always appreciated everything I sent, even when he didn't respond:

Amy: I really hope that sending you things doesn't push you away.

Jonah: I ALWAYS love hearing from you. Every single bit. Your poems are potent. They kill me every single time.

Amy: I'm glad you like them. The way I feel about you inspires me.

Jonah: Yes, please! More please! Any time. When I receive your poems, I wait to read them until I can be in a space where I can take them in. I often begin to respond and then delete it because I struggle find a worthy reply.

Amy: Any tiny word you send me is the most delicious morsel.

But I wished for more. More communication, more in-person dates: a tangible, less ephemeral, connection.

Our second in-person date finally happened in February, *six months* after the first one. The plan was to spend an afternoon together, but he arrived late, and was already apologizing, "On my way out of the office, I found out that I need to be back in an hour." I was disappointed, but still excited. *We were together again, however briefly.* After a bite to eat, we took a walk. We had barely gone a block when he pushed me up against a building and kissed me hard. I felt like he was trying to get my whole face into his mouth. After some intense primal kissing, he looked up, shook his fist at the sky, and exclaimed, "Why do you forsake me?" Then he came back and bit my lip so hard that it swelled and bruised. I loved it. I was happy to be branded by his desire.

... to be continued ...

7

DOWNS AND UPS

Date #40: Something Off On Broadway *February 2016*

Alan and I were a 99% match, but that was common for me, because of the open-to-most-things way I answered many of OkCupid's questions. He was traveling through Eugene, touring with a Broadway show. *Swoon. A Broadway star!*

With Sasha (my golden retriever companion) in tow, we met at Morning Glory. I thought he might like the quintessentially Eugene vegetarian breakfast cafe. Alan was handsome, just like his pictures, with a short, manicured beard, big hazel eyes, and a lithe body. Compared to us casual locals, he looked sharp in his tailored designer clothes. I felt physically attracted to him, but as we spoke, something seemed off about his mannerisms: there was a subtle jitter behind his detached façade. Though I can usually sense people's natures, I couldn't get a read on Alan, and felt thrown off, energetically. Otherwise, our time together flowed smoothly as we compared and contrasted our lifestyles.

He insisted on paying for our vegan omelets. After years of being the one who usually paid for my partners, I loved getting treated. We decided to take Sasha for a stroll before parting ways. As we wound through a neighborhood, out of nowhere, a rainstorm drenched us from head to toe. We stood on a street corner, wet as seals, about to head in opposite directions. The moment was ripe for a classic, romantic-movie downpour embrace. At the end of her leash, Sasha sat inches-deep in a puddle, patiently watching us. Even *she* knew we were supposed to kiss! But instead, we just said, "OK, bye." *End scene.*

The next day, Alan came to my house. I made dinner and then we had sex, yet I still couldn't read his cues. In bed, he was very giving, slipping under the covers after some relaxed kissing. His fingertips slowly, expertly, traced the lines of my clitoris and labia. Then he moved his full lips on my vulva, kissing it gently, repeatedly. He had a skilled tradesperson's approach, as though he had studied and mastered the art of touching a woman. I relaxed into his care and was able to fully enjoy myself. Eventually I had a lovely, unrushed orgasm due to his attentive and patient focus. Lying together afterwards, he talked about life on the road. He was on an ongoing adventure. Over the years, he was establishing sexual connections in various towns, and was putting together a connect-the-dots tour of lovers around the country. I appreciated his ambitious vision.

I asked about a tattoo on his chest. He brightened up and said that it was the chemical symbol for Ritalin, which he had been taking since childhood. Apparently, Ritalin had saved his life. I wondered, *was he hard to read emotionally because he was medicated?*

The next night, I went to see his show. I felt so small sitting in the audience, looking at the guy I just had sex with, now up on that big stage. Considering him from that vantage point, I became existential. He had been in my bed, his face between my legs, and now he was up there, a Broadway actor. *Who was he? Who was I to him? What was I doing with my life, with all of these dates? Why did I have sex with him? Was nothing sacred? Do people just bump their parts together and then go on with life?* I felt uncomfortable. I wanted more than just rolling around with whoever happened to be passing through town.

When the show was over, he gave me a backstage tour, and invited me out to pizza with his buddies, the road crew. He said he felt more comfortable with them than with the other actors, although he didn't seem to fit in with this crowd of brutes either. They were slamming down beers and booming profanities back and forth across the table. I felt quiet among them and was ready to leave early on. After a quick glass of water, I said goodnight.

He wanted to get together again before the show left town, but once was enough for me. I had no interest in a sequel—even with a Broadway star.

Date #41: Breaking the Mold *February 2016*

I love it when life proves me wrong. I had a sweet video date with Sven, from OkCupid. He was a feminine hippie boy with an outdated hairdo and a boyish, round face. Soft-spoken and easygoing, he seemed like someone from my group of friends. But I didn't feel attracted, and he lived over an hour away. Lacking strong chemistry, I let the connection fizzle.

A few weeks after our lukewarm video chat, Sven texted out of the blue on Valentine's Eve. He was in Eugene, and spontaneously invited me to go wine tasting with him. I had no Valentine's plans: *Sure!* We met at a winery and had fun sipping pinot noir and eating high-quality, locally-made chocolate. The feeling was similar to our video chat: friendly, but not sexy.

As we walked to our cars, I asked him if he wanted to kiss goodbye. *Might as well.* I was glad I asked, because *it was an amazing kiss!* I was shocked to discover that when we flipped the physical intimacy switch, we were really well-matched. Our kissing chemistry was electric.

We pulled away, smiling, and I felt suddenly energized. As the sparkly feeling coursed through me, I thought about asking him to come over, but because I had some tasks, I decided to just go home. Later that evening, he texted me from a cuddle party (the reason he had come to Eugene in the first place) and we acknowledged our attraction. I entertained the idea of shifting my schedule to spend the rest of the evening with him. After some consideration, I reneged. It felt good to set a boundary, even when I felt desire. Sven graciously received my floundering, and my "no."

I wasn't super attracted, but that kiss made me think twice! I was open to getting together again, but we never followed up. But Sven broke the mold and knocked me happily off-center. Previously, the feeling of the kiss had always precisely mirrored the energetic feeling of the date. Even though we didn't have romantic potential, our physical chemistry was undeniable. How exciting: with this new dating research discovery, if I were just looking for sex, the possibilities of finding a compatible playmate had increased!

Date #42: My Muddy Valentine *February 2016*

I was thrilled when I received an unexpected message from Ted, a very attractive, fair-featured, Scandinavian artist I had known from afar for many years. On February 15, he texted, saying, "I almost asked you out to Valentine's dinner last night." I was intrigued. I had always been mysteriously drawn to Ted but had no idea he had an affinity towards me. He seemed too airy to be a potential partner but was a brilliant candidate for my "sexually fulfilling lover" category. I imagined our sex might be like him: playfully acrobatic and creative.

Over the following week, we messaged back and forth daily about meeting up. He continued to offer options until I chose to meet him at an early evening event: a free-spirited, DJ'd, well-attended, weekly community ecstatic dance at the Vet's Club ballroom. But when I arrived, he was already deep in his experience and barely acknowledged me. *Was he avoiding me?* Perplexed, I danced with some other familiar people. Once, he came over to me, took my hand and whirled me around, and then spun away. When the evening wound down, he came straight to me, but his words and eyes were darting everywhere, making him seem nervous and distracted. A small group—the folks we had both been dancing with —scooped us up and whooshed us across the street to the Bier Stein for conversation over fries and cider.

After the spirited hang out, Ted and I walked back to the dance hall. Feeling joyful and spontaneous, and disregarding the blatant lack of in-person flirtation between us, I playfully asked if he wanted to kiss. Right away, I regretted it.

Flustered, Ted nervously explained that he couldn't kiss due to a relationship complexity. I felt confused. *Why had he gotten in touch about Valentine's Day? Why did he invite me to so many events?* My sense was that he was struggling and wanted to connect with me, but something was in the way. Despite the momentary letdown from my premature, unrequited intimacy attempt, I felt compassion about his apparent suffering.

We parted in a flurry of awkward mumbles, "I'm so sorry," "No, *I'm* sorry," and after an odd hug, we biked off in opposite directions. I shied away and didn't take the risk to ask for more communication. I would have preferred closure or clarity, rather than the loose strings that remained because we never debriefed.

Since we shared a similar community and frequented the same small organic grocery stores, we inevitably continued to run into each other. The undeniable, warm affinity between us persisted: it's chemistry! Once, a few years after our date, we were both at a music event and he came up to me (I was sitting with friends) and offered to buy me a drink. "I just ordered one," I smiled. His gesture seemed apologetic and I wondered if he was attempting, again, to engage that enigmatic space between us.

I wish I understood Ted. Instead, our relationship hangs suspended in a muddy communication purgatory.

Date #43: The Cute Guy from the Grocery Store *February 2016*

I sent a message to Vince. He seemed rustic, and had smiling, emotional eyes. Before he replied, I re-read his OkCupid bio and noticed that he was bisexual and looking for men. Feeling awkward, I followed up with a second message to apologize. Vince responded, interested in meeting. He shared that he had yet to find a satisfying emotional connection with a man. After a short video chat, we decided to meet up for Thai food at Ta Ra Rin.

In person, the space between us was open and friendly, and we decided to share my two favorite dishes, Pad Kee Mao and Pad Prik King. Vince was strangely familiar. As we slurped our saucy noodles, he explained that he was dating a monogamous man, and that he didn't mind being monogamous or polyamorous, as long as he felt loved. *How endearing ... but why was he on OkCupid?* Crunching on garlicky green beans, he said that he hadn't seen his new exclusive boyfriend in weeks. Evidently, their relationship was mostly through texting, and even those messages were rare. That didn't sound fulfilling to me. It reminded me of my experience with Jonah, except for the monogamy part.

On our second date, we met downtown for tea and then took a walk. We figured out that he used to work at my neighborhood grocery store, fifteen years ago. *Vince was "that cute guy at the grocery store"!* I had lusted after him in his days of skinny jeans, eyeliner and dyed blue hair: to me, he was art in motion. But by the time we became romantic potentials, he had grown softer, and sadder. The realization that he was "that guy" made me more interested in the connection. Plus, like me, he was a Pisces, and I love swimming around with sensitive Pisces men.

For our last date, Vince came to Nia. That wasn't the first time my students got a sneak peek of my dating life, the conspicuous new man in the class. He danced along seamlessly—I had purposefully chosen music he liked (the Cure). After class, we went back to my house, where we ate lunch, sat on my couch, and finally kissed.

He looked at me, and said, "Hmm."

I responded, "Hmm. Try again?"

The second kiss felt exactly the same. We laughed. The contact point of our lips felt thick and stiff. Not needing any more information, we parted as friends, and stayed connected through social media.

The coolest part about the experience with Vince was the realization that you actually can wind up going out with that cute guy from the grocery store. But before you check out, let your lips be the judge.

Date #44: Reservations *March 2016*

Casper was a research scientist and looked cute in his OkCupid pictures. In our messaging, he was responsive. He was a Capricorn, which to me usually means solid and dependable. Everything looked good on e-paper. When we first messaged, he was suspicious that I was a bot because I was typing so quickly. Eventually, he must have decided I was real because we made a plan to meet at Mamé—a super popular new restaurant in the Whit that I had been wanting to try.

When I pulled up, he was waiting at the entrance, a toothy smile beaming from behind a big, bushy beard that had not made an appearance in his online profile. Before I even turned my car off, my radar said *nope, not interested*, more from my energetic impression than beard-resistance. Stiffness took over my body as I parked, and I climbed out reluctantly. Stepping slowly towards the door of the hard-to-get-into, reservations-only restaurant, I was definitely having my own reservations. I thought about my friend Stacy's warning: make short first dates. *Why hadn't I asked for a video date first?*

We entered the overcrowded restaurant. Casper's eyes were wide with excitement; he didn't register my disappointment. I knew that eating at this restaurant meant a long, multi-course dining commitment, and that hours of claustrophobic suffering awaited me. But we slid into the date, and I dropped into question-asking mode. We talked about him, exclusively, for the fourteen-course, two-hour meal. He was not to blame. I dug my own hole and stepped into the pit of suffering.

Although my intention was to practice radical honesty when dating, human interaction can be hypnotizing. I would often abandon my goal, repress my emotions, freeze a smile onto my face, and later, be flooded with regret. I knew there was a better way, but I wasn't always able to achieve it.

I was eventually stuffed with food, information about him, and undigested inner conflict. We wrapped up the endless meal. For some reason, even though he offered to pay for me, I insisted on covering my meal *(at least I didn't offer to pay for him!)*. The bill was $50 each, without drinks. I was miserable because I failed in my quest to be honest, and I guess I "made myself pay" for not embodying the communication queen I wanted to be.

Casper asked me to walk with him to his car, saying that he had something to give me. I felt curious. He handed me a talisman that became very dear to me and still sits on my shelf: a metallic blue, wind-up, knife-wielding she-robot ... *who looks like me!* He chose it for *"Amy the Bot,"* without knowing how badly I needed to be less human. She inspires me to be a cool, detached warrior of truth.

Electra, the knife-wielding robot

Receiving this gift lifted my mood, so when Casper suggested kissing, I said sure. It was a blustery evening, and he pulled me close. As our mouths touched, I felt a cold, wet sensation on my top lip: the mucous that had been accumulating in his thick mustache. I said nothing. Disgusted and bloated, I walked away hugging my robot and wiped Casper's snot off my face.

Date #45: The Effeminate Dom *March 2016*

Neil seemed cute and quirky in his OkCupid profile. When I sent a message, he responded immediately, wanting to get together right away ... NOW! Resistant to his excessive enthusiasm, I slowed the pace and we met up a few nights later at M Bar, my favorite wine bar in Portland.

Before his tail hit the seat, Neil started his pitch, laying the groundwork for the evening: he was into BDSM, and was a dom. "Your signature's lowercase *a* in our messaging was the classic signal that you're a sub." I had already been sized up as submissive, and therefore a match for him. *Interesting.*

As Neil spoke, his mannerisms distracted me. I think most people would have assumed he was flamboyantly gay, yet he purported to be a hetero dom. Red-headed and dressed like a nerd, he even wore an argyle vest. I didn't know what to make of this cognitive dissonance.

We spent a memorable hour together. I have always felt drawn to explore BDSM. Memories arose of a time long ago when I discovered the intensity of relinquishing control and relishing pain. An unexpected relationship with a strong psychosexual power dynamic brought me gratefully to my symbolic and literal knees. My boyfriend's expertly delivered strikes translated into sublime euphoria. It was mind-altering, endorphin-filled bliss to be controlled, marked, and loved by the right hands.

Neil continued refilling his water while I was sipping wine and slipping into a woozy state. As I grew more wobbly, the wine worked in his favor, undermining my stability. Spikes from Neil's eyes penetrated me, tangibly. Suddenly dominant, his lisp disappeared, his tone lowered, and his fluid body turned rigid. Neil was transforming before my unreliable eyes. He was all masculine. His casual reclining had shifted into an erect spine. Facing me squarely, he spoke sharply, directing his comments to somewhere deep inside me. He was a stranger playing with power, but I felt mostly safe. We were in public, and I had absolute conviction that we would not be physical.

I was determined not to submit. He poked around, darting like a dragon, trying to find a way in, testing me for fault lines. I held my center and remained consciously detached. Then suddenly, he relaxed back in his seat and reverted to his effeminate lisp. With a flippy, dismissive hand-waving gesture, Neil proclaimed his final diagnosis:

"You know what you are? *Thwitchy, Thwitchy, Thwitchy!*"

I smiled, victorious. Satisfied with the assessment, I liked thinking of myself as a "switch," someone who explores both dominance and submission. Neil abandoned his hopes of getting me into his dungeon, and shifted gears, moving into a mentoring role. In our parting words, he told me to masturbate while I fantasized about being both a total sub and a total dom. *Maybe.*

As we said goodbye, Neil shrugged his shoulders; I stood taller than usual. My muscles were vibrating with aliveness. Stimulated by BDSM considerations, I wanted to step up and get some leather outfits!

I never did the homework. Even at a distance and no longer in touch, I didn't want to follow Neil's orders. His generous suggestions for my sexual development in his area of expertise didn't stick: he wasn't a match for me, even as a teacher. In order for a relationship to thrive—whether romantic, sexual, client, friend, or teacher—the bond must be strong.

We didn't have chemistry, but this was an entertaining date with a lasting impact: thanks to Neil, I started signing my name with a capital *A*.

And, I got some leather. ;)

Date #46: I Flew Through the Air with the Greatest of Ease
(Told from both perspectives) March 2016

Jarrod and I had a low match percentage on OkCupid, but I kept going back to check out his profile. Tall, with round features and a mop of soft-looking, curly, blondish hair, he oozed gentleness in his pictures. A classics professor and a playwright, he was into yoga, weightlifting, and soccer. After a week of enduring curiosity about him, I reached out. We decided to get together for cider.

In person, everything was easy. Jarrod was a receptive, alert listener, so I felt uncommonly free to talk about myself. The cider loosened us up and our words bubbled about freely. We leaned our smiling faces towards each other across the table. I enjoyed gazing at his big, soft features: his wide mouth smiled like a crescent moon, and his clear blue eyes portrayed depth and intelligence. He was from the Deep South, and called me "ma'am," took my coat off, opened doors, and pushed in my chair: classic movie-style chivalry. I liked it. At the end of the date, he walked me to my car. We lingered awkwardly for a moment, then thanked each other joyfully. I shifted onto my tiptoes to hug him through his puffy down jacket. I wanted to kiss but felt too shy to ask. Later when we were both home, we texted:

Amy: I had such a good time. Thank you.

Jarrod: Wow. I had a great time too. I felt like you were going to say something when I was saying goodbye.

Amy: Yes, I would've asked you to kiss. I'm sorry that I didn't.

Jarrod: I would have loved to! I really wanted to hold your body.

Amy: I should have asked. It seems like things tend to go more smoothly, consent-wise, when women initiate. And like you said, you are from the South, and very polite.

Jarrod: I try to be. It's important to me. Though please don't mistake politeness for lack of desire.

Amy: OK, I won't. 😊

We went out the next night and had more cider, quite a bit this time. Again, I felt great with him. Revving up with mutual engagement and laughter, we had plenty to talk about. We shared memorable nighttime dreams from when we were young. In his childhood dream, there was a lurching, hungry brown bear. I found him quite bear-like and hoped I would get to experience more of his ursine nature.

Suddenly, he wanted to get going. I thought we were going to step out to kiss goodnight, but he invited me to his place—just a few blocks away. It was a classic bachelor pad: a cluttered, unkempt, small apartment with 1970s décor that featured a loft bed perched way up near the ceiling. I would have needed a ladder to get onto it. Instead, Jarrod lifted me high in the air and literally threw me up there and climbed up after me. I wasn't completely ready to have sex but didn't say so. Our bodies weren't a natural fit, and I didn't feel completely at ease. But I liked him so much, and because of the warmth between us, and the cider buzz, it didn't feel bad. Leaving his place, I felt a mixture of giddiness—from the unforeseen surprise of having sex with someone new—and emotional discomfort, from the little things that didn't feel quite right. I wasn't sure what we meant to each other and what our unspoken assumptions were regarding intercourse.

Before that date, he had been very communicative. But after we had sex, several wordless days passed, so I messaged:

Amy: Can we check in sometime today? It feels important to me to connect after having sex with you.

Jarrod: Of course. I'd like that a lot.

Amy: How are you feeling about our night together? I'm tempted to invite you over. Is that crazy?

Jarrod: I'm feeling great about the other night. It was tender and lovely and very pleasurable. It's not crazy at all. It pleases me. I'm tempted to comply should I be invited.

Amy: Ever since we had sex, I have wondered what's going on with us. It felt sweet before that, but now I feel odd about it. Is it just me?

Jarrod: Oh, no, really? It doesn't feel odd to me. Is it because

I've been relatively silent? I've been underwater at work this week. Work, eat, sleep, repeat. What do you think?

Amy: It did feel odd for you to be silent. Something happens to me when I have sex, when I move beyond casual flirtation. Maybe it's a female thing. It's not that I need our relationship to be more than casual. I just like to communicate after sex.

Jarrod: I feel terrible that I've been incommunicado. I don't feel distant but I completely hear what you're saying. We had two great connections—Friday and Saturday—but then very little follow-up. That's probably a strange disjoint. Speaking of connecting ... are you free tomorrow?

Amy: Thank you for these sensitive messages. I really appreciate them. Yes, I'd love to see you.

We went out again, for more cider, of course. Wanting to practice in-person honesty, I again voiced that it hurt me when he disappeared. I needed to be able to speak my truth in a text, on a video message, or face-to-face. Jarrod was disturbed that I was hurt. I generally hope men will get in touch after we have sex, to nurture me by showing their enduring interest. My internal process is, "I opened myself to you and let you inside my body. Please reassure me that that wasn't a stupid thing to do." But how many people don't tell the whole truth about our vulnerability, how we are affected by ghosting, silence, or detachment? Always wanting to be strong, I had gotten used to shutting down and taking care of myself, but true strength for me was being able to look at someone and say I felt hurt. Jarrod listened and cared. I was honest, he was sweet, and the cider was doing its magic. The next thing I knew, I was back at his place, naked, getting tossed back up onto that bed-in-the-sky!

Being with Jarrod was fun and easy, although we only had four or five dates. They all had this same pattern of cider→ tossed up into the bed. He literally charmed the pants off me each time we connected, but once they were off, our sex was sloppy and loose, like his hair and apartment. Maybe it was our different body types, or too much cider. It never felt very sexy, despite our efforts. We liked each other, but in bed, I felt claustrophobic, pressed up near the ceiling with his cider-filled, semi-hard penis, trying to make it all work. We never spoke about our lack of strong sexual chemistry. I usually felt ready to leave pretty soon after being launched up there. The cider helped lubricate things enough to get us into bed, but regular drinking wasn't sustainable for me.

When I met Jarrod, I had been looking for a steady lover for over a year. He retreated to the relationship back burner and moved away a few months later. From time to time, Jarrod reached out for flirty attention when he felt lonely. We sexted a bit, but I was tired of flings that didn't seem to lead anywhere. Once when he texted out of the blue, we processed about our relationship a bit:

> **Amy:** I think you are lovely. But I am wanting to find people to fall in love with, not just sex and fun. I'm more interested in soul connections at this point.
>
> **Jarrod:** I've wanted to revel in our playful personalities. But it sounds like you're looking for something deeper.
>
> **Amy:** Yes, but you brought out a lightness in me. I had fun when we got together.
>
> **Jarrod:** The feeling is mutual.

I wanted sexual passion and soulful love. Jarrod and I didn't have either of those ingredients. I did enjoy the flying, though!

Jarrod's Perspective

> Amy and I were a study in opposites. Settling down at a table, we probably both felt the differences. She was bubbly; I was reserved. She was vibrant; I was contained. She was short; I was (and still am) tall. Yet our connection felt exciting. The first date was a buzz of flirty, quick conversation. As she spoke, fingers flew about her like wild birds. There we sat for

two hours: a lovely wood sprite and one of Tolkien's lumbering ents.

We met a second time at a tiny, low-lit restaurant that glittered with shiny floors and polished brass. As we talked, we edged our chairs nearer. Between us, the energy sparked again. In the shadows outside, I leaned forward as she arched up and we kissed and held each other in the dark. I could feel the warmth of her skin on mine. Did she want to come over? Perhaps ... maybe ... *yes!* Two people from opposite sides of the continent, from different pages of experience, with contrasting natures. These all dissolved later in my high-propped bed as I entered little Amy. After our differences co-mingled, we relaxed, warm and wet, in each other's arms.

The next time we met, we sat even closer. Talked closer. Felt closer. It's nice to remember those sweet days when our paths and persons crossed, but we were ultimately pointed in different directions.

Date #47: The Pragmatic Poet *April 2016*

Jean was a poetry and literature professor. I am "sapiosexual," turned on by intellect, and his OkCupid profile was engagingly erudite; it read like Joyce or Elliot. I had to look up the meaning of his profile name, "Anagnoretic": *the moment in a play or novel when a character recognizes or discovers another character's true identity.* Many of the words he used were new to me. I was so taken that I copied his profile into a document to study it.

When we met for coffee, I found Jean exquisitely handsome. He had pure white hair, deep blue eyes and the rosiest cheeks. Looking professorial, he was thin, wore wire-rimmed glasses, and was dressed in a button-up shirt and slacks. As we spoke, Jean smiled shyly. I had a lot to say, bubbling on about love, relationships, dreams, astrology, music, and writing. Up until this point in my dating adventures, my only lasting attraction was to Jonah. I felt motivated to "lay myself out on the table" so he would get a sense of who I really was. Then, he told me something very private about a health condition, and I was touched by his sadness and vulnerability.

When a quiet moment arose, I asked—as I often do—"How are you feeling about our date so far?" With dull eyes, he noted that our main difference was that I was spiritual where he was pragmatic. From my perspective, there isn't a huge gap between cosmic and scientific. I like to think of myself as a stable blend of the two, but I can come off as "out there" to more logical-minded people.

He added that he didn't want to open his heart to someone who wasn't monogamous. I reserved a small hope that it could be different with *me*. Pushing just a bit, I suggested we could shoot pool and make out sometime just for fun, without any plans to become a couple. At the time, he said that he would consider it, but the few times I reached out, he was "too busy." Jean's reservations were probably wise. *Anagnorisis* ultimately moved us separately on, following our natures.

Date #48: Heartbreak, Wizard-Style *April 2016*

As I looked through Soren's OkCupid profile, something deep in me moved; I was giddy, like a little girl who discovered a treasure chest. His job description was "Esteemed proprietor of a between-the-worlds establishment, serving sacredly enhanced elixirs." Highly intrigued, I sent a message:

> **Amy:** Hi, Soren! I get a really good feeling from your pictures and profile. It sounds like you are some kind of alchemist. I'm very interested in magic. I feel enthusiastic about connecting with you!
>
> **Soren:** Magic is where it's at. I'm open.
>
> **Amy:** Great! Would you want to meet up? Usually I chat quite a bit before meeting, but with you, I feel ready to meet just because of this feeling I have.

Soren: Let's do it.

Soren's pithy texts were like riddles and went under my skin. Desiring to connect, I used a similar, cheeky texting language, riffing with his style. I felt engaged and on edge. He sent directions to meet him at his shop, and when I saw them, my heart jumped: *The apothecary I'd been looking for!* Karezza Boy Chad (with the tea ritual at the Chinese restaurant) had told me about his shop. I had been intently seeking it for months, and now this hard-to-find man appeared on OkCupid! The connection suddenly had more gravity.

We met after-hours. Approaching the apothecary hesitantly, I held my breath. My chest tightened as I stepped inside. He called, "Hey!" as he was moving briskly, cleaning up. After a few moments, he looked up at me and lifted a long arm straight up in the air, as if he confidently knew the answer to a question, then went back to his task, singing.

The shop was empty. I felt like a piece of furniture. Trying to play it cool, I shyly observed him. Then, he paused to look at me and consider my presence more seriously. Everything felt strange. *What was this place?* Time slowed. Our eyes met. There were questions hanging everywhere. In my mind, they were something like,

Amy: *Are you my true love, the one I've been waiting to meet all my life?*

Soren: *Are you planning to steal my soul? Do you think you can handle my medicine?*

His bright green eyes gazed at me steadily from under wild, bushy brows. He had thick hair that was mostly grey, though he was only in his early 40's. Sensuously round muscles pressed through his soft, light blue cotton t-shirt. And the way his brown cadet-style cap was twisted off to the side made him painfully attractive to me.

Staring back at him, I felt weak. Soren hit the exact tuning fork frequency of my "core erotic theme." (Jack Morin coined this concept about formative and lasting sexual triggers.) Soren's brand of boyish cuteness tweaked my entire system and touched my big "YES" button. I had a crush on a similarly cute boy in junior high who had this certain *je ne sais quoi*, and wore baseball hats, and also didn't seem to notice me. Standing there, I felt woozy from oxytocin, dopamine, and pheromones. Soren's aloofness was a hook.

When our eye contact released, he seemed a little more human. He softened, moved closer to me, and asked if I would enjoy a drink. Relieved to have something to focus on besides him, I gratefully accepted. Soren stepped behind the counter to study a long row of elongated, colorful bottles. Looking back and forth between me and the elixirs, he half-smiled and selected a greenish potion from the shelf.

We moved to a small wooden table and he poured tall, slender glasses of the mysterious brew. I tasted honey, herbs, and flowers. Its effervescence was strange and seemed more squiggly than bubbly. When I swallowed, a cool wave rushed down me, followed by a hot sensation that shot from my heels up my midline. I tuned in and imagined my cells were millions of colorful quickly-blooming flowers. Spinning with hormones and altered from the elixir, I was flying. Karezza Boy Chad said he was a "true wizard." *What was in this stuff?*

Trying to manage my big reaction to Soren and the drink, I overcompensated and acted stiff and formal, as though at an interview. He asked me about pottery and my master's program, and I wanted to know about the elixirs and how he became an alchemist. There was a pronounced coolness to his demeanor as he explained the plant extracts. His lips stayed mostly pursed.

Every once in a while, a beaming smile would flash while his eyes brushed past mine in slow motion. Eye contact between us felt loaded, and I wondered, *might he have Medusa-type powers?* There was definitely some magic afoot: in the walls, in the elixirs, and in him.

Though reserved, he was generous. He shared his special potion freely and offered a tarot reading for me as we sipped from our glasses. When he drew the card called "the Angel," his eyes bulged, and my heart moved. He tilted his head, and asked, "Angel, huh?"

Smiling, I shrugged and said, "Aren't we all?"

When I asked what he was looking for with online dating, he leaned towards me and said, "I just want to have a genuine human connection." I thought, *if I could only relax, I'm sure we could have that.* He mentioned, "Outside, at this moment, the Scorpio full moon is rising." I raised my eyebrows and nodded. We both knew that could signify a potent beginning.

I was traveling home to Eugene that night and didn't stay late. When we said goodbye, his hug was quick and stiff. Then he bent away at a strange angle and waved, with what looked like a sarcastic expression. I interpreted his body language as "Time for you to go now," and felt upset.

Because of his detached demeanor, I assumed my feelings weren't mutual. On my drive home, I messaged him. After a short debrief of our time together, I said:

Amy: I found you attractive in many ways. I left with the feeling that you weren't interested in me, but maybe I was wrong?

Soren: I had fun, and I also think you're attractive. I am interested. "The Angel and the Wizard" sounds compelling. Let's get together again soon.

Although his actions had been generous, I hadn't felt any romantic interest from him. A week later, when we met at his shop, there was more warmth between us. He served the same "Dragon's Tongue" elixir we had shared the first time. For dinner, we walked to ¿Por Qué No?, a restaurant on North Mississippi Avenue that we both loved. We found a tiny table and sat beneath low-hanging piñatas.

Soren leaned in to ask, under the noise, how the elixir affected me. "I feel like millions of pink and yellow flowers are exploding into bloom inside me," I answered. With smiling eyes, he nodded slowly, studying me. I felt seen by him for the first time.

Then he wanted to play an energy game and said I should just notice my internal experience. I closed my eyes and my second chakra, in the depths of my belly, felt warm. When I reported this, he closed his eyes softly and nodded, smiling. I was an eager student and wanted more. *Was I falling under a spell?*

After we finished our *pescado* tacos and chips, we went for a stroll. I wished we were holding hands, but his were deep inside his pockets, and I felt hesitant to initiate with this quirky man. But when we arrived at my car, I faced him and boldly asked if he wanted to kiss.

He seemed puzzled, as though I had asked him to speak Swahili … but he said OK. Shifting up onto my toes, I leaned towards him. Our lips didn't match up right. The kiss was *so weird*. It landed on his bottom lip, which had the responsiveness of soggy cardboard. Soren just stood there, stunned, looking straight ahead. Mortified, I scrambled to make it better and tried again, this time finding both lips. I felt a tiny response, as though his lips were asking a question. We parted awkwardly. On my way home, I messaged him to say how strange the kiss felt. I was comforted by his response, "We'll just have to try again, soon."

The next week, he invited me for dinner at his small cabin in the woods. I made a Thai noodle dish that tasted complex and authentic, which was surprising because I'm not a very good cook. *Was I channeling his magic?* It tasted better than any food I had ever made.

After dinner, Soren invited me to listen to music. We sat in side-by-side armchairs that faced an empty wall. He drummed on his body and chair constantly, and announced each artist as the next song came on: Captain Beefheart, Gudrun Gut, Faust, and other obscure artists. I tried to initiate conversation a few times, but he just nodded, shrugged, or shook his head in response. I felt jealous of the music: *how did it so thoroughly capture his attention?* When Soren asked if I was OK, I shrugged and nodded at the same time. Reading my confusion, he looked at me with one big eye and said, "I'm a weird guy." My painful attraction to him made me willing to be an awkward co-pilot to his passionate, hour-long wall-watching music experience. I wished I knew what he thought about me.

When the listening session was over, he walked me to my car. I was hesitant to initiate kissing again. Gently placing his hands on my shoulders, he cocked his head slightly to the side, and with resolve, pulled me to his lips. The kiss was so electric I wondered if it burned my lips. I wobbled backwards. "Getting better," he winked as we parted. As he bounced away, his gait made him look like a proud young boy. During the following week, we texted:

Soren: I had a dream last night: an angel was inside an oven, making elaborate pastries on a pottery wheel. When they were finished baking, she pulled them apart. They were delicious, with angel-light filling.

Amy: Wow.

Soren: Truth.

Amy: Maybe one day you'll invite me to sleep over. I wouldn't say no.

Soren: You are most definitely invited to sleep over. See you Thursday.

The next week, I made us a vibrant platter of sushi with my newfound culinary magic. Afterwards, as we took our places in the armchairs for another session of parallel music listening, I felt a wave of dread. *Would all of our dates be like this, sitting side-by-side, listening to his angular, abstract music?* After thirty grueling minutes, he looked over and asked, "Would you like to lay down next to each other?" My whole body relaxed.

Rolling out a thick foam mat, he made us a bed on the living room floor next to a fireplace. (He had recently moved in and didn't have a regular mattress yet.) We started off lying down, looking at the ceiling, holding hands. It was a new orientation of our side-by-side, and this one felt much better.

In the quiet, for the first time, I felt an emotional connection with Soren. He rolled over to face me, as if feeling it too, and asked, "Would you like to play the energy game?"

I rolled towards him to align our chakras. "A warm swelling in my heart chakra," I told him. He nodded. "Now there's a bright blast in my third eye. Like glittering stars," and then, "Oh! An expansive watery warmth in my second chakra." I was surprised by how clearly I could feel it.

Then he said, "I'm going to send a bubble of golden energy straight in." I felt it push into my solar plexus, my third chakra. I was getting high from being with Soren; I had never experienced anything like it. Feeling playful, I pushed him; he pushed back, and we laughed like kids. Then I went at him with all of my strength, amplified from the charge of our connection, and we wrestled hard, exerting maximum effort, for a minute or two. Eventually, he pinned me, kissed me with his electric lips, and released me.

I climbed on him and pinned his arms above his head. Our eye contact deepened. The world stopped.

After an extended, dreamy moment, I realized I couldn't move. The world between our eyes liquified, and my body became paralyzed, invisibly bound. Tears formed and my whole body trembled in ecstasy. I felt close to orgasm, fully clothed, without even moving or being touched. It was exquisite, perfect power. I felt an overwhelming urge to surrender, to experience everything possible with him.

He released me after some unknown amount of time in this "chakra lock" (the name I invented). I cried in his arms. We cuddled and kissed and rolled around like kittens. I fell asleep on top of him, solid and safe on his heart. My ear was folded and numb when I awoke.

Soren must have awakened at the same moment; his voice was strangely loud, filling the dark room like an intercom announcement, "Do you have everything you need?" His quirky delivery was strangely nurturing. Throughout the night, I woke and slept again, each time shifting my chakras towards his, re-aligning our energy centers. At one point in my light sleep, he kissed my neck, and I thought, *I could linger in this moment for the rest of eternity.*

When we awoke in the morning, he dubbed us "survivors of the first Angel-Wizard slumber party." I was glowing. I asked if I could touch his penis, and after a thoughtful pause, he said, "That would be OK with me." He pulled his boxers down and was erect. I felt strangely drawn to his cock, admiring it like art; I had never found a penis truly beautiful before and spent quite a while adoring it. I first used my hands and then my mouth, moving slowly and carefully as I caressed the sacred limb of this most special being.

And then, with feather-sensitive fingers, his meditative touch floated me into an orgasmic stratosphere. Moving slowly and precisely, he ushered me to a sexual height I had never before experienced. He kept me lingering way up there for a very long time. It was an elongated climax that soared over a cosmic mesa.

In the middle of my orgasmic transport, someone knocked loudly at his door. Afraid I may have disturbed the neighbors, I whispered, "Was I being too loud?" No, he'd promised to lend a quick hand to his neighbor.

"Be right back," he said, kissed my forehead, and dashed out. Shaking and electrified, my orgasmic state continued. I wandered naked through his place, touching the ceiling—*little me, touching a ceiling! How did I get so tall?* It was the magic: sex magic, wizard magic. I circulated around, stretching upward in a wandering, ceiling-touching orgasm, reveling in the highest sexual high I had ever felt. Somewhere in the space-time continuum, that orgasm is still happening.

Soon, he returned; we crawled back into bed to relax into a mystical sex afterglow. The sweet spring morning poured through his window. Some time passed, and then he made us coffee. We sipped the strong brew sitting in the floor-bed and talked about relationships. I asked him, "What do you think about me being polyamorous?"

"I'm not clingy and weird or anything," he said.

"I think I might be clingy and weird."

"Better than the alternative: clingy and NOT weird," he joked.

We laughed. *Was I falling in love with his weird self?* I felt nervous when he flippantly said, "I've always been monogamous, but I could be polyamorous, no big deal." For me, it was a very big deal. I wanted to have as many of those orgasmagical experiences as I could. He gave me a bottle of the magical Dragon's Tongue, and I was thrilled to have something of his to take with me, and into me.

After our otherworldly night, I felt confused. I questioned my assertion of being polyamorous, willing to bargain to secure our connection, to hang on to this magical wizard. I stopped putting energy into dating, focusing only on the Wizard. Even when ghosty Jonah reached out, I wasn't very responsive.

I wrote poems, trying to grasp the ineffable. We continued to have sleepovers weekly when I was in Portland. Sometimes we would go out to eat, or to an arcade or a movie. Each date started with elixirs at the shop. Between dates, we flirted through texts:

Soren: Our fields are starting to mix.

Amy: How do you feel about that?

Soren: I love a good mystery!

Amy: I really like your field.

Soren: You're a fucking magical universe!

We kept the rhythm up for a handful of weeks, but it was never as sexy and magical as that first night together. My difficult feelings from our very first date still lingered; I was afraid that he didn't like me, that I wasn't special enough for him. I craved more time with him, and when I asked about spending two nights together, he said, "one night feels abundant." His interest seemed to fade, and as it did, I grew more hooked in. Our conversations, both from a distance and in person, were fraught with confusion and misinterpretations.

When it was good, it was profound and addictive. In the arms of the Wizard, in the bed of the Wizard, I was a toy, a puppet, whatever he wanted from me. *Was it obsession or love?* I didn't understand his reserved, internal style, and felt fractured inside. I ignored the red flags. Wishing the relationship could work, I was willing to put so much into it, to lose so much, including my pride. I made myself crazy and couldn't figure out how to relax and just be myself with him. I kept going back to him, entranced, full of little girl hope.

One time when we woke up in the morning, after some mutual sensual touching, I climbed on top of him and pressed my vulva against his hard penis, putting our genitals in skin to skin contact for the first time. With his cock against his belly, I slid my wetness up and down along the shaft extremely slowly. Although I wanted to, we hadn't had intercourse yet. Soren had set a boundary against penetration, and I wasn't sure how he would respond to this "almost" state. He smiled softly. Intensely energized, I was elated to finally experience this contact, and yearned to take him into my body. Then, Soren suddenly gripped my throat firmly, choking me gently in a way that sent an orgasmic wave of ecstasy flooding my entire body. Afterwards, we had a sweet breakfast, and said goodbye. Later that morning, my vagina was burning. I texted Soren:

Amy: My yoni is on fire today. It's distracting.

Soren: I'm in a similar position.

Amy: On your back with your legs up in the air?

Soren: If necessary.

Amy: It's intense.

Soren: Me too. Very warm.

Amy: Is it just energetic? Was I rubbing against you too hard?

Soren: I don't know what to think. I'm feeling a lot of heat. We weren't doing anything hard or rough.

Amy: I would feel awful if I gave anything to you.

I was scared: *was it the herpes that "couldn't be transmitted" from Ivan's big, condomless penis?* Petrified that I had given him an STI, I went to get tested right away. I thought he would end things with me if I had positive results. Soren's communications that week were short and distant. He said, "I'll know what I need to do when your results come in." *Not very reassuring.*

Both of us had burning symptoms that lasted several days. At the end of the stressful week, I got my results: all negative. *The burning must have been the magical sexual kundalini fire between us.* I wished he would see it that way. But the week after I shared my results, I barely heard from him. I texted:

Amy: Tonight?

Soren: We can hang out. I don't think I'll be up for putting out.

Amy: Putting out?

Soren: Making out.

Amy: Ha ha. We don't have to make out.

We drank elixirs and then took a long walk and talked. He saw the burning as an omen. The space between us felt sober. I knew I should go home, but I slept over. When I tried cuddling up to him, he barely responded. In bed the next morning, after a distant night, I told him that I thought I loved him. He said, "Love is strong."

You know that amazing feeling when you can tell that someone loves you and you can feel the wash of their love? The high you feel from the shared magnetism? Well, that was the feeling that was NOT there. I devoured his crumbs like chocolate cream pies. I was lost in the dream of his magical powers. I didn't know how to capture his attention.

On our date the following week, I initiated sexually by going down on him. But Soren just lay there stiffly. When I asked if he was OK, he grabbed my thighs, and pulled my crotch to his face. Suddenly we were in the "69" position for the first time, and he started going at me with a primal voracity. I had never experienced such fierce sexual attention before. *He was angry.* It was painful, soul-painful. Closing my thighs, I climbed off him. After a long, stale silence, I said that things were feeling off between us. "Mm-hmm," he replied, then turned his back and was soon snoring; I barely slept at all. In the morning, Soren had to get to the shop early. We hurried out without much conversation.

The whole next week, my body felt like it was getting stabbed, wrenched and beaten. Wishing for access to the deepest, most magical intimacy possible with him, I strategized. I needed a grand gesture and decided to be wild and spontaneous: I made an audio recording of myself having an orgasm, and quickly sent it to him. *No response.* After three more days, I reached out to see if he still wanted to get together that week. He replied, "Sure."

That last time, the food I made was mushy and disgusting. It couldn't be ignored that we were overcooked. We smoked some strong marijuana and our conversation was strained. When I eventually said, "Did you get my recording?" he grimaced. He was angry. Shaking his head, he said that he knew it didn't make sense, but he experienced it as "abusive." I apologized, but also felt confused that my vulnerable act had upset him, *the exact opposite of my intention.*

When it was time to go to sleep, Soren lay down next to me and curled up with his back to me, shut down. In the morning, he used his loud announcement voice to say that he wanted to stop our sleepovers and was no longer interested in a romantic relationship. I sat up, stunned, and looked straight ahead at nothing. I felt embarrassed to be in his bed when he didn't want me there. Shaking my head, incredulous, I said, "I can't believe my orgasm killed the relationship." I bagged up the toiletries I had been leaving there, along with the remnants of our disgusting dinner. For the last time, he walked me to my car. As we said goodbye, he said, "Don't worry. We'll talk soon."

I hoped that meant he would reach out, but he didn't. After a few months, I messaged to say I thought we were going to stay in touch. Soren was defensive, but invited me to meet him at his shop, during business hours. Needing closure, I went. We were strangers. His vacant eyes looked away, like a boy in a timeout. Rejection filled me like lead, and I said my final goodbye. I needed to break the spell.

This chapter with the Wizard carved a hole in my heart, and I climbed in to slowly lick my wounds. Soren exposed me to what was possible in the realm of sexual magic. *Would I find that again? Could I settle for less?* Though I continued to date, over a year would pass before I could open my heart again.

8

BURNED BY MAGICAL FLAMES

Date #49: Not Sleeping in Seattle
(Told from both perspectives) June 2016

Before I met Soren, I was chatting with Nikolas on OkCupid. He lived in Seattle (five hours away) but our flirting felt fun and easy—*why not?* Although both of us preferred dating locally, we continued texting. Nikolas seemed so handsome—with tanned skin, dark hair, and crystal blue, diamond-shaped eyes. He loved to text and sent lots of emojis—not too cool to be cheesy. Communication flowed, our hearts happily bumping.

His profile featured his most prized possession, a sailboat, and I thought, *maybe I should sail around the world with Nikolas.* We joked that he could set sail down the I-5 freeway and pick me up en route. I saw an image of him: brave and determined at the helm, underway, weaving through the car-filled highway.

I stopped flirting with Nikolas in April, after Soren swept me away. But by June, for my sanity, I decided I should date again. *Maybe seeing someone else would stabilize my fracturing heart?*

∽

The day after my mother died in 2013 was my daughter's fifteenth birthday. She had always been unhappy in my five-woman, mixed-family house, and her father was in love with a woman in Port Townsend, Washington. She and her dad had been traveling up there every other weekend, and that was where she met her first boyfriend. I really liked him, and felt so happy for her, that when she asked me—on her birthday—if she could move to Port Townsend, we both cried as I said yes.

~

I was heading north to her high school graduation and made a last-minute plan to meet Nikolas for tacos on the streets of Tacoma. As we were walking towards each other, he waved to me from afar and it was immediately apparent that the image I had conjured had been a projection. *Ugh! Why had we not done a short video call?*

Nikolas was flirty but awkward. He was a sweet Pisces, and we jived conversationally, as we had through messaging. As we ate, he admitted that he was naïve in the relationship world: he had been in only three committed relationships. After eating, he asked to kiss, and our lack of chemistry was confirmed. Kissing can make me tremble, ushering me into an altered state. But some kissing feels mundane, or worse.

After our flat kiss, I drove off, feeling low and embarrassed that I had dreamed Nikolas could be a magical balm for my open Wizard wound.

Nikolas's Perspective

I met Amy on OkCupid. She was professed poly and I was poly-curious. Amy was so fun to text with that I broke my rule of not communicating too much before meeting.

Our texting was exciting. I couldn't stop. It was also a bit frantic for me, because she was so fast. She had a quick wit, and I did everything I could to keep up. As we continued to text, we were increasingly sweeter with each other. Soon we were sending kisses goodnight and such.

She was understanding when I expressed my nervousness about her being poly, and unconcerned that we lived many hours away from each other. I was intrigued, but hesitant, not wanting a long-distance relationship. We decided to meet. It was funny to be in a town neither of us knew, checking each other out. Conversation flowed. A great kiss too. *Rats!* I thought. *So far away.*

Sadly, our connection faded. Our texts trailed off. When I reached out a few times, Amy sent "good to hear from you" messages back, but not much else. We agreed that we were each in a romantic lull. We never re-lit the fire under us, like the original texting frenzy. I'm not sure why Amy didn't respond much. Perhaps she didn't like me that much, or she sensed my hesitance, or she met someone else. I was not very drawn to a long-distance thing but would have loved to keep a friendship.

I'm sorry that I wasn't more direct about my lack of attraction. Though I fell short in my goal of radical honesty, I told myself: *Patience, young grasshopper. You'll get it, eventually.*

Date #50: Sex in a Temple
(Told from both perspectives) July 2016

My world changed when I was invited, with one of my teachers from my master's program, to present Processwork at "Summer Camp," an annual retreat for adults where sexuality is openly embraced and expressed. I had been hearing about Summer Camp for years, but it had always sounded too touchy-feely for me before this current dating phase of my life. An organization called Network for a New Culture hosted it. On their website, www.nfnc.org, I found this mission statement:

> "Summer Camp is co-creating the transformation of our culture into universal love in the deepest sense. By universal love, we mean deep intimacy, transparency, honesty,

spirituality, genuine equality, compassion, and sexual freedom all through the context of community."

Unsure of how I would respond in such a sexually open environment, I chose to dip my toes in and stay for only three nights (most people stayed for one or two weeks). I arrived at night, mid-week, and found the tent they had set up for me. The next morning, walking through the dew on a grassy wildflower path, I had a wordless, magnetic attraction with an intriguingly bright man with thick, dark hair, penetrating eyes, and a huge grin. Time slowed; we passed each other with a lingering gaze. At breakfast, I spotted him sitting with a few others and decided to ask if I could join his table. Our smiles were uncontained as I took my seat.

He warmly began introductions around the table, noticing out loud that I must be new to camp. Looking into my eyes, he said his name was Sylvan. I introduced myself to everyone and mentioned that I would be presenting Processwork the next day. I gave them my elevator speech: "The foundation is an attitude of 'deep democracy,' where all parts of all people are valued, especially the parts that society tends to marginalize. We'll do exercises to unleash these repressed parts of ourselves, which often hold our greatest gifts and powers." Sylvan's eyes traced me as I spoke, and goosebumps rose in the wake of his gaze.

The friendly folks smiled and nodded with interest. I added that the camp organizers had asked me to come a day early, to get a feel for the scene and integrate with the campers. Sylvan shared that he too had been a presenter in the past but was attending as a camper this year.

After breakfast, over 100 of us filed into the Dome: a big, central tent. Looking around, I noticed familiar people from Eugene, and several of them came up to welcome me enthusiastically. I felt exhilarated when Olive, a woman I had always been drawn to, screamed with delight and ran to pick me up and whirl me around. *Wow,* I thought. *These people really know how to show love.* I was surprised to feel so comfortable in the open, touchy-feely atmosphere. Many of the campers were only partially dressed. It felt like an adult fairy land.

As the organizers asked for our attention, my eyes scanned the crowd. I spotted Sylvan sitting on the opposite side. An attractive, dynamic man welcomed us, gave remarks about the upcoming day, and then led a group exercise called *What's in the Field Between Us?* The direction: approach someone and give voice to the unspoken.

The circle suddenly broke and transformed into a swarm of communication seekers. Sylvan and I eagerly signaled to each other from across the room. Pairs formed and slowly dropped into seated dyads. We climbed across the sea of bodies to finally sit cross-legged, facing each other, holding hands. We confirmed our mutual attraction and made a plan to eat lunch together. As the mingling continued, a few people approached me to express assumptions about me. By the end of the exercise, I was relaxed and energized from the crucible of honest, open communication. This training ground for radical authenticity was exactly what I'd been longing for. I was quickly becoming a fan of Summer Camp.

After the connecting game, there was a workshop on Nonviolent Communication. Sylvan didn't attend, and when I walked out of the Dome afterwards, he was waiting for me near the outdoor dining area. We served ourselves from the buffet line, and then dove into our food and each other. Right away, we were close. His long-lashed eyes beamed with desire. I was melting. Continuing with transparent communication, he invited me to sit in his lap. After feeding each other bites of vibrant salad and marinated tempeh, we lay down in the soft grass, held each other's faces, and playfully rolled around, kissing and laughing. *How extraordinarily wild to be tender and close so fast.* It was only the beginning of my first day there, and already, so much had happened!

During the afternoon session, Sylvan and I sat together for the group forum. I moved behind him to massage his shoulders, and sometimes leaned into him from behind. We playfully kissed some more. Later that night, he invited me for a cuddle date in his very large, canvas Bedouin-heaven tent, decorated with tapestries, rugs, incense, tarot cards, and music. Fully clothed, we effortlessly talked, kissed and touched. High-level sexual communication was my perfect medicine. Needing a good night's sleep because I was teaching in the morning, I said goodnight before it got too late. Floating back to my tent, my legs felt like clouds.

The next day was my first time teaching a large group. Free expression of sexuality was certainly the stand-out feature at Summer Camp, but there were many other focuses, including communication, boundaries, rank awareness, racism, sexism, transphobia, personal growth, accountability, etc. You didn't have to be a wild sexual exhibitionist to thrive at Summer Camp, and I learned that many campers were monogamous and came for the community, workshops, and open feeling.

I was excited to be teaching Processwork to the receptive group, but noticed Sylvan sitting with a beautiful, young, topless woman who had intoxicatingly sexy breasts with huge, enticingly luscious areolas. Throughout the day, it wasn't easy for me to ignore the two of them, especially when he addressed me with direct questions while massaging or cuddling her. *Was he testing me?* By the end of the day, I felt uplifted and energized, having mostly taken the big-nipple situation in stride.

My long day of teaching ended after 9 p.m. Exhausted but also excited to see Sylvan again, I took a quick shower and then we reconnected. He enthusiastically escorted me to "Aphrodite's Temple", a two-story cabin set back in the woods. The Temple was the camp's haven for liberated sexual exploration. I had missed the mandatory Temple orientation, but Sylvan was one of the "keepers" of the Temple, authorized to give me a private tour. There was a lot of buzz about the Temple. I felt shy and nervous.

Sensitive to my hesitation, Sylvan and I lingered in the shadows outside and made out in a parked golf cart. As he explained some of the Temple rules and etiquette, pleasure moans filled the thick July air. When I felt ready, he guided me by my fingertips. We tiptoed out of the cedar forest and into the Temple with childlike wonder. Inside, it was surprisingly beautiful, every surface wrapped in jewel-colored fabrics. The first thing I noticed were bowls overflowing with condoms, lubes, and dental dams, boxes of cleansing wipes, stores of whips, ropes, floggers, and paddles, and stacks of clean sheets, with separate bins for laundry. Off to the right, up against a wall, Sylvan pointed out the momentarily uninhabited St. Andrew's Cross. Earlier that day, one of the campers gave me a tip, "If you want to have an exquisite experience, find the man with the flogger." I imagined being tied up there, with him, or a mini-harem of my choice, behind me. *Maybe, one day.*

The ground floor was mostly wall-to-wall mattresses, for cuddling and sensuality. A few naked couples were gently caressing. It seemed sweet and slightly edgy, *just my speed.* Above, we could hear the sounds of boisterous fucking.

Sylvan grabbed my hand. My eyes must have spoken for me: *What? We're going up THERE?* because he nodded with confident excitement and led me up the ladder. When we emerged upstairs, familiar folks were sitting on couches, naked, some of them casually touching themselves, gazing at the pile of people who were bucking, moaning, and repositioning on an enormous bed. It was shocking to see sex so out in the open. Even though voyeurism was encouraged, a voice in me said, *Isn't sex supposed to be private? What would their parents think?* I let myself take a closer look. A voluptuous woman had three men serving her. Everyone was aroused in a tangle of body parts that were thrusting and thrusting, while this incredible woman moaned and moaned with pleasure. Her tremendous sexual power imprinted on me. *Wow, that was my classic fantasy, the one I'd envisioned over and over, and here it was in real life! Would I ever be that woman on the bed, having my own "ritual of abundance," as I overheard one older woman call it? Could I?*

I held my breath, unsure of what was going to happen, when Sylvan grabbed my hand and led me straight up to—and then past—the scene. *Phew!* There were five small "rooms" surrounding the carnal display, each separated by a lacy curtain for faux privacy. We went into one of the tiny antechambers. It had a beautiful bed with a purple satin bedcover. He gently removed my summer dress and then my panties, sliding his finger underneath the elastic, slowly, as if unwrapping a present. I watched in heightened anticipation as he undressed. With confidence, he guided me down onto my knees, centering my head in front of his throbbing cock. Suddenly, we were participants in the Temple festivities. I shivered.

Then, he said: "Have you ever deepthroated?" I shook my head.

"Would you like to try?" Smiling, I nodded. "Stick your tongue all the way out. Relax the back of your throat. Look into my eyes."

It was sexy and wild, a fantasy. I liked that others had watched us go in and could see and hear us through the gauzy curtain. I was a teacher, Temple-goer ... and a deepthroater! *What else would happen to me in this wondrous space?*

I liked submitting to Sylvan and was surprised that there was a trick to deepthroating. Sylvan was an authentic alpha. I absorbed the experience with gratitude, but also felt conflicted; the deepthroating hurt a little. Sylvan was enjoying fucking my mouth, which seems to be a common male fantasy ... but I couldn't ignore the burning in my throat.

We slept together in his tent that night and had sex. But it felt a little too much like fucking, not emotional and connected enough for me. *Oh well.* In the morning, we had breakfast, and then it was time for me to leave. We spent a long moment together standing next to my car. "Thank you for spending so much time with me," I said. He kissed me one last time and gazed into my eyes. "Thank *you.*" Lingering and not wanting to say goodbye, a spontaneous plan arose: he would come visit me on his way back to Idaho. Warmth and colors swirled through my core as I drove off.

Winding through the sunny hills of Southern Oregon, I reflected on my time at Summer Camp. Not everyone there was polyamorous or felt sexually free. It was sex-positive, but not a huge orgy. Just like in the real world, everyone had their own level of comfort and openness. There was more nudity and general body-positivity than your average retreat, but it wasn't a constant Dionysian freak-out. My final verdict: *Summer Camp is good for the world.*

Sylvan arrived in Eugene a few days later. I felt comfortable with him, but sexually, what was exciting in the Temple seemed foreign in my bedroom. Away from the buzzing communal high, our connection was more mundane. Plus, my raw throat—that would take weeks to heal—was getting worse. We weren't a perfect fit. I didn't articulate what was bothering me; the wound in my communication center became an unrelenting reminder that I hadn't voiced what I didn't want.

Sylvan's Perspective

Meeting Amy was beautiful. Walking to breakfast, early morning, I passed her on the path. *Damn, she's cute,* I thought, and looked back over my shoulder to see her looking over her shoulder at me. It was like magic, a sweet "I see you!" moment of recognition. The spark between us was clear.

Later that morning, during an exercise, we beelined for each other, like, *I need to talk to you!* Campers spend the first two days doing consent training, which creates a safe container for people to speak from their hearts. We practice asking for what we want, and we practice saying no. Even though the camp environment is so open, I was still a little shocked when she said, "I could kiss you right now." I thought that sounded awesome.

At lunch, we were sitting in the grass and Amy straddled me, facing me. We were suddenly making out with a hundred people walking around us.

The next night, we went to Aphrodite's Temple. The New Culture movement has this unique offering of sexuality integrated as a constructive part of community. At Summer Camp, the organizers cultivate a really impressive level of consciousness, integrity, and transparency. I have learned through my many years at Summer Camp, and other alternative living gatherings, that when eros is at the center of a community, people act way less violent towards each other than in mainstream culture. Transparency is really an amazing thing, and a central element of that is this Temple. Amy and I had some beautiful, playful explorations in the Temple.

Our reunion after Camp at Amy's house was super sweet and kissing and cuddling on her bed was yummy. It was sunny and warm with the windows open and Amy was moaning at full blast. I felt self-conscious about the neighbors, but she said it was fine. We had one night of romance together, and when the time came, I didn't want to leave.

I feel some sadness and tenderness that we didn't get a chance to continue. There's still a little longing and tugging on my heart strings. I have a partner I'm crazy in love with, so it's not like I'm lonely; I just cherish Amy. When we met, I had just ended a 22-year monogamous marriage. I went through a lot in that break-up, and Amy was a big part of my sexual healing and healing my heart. I feel grateful to her for that.

After Sylvan left, the burning in my throat pressed me to be honest with him. We had several video talks over the next week, sharing our feelings. I revealed my ambivalence about the deepthroating and let him know that I wished I had stopped it at times. When I told him about the lingering pain, his whole face softened. I was impressed by his utter lack of defensiveness. He offered a piece of Summer Camp wisdom: a good consent rule for oneself is,

If you're not a "fuck yes," you're a "no."

Despite the ease of our processing, time revealed that we didn't have the chemistry to sustain a long-distance romance. Reality woke me from my dreaminess, and with our feet back in our own lives, we moved forward as warm friends.

Although I loved dating, the rollercoaster ride was sometimes grueling. *Did I have to carve myself a brand-new personality to finally become radically honest?* I wanted to evolve so badly, but it was proving hard to shake my old, entrenched patterns. Although the experience with Sylvan was unique, I felt low because of my sexual silence. I folded inward, the heartbreak from Soren still echoing.

Date #18, Jonah Continued: You Can't Put Fog in a Jar
August 2016

It had been eight months since my ultra-short, lip-biting, second date with Jonah. Our pattern of silent gaps, canceled plans, and fits of racy, romantic texting continued. On one of our many thwarted evenings we had this exchange:

> **Amy:** Today is one year since our first date. Happy anniversary! LOL
>
> **Jonah:** Holy! Wow. Time ... swift.
>
> **Amy:** Maybe for you!
>
> **Jonah:** Geez ... wish we could consummate it ;)
>
> **Amy:** I have a gift for you.

I sent a video striptease message for him on Marco Polo, my favorite video chat app. I could tell he was watching. I loved to dance for Jonah.

> **Jonah:** Ooohhhh. I can hardly contain myself when you send me videos. I am so turned on right now. It makes me that much more bummed to miss you this eve. The longing is exquisitely painful. It almost frightens me.
>
> **Amy:** What are you afraid of? My lessons with you are patience and acceptance. Do you know what yours are with me?
>
> **Jonah:** You've got me at the edge with that video, but I'll pause to consider my lessons. Between us is a level of clarity that makes my heart swell for you, mostly because of your acceptance and love. I'm inspired by your ongoing openness to me in spite of logistical and emotional setbacks and

disappointments. Your full receiving of me is dear and enlivening.

Amy: I trust in timing and the perfect unfolding of things. And I trust you to be true to yourself.

Jonah: I am watching your video on repeat. I am painfully turned on and can barely contain myself.

Amy: I'm lying down in my bed now. I'm going to slip my hands into my panties and won't be surprised when I find I'm very wet.

Jonah: Wow wow wow. Watching your video, indeed I have fallen in love with your face, your voice, your heart, you. Feeling my cock hardening and pulsing and watching and wanting you, to be inside you, to fill you, penetrate you, and hear and feel your warm excited breath in my ear, on my skin. Amazing how you ignite such passion and yet hold me in such a way, whether up close or from such distance, that allows me space and comfort to soften and break.

Amy: I'm so tingly inside, in my yoni, swollen and pulsing and so, so, so wet, dripping, my heartbeat quickening and my breath getting shallow.

Jonah: I'm putting my phone down next to me now. I need to touch myself and think of you.

(A little later) **Jonah:** Thank you 🤍

Amy: Thank YOU! Funny, I'm strangely excited that we *almost* had an amazing date tonight. LOL

Several months later, for our third in-person date, Jonah planned to drive down to spend a long afternoon in Eugene. We were going to meet for lunch and then head back to my place. Singing and dancing, I changed the sheets and cleaned every inch of my house. Finally, I dressed up and felt flowy and beautiful, whooshing out to meet him at Tacovore on a perfect, sunny fall day. I imagined us hours later slipping into bed, seeing and feeling his bare skin, his hands moving on my thighs, our heart-body mystery finally unfolding.

My heart flooded when I saw Jonah waiting for me outside. We had a bright, warm hug, ordered, and sat down in the courtyard. Looking at him I thought, *wow, Jonah actually drove here to see me.* But before the tacos had even hit the table, a call came in. My psychic efforts to will him to ignore the call failed. On the phone, his face darkened and his whole being slumped. Hanging up, he vacantly reported that his son's childcare had fallen through. We ate quickly under a heavy cloud. After a sad kiss, he was gone.

I stood on the corner of Fifth and Blair, shocked, and heard the voice of an iconic, disgruntled, ex-Lane Transit District (L.T.D.) bus driver approaching in the distance. Knowing what was coming, I watched for his bicycle. The mantra grew louder as he came into view. Flags and streamers flew around him, and he was dressed as usual in ridiculous, colorful rag layers, with rainbow knee-highs and a pink tutu, like a Technicolor bumblebee. He screamed his repeated war cry into the air for the world to hear: "L.T.D. can lick my big, sweaty, smelly NUT-SAAAAAAAAAAAACK!" The acoustic vibrations of his expressive emotionality shook off at least a little of my disappointment.

After another six months of proclaiming my undying love in poems, songs, and orgasmic audio recordings, and Jonah's predictable, intermittent silences and last-minute cancelations, we had our fourth in-person date. On my way to Portland, I drove an hour out of my way to see him at his office. Between clients, he scooped me up, placed me on the massage table of his Zen-feeling room, and we stared into each other's eyes. I unzipped his pants, looking up at him to make sure it was OK. When he smiled shyly, I touched him through his boxers. We kissed breathlessly, grabbing and pulling hungrily at each other, for ten minutes, when his next client arrived. Slipping out the back door, I was flooded with poignant exhilaration, knowing it would probably be months before I'd see—maybe even hear from—him again.

Our four dates in two years added up to less than five hours together. Each in-person meeting was both delicious and tormented: full of anticipation, lust, and ultimately, crushing disappointment, as reality eclipsed every date.

I was up against big opinions that I should cut it off out of self-respect: "Don't accept his disappearing," "Stop pouring your precious energy into the connection." Friends and mentors discouraged me; my astrologer said that Jonah was "like fog, and you can't put fog in a jar."

But along with the disappointment, there was lots of juicy longing and a lingering, mysterious magnetism. Jonah was unreliable, but he always eventually showed up. As time went on, I learned detachment from him and initiated less.

If I had been pining for Jonah as a primary partner, I would have been miserable. Polyamory created a container where he could be however he wanted. I continued to pray, romantically, that our bodies would find and discover themselves with each other. I dreamed of a time where we could be exceptionally, wildly free together. Sexually, I imagined we would be otherworldly and primal. Over time, the muscles of my teleological trust in the divine order of the universe were challenged and fortified.

The limitations of the relationship with Jonah forced me to grow, and the insatiable romantic in me was continually fed. Eventually, I cultivated sustained gratitude and complete openness to whatever might manifest between us, following the flow of life, and receiving his silences more like Mount Hood: glorious and impersonal.

... to be continued ...

Date #51: Falling for a Tree *September 2016*

One evening at a house concert, my musician friend introduced me to a dreamy tree of a man, saying, "You and Hugh should know each other." Hugh had to bend way down to talk to me. With a rich

French accent, he said, "Hello, my dear. I am fully enchanted to make your acquaintance." *Oh, that voice!* Time slowed; each of his words was thoughtfully chosen.

Hugh was a carpenter with the warm eyes of a mystic. Showered by his profoundly rich, scholarly word choices, I was impressed to the point of being ungrounded. My heart tumbled around inside me and I hastily changed my rule about height. When I later described how tall Hugh was to a friend, I swooned, "6 foot 20."

Back home after the event, I wrote a few poems and sent them to him. He responded with an invitation to dinner the next night. We sat cross-legged on his cold, dirty floor—he lived in a converted garden shed. He fed me a harvest stew, cooked to perfection, filled with colorful root vegetables he had grown. As we ate and talked, he thanked me for the poems, and explained that he was "chaste of heart." I assumed that meant "chaste of body." *Ugh, he was monastic.*

During our dinner, Hugh leaned in towards me, made eye contact and asked poignant questions. He called me "my heart." The evening felt as romantic as possible without the potential of sex. As I was leaving, I said that I would love to spend more time with him.

Over a few more meals that autumn, our interactions continued to be flirtatious and warm. We were affectionate, often massaging or cuddling at social gatherings. People who saw us together asked if we were dating. I felt satisfied and loved the snuggly way we bonded. But then Hugh moved to a farm somewhere in central Oregon.

The following summer, Hugh reached out to let me know that he was back in Eugene and had changed his mind about abstinence; he was newly interested in exploring sexual relationships. We took a few romantic outings: picnics, swimming, and wine tasting. I was surprised to feel reserved. He used to seem so earthy and grounded, but when he looked at me through "Are you my potential partner?" eyes, I felt guarded. Spending time together had been strangely different when I couldn't get enough of him. He spent the night once, but we both stayed fully clothed, and slept next to each other like friends. I wasn't ready to be sexual with him, and neither of us made a move to kiss, or even cuddle.

Opening to the possibility of an intimate relationship after a long period of chastity seemed to bring up a lot of Hugh's emotions.

Some negative assumptions about women surfaced that made me recoil. He said things like *"women always ... " or "I hate how women .... "* I didn't want to wrestle with his myths and limiting beliefs. I needed to be with someone who took responsibility in relationships.

As souls, Hugh and I still always connect on a deep level. A few times, I ran into him with a beautiful, new, young woman, and hoped he was finding what he needed. Once again, my initial excitement and longing weren't grounded in reality. Too often, I put people—not just monks—up on unnecessary pedestals.

Date #52: The Shaman *October 2016*

In 2015, I went to a retreat center on the Oregon coast for a few days and was powerfully drawn to Raphael, an incredibly beautiful Ecuadorian shaman. He was leading a workshop, and we kept bumping into each other. Each time, I thought I felt a mutual sparkle. I longed to know him and tried to make my desire obvious by engaging whenever we met. He had long black hair, rich brown skin and big, laughing eyes. I guessed he was around my age, though he seemed beautifully ancient. His body was muscular, but the beauty that moved me was in his deep presence, and his meditative spirit. In one of our chance meetings, he asked where I lived, and we realized that we both knew Geraldo, a good friend of mine in Eugene. Though nothing manifested, I sensed a special connection. He had no ring, but because he wasn't flirtatious, I wondered if he was married.

A year later, Geraldo randomly messaged me: Rafael was looking for a ride. I happened to be driving from Portland to Eugene on this day. Like a happy puppy, I sprang at the opportunity. We met in downtown Portland, and I was tickled that he literally jumped when he recognized me. Again, I sensed our undeniable chemistry. At a cafe, we shared a biscotti and latte as we recalled our encounters at the retreat center. His eyes scintillated underneath wild, playfully jumping eyebrows. His gaze danced all over my body and face. *He was checking me out!* I liked his honest flirtation. In my experience, Latin American men generally seem more sexually uninhibited than men from the States; I find it refreshing.

Our two-hour drive was tender. We swayed together, singing loudly, "*Country roads, take me home* ...." He told me poignant stories about heartbreaks and deaths. As I drove, he fed me sweet little morsels of mini rice cracker sandwiches with grapes and goat cheese, slipping them between my lips. Nothing could have tasted better. Rafael said, "Do you know what I'd really love to do with you tonight? *Dance!*" I was sure we could find something. *Dancing with the shaman?* I was ecstatic, animated, and tapped into my true nature. I breathed the nutritious moment in, tasting the richness of existence.

We landed at my house, and while I searched online for dancing possibilities, Rafael made himself comfortable on my sofa and was studying me, smiling. I felt happy but shy. Once I had chosen a blues fusion event, he made a soft, inviting gesture, playfully patting the cushion next to him. I stepped carefully towards him, aware of my every movement. The potency of our connection made me feel light and woozy. *Was I dreaming?*

When I sat down, Rafael moved closer until our legs were almost touching. I turned to face him and lifted my shy eyes to meet his. Ever so slowly, his face moved incrementally towards mine. When our mouths crossed an invisible threshold and made contact, we were startled by a strong electric shock—strong enough to hurt my lips! His large, laughing eyes opened wide with surprise. And then his ancient face melted, all smiles, and he pulled me in, close.

As we kissed, Raphael's tongue darted, wild and unpredictable. Subtle electric pulses like little shots of lightning came through his kiss, and I imagined a powerful snake spirit threatening to dart out of him and into me. *Was he wrestling between his primal and spiritual natures?* Our kissing was expressive, edgy, and alive, but also strangely complicated. I felt hesitant to go further, or even continue much longer.

Sensing my turmoil, Rafael pulled away slowly. His eyes were round with compassion, and his big face softened. Then, he intuitively placed his head gently in my lap. I relaxed, able to breathe again, and found solace in combing my fingers through his long hair and massaging his head, neck and shoulders. *Nurturing and intimate: perfect.*

Later, we went to Salseros Dance Studio. It was huge, and I thought, *this place would be perfect for relocating my Nia classes*. Not knowing any blues fusion steps, we had so much silly, wild fun doing our own version of unleashed dirty dancing. We came up with signature moves, twisting slow-motion down low and exploding in uncontained laughter. Rafael's laugh was full-bodied; he vibrated joy throughout the room. At one point, another man approached us and invited me to dance, and I said, "I can't, I only have this one precious evening with Rafael."

He was in town just that one night. After dancing, I drove him to Geraldo's house. When I parked the car, he asked to come back to my place instead. But I wasn't ready for any more interactions with his snake, especially in bed. I said, "I feel complete for tonight ... but maybe next time?" Nodding and smiling, he respected my boundary with grace.

We got out of the car and kissed goodbye, both smiling widely as we parted. I drove off towards the full moon. It was perfect.

... to be continued ...

Date #53: We Should Really Hang Out ... *November 2016*

Guarded after my experience with Soren, I had pulled back from OkCupid. My bar was set higher than when I originally started dating. Slightly curious, I signed up for a 48-hour free trial on an expensive "Dating for Spiritual People" site and messaged there with Felix. An attractive veterinarian, he was new to town, with piercing blue eyes. His interests included sacred plant medicine rituals—ayahuasca, peyote, mescaline. In our messaging, he was kind and communicative. We decided to meet for drinks.

In the crowded entrance to the cider house, we waved and pushed through strangers. *He was cute!* Happily surprised that he matched the energy of his profile, I said, "I like you!" which evoked a huge smile. We settled in, split a huge, fresh salad and chickpea fries, and sampled a colorful flight of local ciders. We shared many personal, vulnerable stories, and lots of laughter ... for three hours!

Over the course of the evening, my excitement waned. Even

though he checked several of my main boxes, I ironically lost steam. By the end, my engine was completely drained. When he walked me to my car, I didn't initiate kissing. Neither did he. We just said goodbye. Not kissing felt like the final verdict.

Felix and I messaged a few more times. My last flicker of hope quickly petered out in our uninspired messages. It felt like the kind of friend where each time you run into each other, you say "we should really hang out." But that same line repeated a few times gets embarrassingly awkward, revealing that neither of you prioritizes the relationship. My free trial expired, and I sank back into my uncomfortable hole.

Date #54: Too Many Frozen Sausages *January 2017*

I met a sweet hippie at a Zegg Forum facilitator's training. Cameron was ten years younger than me and seemed dreamy and sensitive. He had long, straight, dark hair, round eyes, and a constant shy smile. During a lunch break, we were both loading up at the salad bar at Sundance Natural Foods. Twice over the weekend, we stood in the bathroom line together and chatted. On the last day, we parked our cars right next to each other. *Was the universe putting us together?* When the workshop concluded, we spoke in the parking lot about our obvious magnetism.

Cameron let me know that he was in an open relationship with a woman in Eugene but lived in Portland. We traded numbers and texted for a few weeks. Several days would pass without a response, but when he did reach out, he was expressive and enthusiastic. Eventually, he invited me to his home for a meal.

Dinner with Cameron was my third date that day (the first two were uninspiring). The night before, I dreamed that I was overwhelmed with thousands of tiny frozen sausages, everywhere! In the dream, I had filled my freezer and resolved to feed them to my cats. Those little sausages were taking up way too much space.

I often stacked my Thursday Portland dates, like when I saw Cardboard Christian for breakfast and Kelly the Leprechaun for dinner. Between dates and clients on this triple-date-day, I laughed with a therapist friend about my dating merry-go-round and my sausage dream-noir.

Then, when I arrived at Cameron's house, the world and my dream collided: he was preparing sausages for dinner! I thought optimistically, *at least these sausages are big and fresh.* (For the record, I don't have any specific size preference when it comes to "sausages.")

Cameron moved slowly and deliberately. I felt comfortable in his well-cared-for space. Our dinner conversation was intellectually stimulating; Cameron studied alternative energy, and we shared creative, sustainable living ideas. The space between us felt alive. And the sausages were delicious.

We kissed playfully after dinner in his minimalist kitchen. When we pulled away, smiling, we planned a cuddle date the next week at my house. I looked forward to it, and we sent a few messages.

A week later, Cameron arrived on bike, out of breath and sweaty. We went up to my room for our cuddle. With our clothes still on, we laid down; his strong odor and sticky, clammy body weren't drawing me in. I wanted less, not more.

Not able to fake it, I said "I can't get comfortable." We sat up and talked a short while, and soon I thanked him for coming over and suggested we check in later that evening. When we spoke on the phone, I said that I was in a dating hole—which was true. But of course, I would have dug myself out if the feeling were there.

I decided that the next time I dreamed about an overabundance of unwanted sausages, I should probably delete my dating apps for a while ... or at least clear my schedule for a day!

Date #55: Plane Attraction *April 2017*

In a basement gate of the San Francisco Airport, it was almost time to board my delayed plane to Istanbul. Looking around the overcrowded waiting area, I spotted what seemed to be the last seat available. I did a double take when I noticed the attractive man sitting next to it.

I took a breath, rolled my luggage over, smiled at him, and sat down. Checking his fingers, I wondered about a potential wife. *No ring.* I fantasized about blurting out an invitation to make out right there in the airport. Why not? We would never see each other again. It seemed like a perfect romantic movie-esque thing to do.

When it was almost time to board, I struck up a conversation. We were on the same flight. Noticing his accent, I asked if he was going home. *Yes, to Israel.* I introduced myself, said I was Jewish, and he told me his name: Yoav.

We continued chatting while we waited in the unmoving line together. Yoav was just a little taller than me, which made standing together feel comfy. I explained that I was heading to Greece to attend *Worldwork,* a Processwork conference that is held at a different political hotspot every three years. I was going to teach a workshop, see clients, and participate in large group processes where hundreds of people (from over 45 countries) work together dynamically to explore global issues from all possible sides. I learned that Yoav worked for a big tech company and lived in the Bay area with a wife and kids. *OK,* I thought: *just friends.*

As the line began to move, we pulled out our seat assignment stubs ... and his seat was *right next to mine!* On this eleven-hour flight, with over 500 people, Yoav and I were going to be sitting together?! We were both shocked. With big smiles, we shuffled to our seats. A lovely flight attendant wearing a tightly-pulled bun was waiting for us. She reached for my bag and said, "Your suitcase needs to go up to the front of the plane; we have limited space in the overhead compartments." Yoav boldly responded, "Can we move up to sit with our luggage?" trying to get us both—*like a couple*—relocated to first class. It didn't work, but how cute that he tried.

Thank God I didn't ask him to make out back in the lounge! It would have made for a very awkward, long plane ride.

Once we settled in, the Turkish Airlines flight attendant offered us much appreciated warm cotton washcloths, then the dinner menu, which included fillet of salmon, hummus, double chocolate cake, and homemade lemonade with fresh mint. We were thrilled. Our arms gently touched as we settled into our seats. Eventually, after hours of reading books and watching movies, he looked at me, and said, "Maybe we should get some sleep." I agreed, he turned the lights out, and we said goodnight. The contact point between our upper arms softened as we relaxed into each other. I tuned in, matching the pacing of his breath and we drifted off. It was profoundly moving to indulge in the tender intimacy of breathing together. Hours later, when we awoke messy-headed, I took a selfie of us. Unfortunately, he wasn't on Facebook, so I gave him my business card.

Emerging from the plane in Istanbul, an ocean of wall-to-wall bodies confronted us. Sleepy-headed, Yoav wanted to help me with my connection to Athens, but I knew I needed to race if I was going to make the flight. We had a way-too-quick hug, and I barely squeaked out, "Email me!" before dashing off through the crowded, humid airport packed tight with families, tired old women wearing floor-length dresses, and weary, unmotivated travelers leaning on appliance-sized luggage. It was a long race to my connection, continually swerving my heavy suitcase through walls of bodies, calculating if I would make it as I ran. When I finally arrived at the gate, sweaty and exhausted, the "Final Boarding" sign was flashing red, and I was the last person to squeeze through.

I never did hear from Yoav, but I treasure the memory of breathing, sleeping, and dreaming with a familiar stranger.

Date #56: Boxers Do Not a Proper Swimsuit Make *April 2017*

Partway through the Processwork conference in Porto Cheli, in the Peloponnesian Riviera, I noticed a very sweet Dutch man. He wove freely like a butterfly through the space, a self-appointed host, connecting with the conference participants. His apparent emotional abundance intrigued me. Physically, he wasn't my usual type; he had a tousle of curly blond hair, a round and soft face, bouncy energy, and a big, bright smile. He reminded me of a crazy young scientist and would have rocked a white lab coat.

Towards the end of the week, I taught a workshop called *The Ancient Art of Self-Love*. Luca was the first to arrive. Grinning widely, he approached me directly and stepped right into my personal bubble, his face suddenly unusually close to mine. *Cultural diversity?* In a thick Dutch accent, he offered, "I massage you?" bounced behind me, and dug deftly into my tight shoulders, causing an eruption of sighs and moans. When some participants arrived, he sat down next to me, satisfied. He was amusing, sweet, and I thought I saw a glimmer in his eye.

The next day, flirting, I invited Luca to sit together at lunch. As we ate, I casually slipped "I really like you" into a moment of silence. He stiffened, and I asked about it.

He related this: "A few years ago, I had a crush at a similar conference, and she rejected me." His eyes darted around the space as he spoke, as though the woman's ghost might be lingering. We shared a long quiet moment together, acknowledging his deeply-carved pain.

The following morning was the final session of the week-long conference. Luca and I found each other afterwards and decided to spend the afternoon together at the beach, just a short walk across the street.

While we both reclined in lounge chairs, I couldn't help but notice the tip of his penis sticking out of the little slit of his makeshift bathing suit (boxer shorts). *Should I say something? We were just getting to know each other!* When I couldn't help myself and stole glances, it reminded me of a baby: soft and innocent.

As Luca vulnerably shared stories of childhood trauma experiences, his penis seemed to be looking to me for reassurance. He spoke with a nervous, bubbly demeanor; his story was actively popping out too. I was relieved when he finally shifted and pulled the tight boxer shorts down as though to clear a wedgie, except that his penis migrated along, and the tip, like a relentless whack-a-mole, now squeezed out the bottom. We lingered at the beach for about two hours; it wasn't easy to avert my eyes for such a long period of time. Boxer shorts were clearly not a functional replacement for a bathing suit.

Exhausted, we went to my hotel room to cuddle, clothes on. I relaxed into Luca; his physicality was medicinal. It had been a long week of intense emotional processing, and the physical contact brought unexpected tears. Once my feelings had run their course, we took turns sitting up to massage each other. My muscles surrendered freely to his intuitive touch, and gratitude flooded my system.

We had plans to meet up with friends from the conference for an early dinner, and after a while, I was ready to leave the emotional cave of my hotel room. Holding hands, we walked with the group in the fresh Aegean air, publicly affectionate. When we took our seats at the outdoor restaurant, his bright, boyish face beamed as he said, "I invite you!" which meant, "I want to pay for you." Touched, I accepted.

After dinner, Luca and I returned to the hotel. We ran into some other conference friends and hung out for a while. I would have preferred solo time with him, at least to have a nice goodbye. Soon, I was exhausted and had to catch a ferry before sunrise. We had a sad, clunky hug, then parted. *So anticlimactic.* As I walked away, down a long hallway, I heard feet running towards me, and in his sweet accent—*"Emmy, wait!"*—Luca called to me for a more satisfying goodbye.

We shared a long hug, feeling each other one last time, and then looked into each other's eyes. The space between us liquified, our faces came close, and my lips softened, ready for a kiss. We were awakened out of the dreamlike state when his drunk friends crashed loudly into the hallway, coming to fetch him. After one final squeeze, he was gone. It was the perfect conference near-romance.

Part III
EROTIC EVOLUTION

9

SEXUAL CHRYSALIS AT SUMMER CAMP

Sexual Healing *July 2017*

I was thrilled to return to Summer Camp to teach Processwork again. After a year of unintentional celibacy and wound-licking from my dip with the Wizard, I planned to stay the whole week this time. Sylvan, my Temple escort and Camp mini-romance, was the last person I'd had intercourse with. Other than a few short-lived crushes and kisses, my dating life had felt mostly dry and dull. By returning to Summer Camp, I was basically saying, "I want to have sex!" There would be workshops every day, dances and other movement experiences, talent shows, the Temple, my teaching experiences, community forums, delicious vegetarian food, and those radical honesty exercises I loved. My biggest excitement was the potential of finding a new lover—or lovers.

On the first night, the entire 120-person group was playing a social game in the Dome, where most of the workshops and group activities were held. Our instruction was to find seven-minute, low-pressure dates. I looked around. *Where was Vaughn, the sex therapist?* I had met him briefly the year before, and he was recommended by my friend Olive, who had worked with him both in person and online. I found and approached him. Amidst the buzzing sea of excited campers, I told him that I was curious about working with him on my sexuality.

Vaughn was a towering figure, but as we spoke, he somehow shrank down to nearly my size. As he softened towards me, he seemed to be conjuring a forcefield around us; it was suddenly just the two of us in the whole Dome. *Was Vaughn another wizard, slowing time?* He had the most caring demeanor, with eyes that listened. Everything about him was round, including his big bald head. He was in his seventies.

Vaughn called himself a "relationship and pleasure coach" and a "yoni whisperer." He said that his mission was to make as many yonis as possible feel safe and loved—quite a life purpose! Yoni is a Sanskrit word for vagina, which translates to "sacred space." As a child, I was embarrassed by the word "vagina." People always said it with a whiny voice, in a way that still feels like a jab. "Yoni" is a reverent term that honors a woman's genitals as a spiritual gateway for divine procreative energy. The word is soft, gentle, and loving. Each time I hear it, a part of me gets healed.

I let Vaughn know that my interest in working with him was partly personal—for my own growth and healing—and partly professional, as I dreamed of becoming a sexual healer. Enthusiastically, he suggested a "yoni massage," and we planned to meet the following afternoon. My homework was to think about what I would like to get out of the session. When I asked about money, Vaughn replied that he never charged for his services. All his sexual healing sessions were free. I was grateful, but also cautious about an unequal exchange, especially in the realm of intimacy.

My whole body and spirit were starving for the nutrients I imagined a yoni massage could provide. My strong inclination towards kissing, dating, and sexual exploration didn't necessarily mirror my sexual self-esteem. Even during highly sexual phases in certain past relationships, I didn't feel sexually complete. I focused on pleasing others, and had a hard time receiving physical attention from most of my partners. A yoni massage, where I could simply receive sensual touch, sounded medicinal.

When the social game was over, outside the Dome, Vaughn introduced me to his wife, in case I wanted a feminine presence for our session. She was earthy, quiet, and soulful and it was obvious how much he loved and adored her, though one-on-one seemed best for me.

The next day, Vaughn met me outside my tent. We sat in chairs and I told him that I wanted to increase my pleasure tolerance, amplify and lengthen my orgasms, and ultimately have a whole new kind of orgasm. Most importantly, I wanted to practice asking for touch that brought me pleasure and saying "no" when I didn't enjoy something. He framed my intention as a therapeutic sexual focus, and said, "You are free to change the focus at any point during today's session. And, any boundary you set will be honored throughout."

Before we went into my tent, he put his hands out for me to examine. It was a sweet, calm and simple gesture that imbued me with a deep sense of safety. Too many times, I had silently endured discomfort from someone's unconscious fingers. Vaughn's fingers, however, were well-groomed and otherworldly-baby-soft.

In the tent, I took my clothes off at his invitation; he kept his on. I slipped under a sheet while he put on music—he chose a playlist with Enya, Bliss, Morcheeba, and Zero 7. When I was settled, Vaughn held my hands, looked into my eyes, and shared his excitement about my journey, saying that he welcomed the unexplored parts of my sexuality and that my openness impressed him. He then gave me a full-body massage, starting with my back. His wise hands worked slowly, paying extra care to areas that elicited louder moans. When I turned face-up, he asked about potentially sensitive areas. "Would you like me to massage your breasts? Are your nipples sensitive?" He cupped my breasts, then gently moved long fingers in sweeping circles, avoiding my nipples. *Amazing.*

"Are you ready for me to touch your yoni?" His questions helped me practice using my voice at every step. I said: "Yes, thank you." Receiving and vocalizing felt so new. *What a gift.*

It was hot, and Vaughn took his shirt off, leaving his sarong tied around his waist. He pulled aside the sheet that partially covered me. Sitting between my legs, he started by touching the external parts of my yoni, naming them and asking about my sensitivity. "The outside area of the vagina is called the vulva. It includes the inner and outer labia, the clitoris, and the entrance to the vagina, which is called the introitus. And here is the opening to your urethra." He touched each part gently and slowly, reading me closely for cues of potential distress.

Next, he asked if I was ready for him to put his finger, with or without gloves, inside me. I was ready; my yoni was relaxed, and I opted for no gloves. Using lots of lube, he entered me gently. He inserted his finger palm-up. "I'm going to be moving my fingers to different locations. This is called yoni mapping." Vaughn guided me on a sensory tour: "Here is your G-spot, just inside the vaginal opening, towards the front of the body. The skin there has ridges. It might be sensitive."

"Oh, yeah, that hurts a little." Like a mute person who finally speaks, a wave of complex emotion rushed through me. I felt overcome from giving voice to my sexual discomfort, maybe for the first time ever. The physical pain went away when he adjusted the pressure. "How's that?" I replied, "Better. That actually feels kind of interesting."

"Yay!" he cheered brightly. "You just told me something you don't like!" We were both beaming, and he decided to celebrate aloud each time I asked for a change.

Vaughn continued, "The G-spot is the area that stimulates female ejaculation, or amrita. It's often ultra-sensitive when you aren't aroused, similar to the clitoris." I joked, "OK, maybe we can try that later."

All smiles, he said, "Sure! I'm going to move deeper now, to your A-spot." He palpated the spot and I felt a deep rush of pleasure. Last, he rotated his finger and pressed towards the back. "This is your P-spot," which stood for posterior, towards the spine. "Woo! Wow!" Those portals of pleasure had never been touched this way before. I treasured the education, training, and rare opportunity to focus on the subtleties between these different pleasure zones.

After the mapping, Vaughn began the massage using a wide variety of strokes and techniques, both internally and externally. He used some toys, which (unlike my past disinterest) was actually fun. With plenty of lube, he touched me with such spaciousness and slowness that I was able to focus completely on receiving sexual touch for the first time in my life. It was completely different from a mutual sexual experience, where I usually focused on the other's sexuality. *What a deep gift.*

One of my favorite Summer Camp sayings, which I had learned from Sylvan the year before, is: If you're not a "fuck yes," you're a "no." If a person isn't enthusiastically a complete and total yes to a connection, a kiss, a sexual experience—anything that involves consent—then it's a no. *What a relief.* I wanted to tune permanently into consent, to prevent further sexual regrets. Vaughn was a devotee of this sex-positive, consent-based practice, acutely attuned to my facial expressions, twitches, hesitations, and subtle recoilings—to anything that didn't seem like a "fuck yes." He kept cheering each time I gave him any negative feedback or clear direction.

Some time into this catharsis, I began to feel sexual and asked to shift the focus to arousal, to explore my orgasm goal. In the past, I had almost always pressured myself to orgasm quickly, so whoever was trying to please me wouldn't have to work too hard. It was a feat to simply sense what was happening, to remind myself that there was plenty of time, with no expectation for me to be or do anything for anyone, and that I could trust Vaughn to take care of himself. He supported me in this by continually encouraging me: "Just relax and receive, you deserve it, just be in this moment. Luxuriate in your sexuality; don't worry about me. For me, this is about as much work as eating ice cream." We both laughed. I was able to let go and felt grateful for his support.

Once I finally settled in, my inner dialogue quieted and I lingered in a state of arousal for a long time. Eventually, I was overtaken by a silent, full-body orgasm. In a deeply altered state, it felt like my energy field expanded into the ground below me, sending rumbling roots of fresh growth, infusing the earth with the inspiration of new potential. It was common at Summer Camp to hear wails of ecstasy pouring out of tents, and I wouldn't have held back if my orgasm inspired sound. But this went a different direction, down and in.

After the blissful state abated, Vaughn asked to lie down with me. I was surprised. It felt odd, but I said "sure" and he held me, telling me how much he adored me. When he whispered, "I'm in love with you," I recoiled. My afterglow was interrupted by the mention of his personal feelings.

Sensing it was time to wrap up, Vaughn soon gathered his things and left me to rest. I thanked him and we agreed to check in soon. I stayed in my tent for some time, in deep relaxation, happy to be alone again.

Later that day, I found him to check in. "It was amazing for me. But to be honest, I was taken aback by your declaration of love."

Vaughn looked directly at me and said, intensely, "My feelings are my feelings and they have nothing to do with you. You are not responsible in any way for my feelings." He said that he falls in love often, and that he had already fallen in love with four women that year at Summer Camp.

That was a relief. As a therapist, I had boundaries around sharing deep, unsolicited affection with my clients. *Was it safe to have a sexually therapeutic, one-way relationship with "in love" in the mix, and no payment or other compensation?* Out of my territory, I proceeded with caution.

We planned a second session a few days later at the Temple. Out of everything I had experienced the year before at Summer Camp, my wild time in the Temple with Sylvan made the strongest, longest-lasting impression, and I was both excited and nervous to return. But the Temple was mostly empty that mid-afternoon; there was a couple in one of the small rooms making cooing sounds. A woman in her mid-70s was sitting alone on a couch, looking out the window and gently touching herself. We chose a small, lacy chamber. Vaughn asked about my focus, and since the first session had felt so profound, I chose to focus on therapeutic healing again.

He started by massaging my back, which felt very nurturing, and then the front of my body, and finally, the yoni massage. Using clear cues for what I liked and didn't like, I asked for specific shifts: "Not right on the clitoris," "Long, gentle strokes," or "Could you use two fingers?" Vaughn was enthusiastic.

Again, I eventually wanted to shift the focus to arousal. This time, I allowed myself to release into pleasure more deeply. I felt free to explore and experiment in the Temple's nurturing and encouraging sexual atmosphere.

Then, Vaughn told me that he was getting aroused, and said that it was my choice whether he brought his own sexual energy into the experience. Curious, I invited it. He started moving his body, rocking front and back as he touched me. He made eye contact with me. Nothing else really shifted except the way he did what he did; there was more energy, enthusiasm, and mutual participation.

We were suddenly both being sexual, even if the touch was still one-way. As we built sexual energy together, my pleasure increased. It felt kinky to enjoy being sexual with this man, so much older than me. Imagining myself from an onlooker's perspective, I noticed my unspoken judgment about our age differences. Going over my edge to have mutual sexual contact with Vaughn loosened a prejudice in me, shifting my ageism.

I soon had an orgasm. Then we cuddled briefly, but I had another date and had to get going. The cuddling part felt strange; it was more for him than me. This was an inner conflict that I wasn't sure how to navigate. Vaughn was giving me so much, and it felt wrong to not want to cuddle. I knew I would have to bring this up in the future. After he walked me to my next date, we parted with an affectionate hug.

I had attractions to a few older men at Summer Camp, and the experience with Vaughn helped me feel more open to them.

Date #57: Easy on the No's
(Told from both perspectives) July 2017

I met Theo briefly the year before on my first night at Summer Camp. I was walking around alone and felt drawn to join a circle of people playing a game. Like a large, friendly hobbit, he welcomed and folded me into the group, quickly teaching me how to play. My first impression was that he seemed like a uniquely emotionally available man.

On the first day of this year's camp, I sat next to him in the big group circle and felt happy when he asked to put his head in my lap. Instinctively, I massaged his head and neck, and he moaned. When I touched some acupressure points, electrical impulses moved through his body in surprisingly strong kundalini jolts. At one point

Theo said, "You know this is making me fall in love with you." It seemed that "falling in love" happened often, and easily, at Summer Camp!

Later that evening, there was a blindfolded contact improvisation dance experience, and Theo encouraged me to go. He had been doing contact improvisation for years, but I had only tried this twice before. Not usually drawn to physical contact with strangers, I went, reticently. A wise, older woman guided the experience, and her cues calmed me. She gently invited us: "Just relax, be curious, explore new expressive movements." The blindfold helped me stay grounded, and I found grace as I circulated. At one point, as the group moved slowly on the floor, crawling and slithering around, Theo and I found and recognized each other—first through contact, then confirmed by humorous whispers and mutual peeking. We sank in together and went back and forth between being acrobatically playful and sweetly cuddly. He felt like a slightly stiff teddy bear.

The next night, a large group gathered in the Dome for a Tantra 101 workshop before the ritual opening of Aphrodite's Temple. We changed partners in a series of exercises that built slowly from sitting back-to-back and breathing with a partner, to eye gazing or hand holding, to more potentially erotic positions. When I paired with Theo, we were instructed to "yab yum."

I straddled Theo and got into position; he immediately broke into a sweat. His body started to buzz. *Was he scared?* We were awkward and stiff, and the moment felt complicated. As I rotated on to my next partner, I wondered why our yab yum felt so weird.

After the workshop, the large group prepared to walk pilgrimage-style up to the mandatory Temple orientation. Theo approached me and asked me to go with him. *Like, a date?* I wondered. "OK, sure," I said casually.

As we walked, we shared our boundaries, fears, and desires. I said, "I don't want to be sexual, but I'm enjoying our connection." One of his desires was to cuddle, and I said, "Let's see how we feel." It felt good to enter with boundaries.

The Temple priestesses welcomed us all by simply, clearly, and lovingly explaining the consent guidelines. Then, one of them, a buxom tantrika draped in layers of black and red lacy shawls, beads, and bells, stood tall and shared this moving prayer:

"Yab Yum" tantric position

"Sexual pleasure is every human's birthright. We are all at different comfort levels, each of us responsible for our own experience. Let's take care of ourselves and each other in this sacred space. If you need help, ask for it. We stand at the center of a vortex, a swirling consciousness of pleasure and healing. We can visualize waves of global sexual healing transmitting out from this Temple and into the world. Sisters and brothers, welcome to your Temple. May you have an experience that is most nourishing to your spirit. Namaste."

We were ceremoniously invited to commence. While some of the campers began disrobing, touching each other openly, and diving straight into various celebrations of sexual contact on mattresses in the center of the room, Theo and I retreated to a cozy, semi-private corner.

Exuberant sexual activity was all around us and focusing my attention on only Theo was safe yet challenging. In a quiet voice, he confessed feeling shame around his sexual fantasies. I asked if he wanted to describe them, and when I said they sounded exciting and totally normal, he seemed relieved. *Maybe Theo would make a good one-way sexual healing practice client.* After we talked a while, he suggested that we trade massages. As I was rubbing his back, he asked about cuddling. "Actually, I don't feel like doing that," I said, feeling matter-of-fact and not overly concerned about hurting him. My experience with Vaughn had already helped my throat chakra open; I felt more relaxed about setting physical boundaries. There was a lot going on at the Temple, and I liked where I was sitting. I had a strategically good view of the center area where some very compelling, exhibitionistic activity was happening, involving a different camp flirtation of mine.

For the rest of the week at camp, whenever Theo saw me on the path, he would playfully grab me, pick me up, and sometimes kiss me. He wanted a deeper connection. I enjoyed having a buddy, and knew there was something for us to explore, but I didn't feel sexual. Gentle kissing pecks were the most I wanted with Theo. When he vulnerably expressed his desire for more contact, I listened but chose otherwise.

My steadiness with Theo was a personal success. Maybe it was the culture of camp, or his ability to accept my limits, that nurtured a wonderful ease between us. Or maybe I was just getting better at voicing what I wanted and didn't want, saying no when I wasn't a "fuck yes," and moving closer to my goal of radical honesty.

Theo's Perspective

Boy, was I flattered and excited when Amy came up to me after an early summer performance (I'm a musician) and expressed interest in me. I recall it felt rather forward, or at least much more than I was used to from a woman; something like "I really like you," or, "I'm seeing more and more of your essence." I had met her briefly the year before at Summer Camp 2016, when I was a new kid on the block and Amy was "Big Man on Campus" (and very cute).

At that point, Summer Camp 2017 was only two weeks away, so when we encountered each other at camp those comments were still fresh and they allowed me to communicate my desires freely with Amy.

Summer Camp 2017 was a significant opening for me; a coming into confidence and an ability to feel, which I'd been lacking. I am definitely a late bloomer.

It was glorious to be upfront with Amy. To be able to say things like "I think I'm falling in love with you" and know that we both knew these feelings were more about *my* opening than any reality as to our future relating. Still, I was disappointed that she was not available for more "getting to know each other" time. Amy was faster than I was at figuring the chemistry of possibilities available to us. At the time, this was hard, but I thank Amy for modeling how to be open, playful, and honest. I have carried this spirit into all my dating adventures.

Date #58: The Snake Charmer *July 2017*

Spencer was one of the tantra educators at Summer Camp. My first impression, from the way he interacted with others, was that he was very self-possessed. He was strangely familiar to me although I couldn't place him. *Had we connected on OkCupid? Had he ghosted me? Did he recognize me?*

I felt shy because of his mysterious familiarity and the possibility that he had rejected me. Crossing the edge, I made my attraction explicit during an "airing what is unsaid between us" exercise, when I said something real subtle like, "I'm totally attracted to you." At that point, our connection changed completely. Going over my communication edges almost always results in something interesting.

Spencer reflected my attraction, and from then on, our flirting happened wordlessly in our distant glances and facial expressions. Whenever he saw me, especially if I was flirting with someone else, Spencer seemed ecstatic. Once when I was kissing Jaco, a cute camper, he and another musician arrived on the scene. Spencer played the harmonica like a flute player seducing a cobra out of my basket. Our sexual chemistry kept building.

One day, Spencer led a yoni massage workshop. After all the strokes had been taught, and I was all juicy, he guided us to wrap it up. *What?!* I caught Spencer's eye. Not wanting the workshop to end, EVER, I playfully drew my hand strongly across my neck. His dancing eyes smiled. I begged my attractive dyad partner to ignore his cue, but we had no choice; another workshop was going to start soon.

Eventually, Spencer cutely asked me to have a "cuddle date." I accepted enthusiastically, and we decided to have ice cream. On a very hot day, he filled a large bowl with delicious mounds of vanilla and caramel. We sat on a couch in the Lounge, my legs draped across his lap as he fed me. Our flirtation had been building, and now, it wasn't him watching me with *other* people. I gratefully savored each spoonful he placed upon my tongue.

When Spencer surprised me by following a spoonful with his lips, I responded eagerly, my tongue reaching for his mouth. He jerked away. With big, sad eyes, he explained that he couldn't share any body fluids. His partner was unusually sensitive to STIs transmitted through saliva. Apologetic and conflicted, he added that we wouldn't be able to connect romantically after Summer Camp because of an agreement he had with her that he would not have any other lovers in Eugene.

Not kissing Spencer was fine with me. I appreciated integrity in this wild sea of openness and liked that he was protecting his partner's health. I wondered, *how did she feel about me and the other women Spencer flirted with? Would she and I ever talk about these things?* In my polyamorous future, I hoped to experience more compersion and less jealousy. Spencer and I had something sweet, but not a burning need to be sexual. Flirting was fun. I liked our playful relationship, boundaries and all.

Soon, some of my other "dates" happened to join us. The couch filled up. It was a delirious delight to be surrounded by a group of men who I was interested in, especially when someone took a picture of us, my legs extended over the row of them on the couch. After the photo, Spencer shooed the others away so we could finish our date. I finally realized that I *did* recognize Spencer from OkCupid.

I had recently checked out his profile, but didn't reach out because at the time, I thought he was too old for me. My initial odd feeling made sense: I had been conflicted about Spencer's online profile, attracted but ageist. Connecting with Vaughn helped me grow out of that.

In the following years, when Spencer and I would run into each other around town, we were always warm, but not romantic.

Finding even one lover was eluding me. Until I had a stable connection, I was just an *aspiring* polyamorist.

Date #59: The Wildest First Date
(Told from both perspectives) July 2017

Jaco was the first person I saw when I arrived at camp. Wearing makeup and a skirt, he reminded me of a doll: colorful and feminine with blond hair, blue eyes, and a pretty face. I felt a familiar, uncomfortable attracted-scared combination. After a few days when I loosened up, it became much easier to approach people. I kept running into Jaco and was curious about him.

Summer Camp was a "hunt or be hunted" situation, and if I didn't follow my attractions, I was too open to ANYONE. I much preferred pursuing a potential mate than floating vulnerably among the sea of hungry seekers. I didn't like rejecting people, and it was easy for me to initiate because if an attraction is authentic, the other will usually reciprocate (especially in the Summer Camp environment). Even if they aren't interested, I won't be left wondering what might have happened.

On the third evening of camp, we did a "hand-on-heart" exercise.

Campers lined up in two concentric circles, facing each other. The outer circle, where I was standing, stayed in place while the inner circle, where Jaco stood, rotated. I saw him coming down the line and my excitement built with every rotation. *Finally, we would be standing in front of each other, making eye contact with our hands on each other's hearts.*

But when Jaco had almost reached me, a large man grabbed me by my shoulders and moved me out of place, planting me in the moving inner circle!

I repurposed this strange fate into a flirtatious mini-tantrum and protested *"Nooooo!"* Looking down the line, I melodramatically gestured at Jaco, exclaiming loudly, "But I wanted to be with HIM!" Jaco's eyes brightened, and his whole body wiggled when he laughed. When the exercise was over, he found me and we enthusiastically planned a lunch date the next day.

We brought our food to the outdoor Lounge, a favorite hangout area among campers, and it was mostly empty. Over quinoa salad, I learned that Jaco lived in Seattle, and had a few lovers in different states. After just a little flirty getting to know each other time, he suggested we could share our sexual boundaries, fears, and desires—"just in case." We were both very open to what might occur between us, and this verbal foreplay turned me on.

When we were done eating, Spencer the snake charmer arrived, playing his harmonica, his smile burning underneath as he took a seat on the couch next to ours. Jaco and I were awash in giddy flirtation from our pre-sexual connection talk. Soon, a sensual, red-headed, full-breasted, topless woman playing an accordion sat down next to Spencer. Together, they launched into spirited song.

Flirting with both men at once, I set our plates down on the ground and climbed on top of Jaco. We started playfully making out while moving to the music, getting more voracious and wild as the intensity of the soundtrack crescendoed. I gyrated with abandon and kept kissing Jaco. When the lively song ended, I flung myself backwards onto the couch with a dramatic flourish. A chorus of excited whoops, whistles, and applause erupted from the large group of onlookers who had silently gathered. I squealed in ecstasy and horror at my exhibition, then dissolved into a puddle of girly laughter.

Next, nodding comically, Jaco said, "You know, I think we really need to take a shower because it's so hot out." The sexiness of our date ramped up. The water was cool, but our shower—like the weather—was extremely "hot," with lots of soap-enhanced exploration. Mid-day, in the open-air group showers, he lathered me up and down. I felt a rush of ecstasy when Jaco's fingers slipped in and playfully, gently, teased my most intimate zones.

We toweled off, found a hammock in the woods, and climbed in. Trying to orchestrate a comfortable position together, naked, was hilariously awkward. Eventually, we scissored our legs across each other and found an intimate configuration. One of Jaco's lovers was at camp, and serendipitously walked up to us with a huge smile and two popsicles that she gave to us. Her face shined with joy. *Compersion in action!*

Moments later, one of my other camp flirtations walked by. When I waved to him enthusiastically, Warren came over to the hammock. Straddling Jaco, butt naked, I leaned over and kissed Warren. *Who was I?* This was the wildest first date I'd ever had.

Thrilled, Jaco and I planned a sleepover a few nights later. I hadn't had intercourse in over a year and began to have some anxiety about our date. Jaco seemed extremely sexual and flirtatious. When the evening arrived, I dressed up in the sexiest outfit I had brought with me: a short, black and pink ruffly dress that was skin-tight on top, and my "lucky undies." Our plan was to meet up later, but when I bent over to wash my dinner dishes, Jaco appeared behind me, lifted my skirt and spanked me loudly and playfully, showing my polka-dot panties to passers-by. It was kinky, and I played along, but was starting to worry about our sleepover. *Would he expect to have sex? Did I want any more than just teasing?*

My inner conflict escalated as our date drew near. *I wanted romance.* Jaco was edgy and extreme. The part of me that wanted to be sexually wild and free was the one who had set up the date. I felt woozy.

I found Jaco in the crowd and told him I was having second thoughts; I didn't feel up to a lot of emotional processing, and my cancellation came out on the abrupt side. He was visibly disoriented. I felt selfish for ditching him at the last minute but was also relieved.

We talked briefly the following day and were more distant after that. Jaco stopped making eye contact with me. I felt low, having lost his trust. He was an incredible communicator with a sensitive heart, and I hoped our story wasn't over.

Managing several connections at camp was getting overwhelming; I didn't feel adept at being polyamorous.

I later learned that because of my cancellation, Jaco spent that night with my friend Olive, and they started a relationship! Later that summer, he came to Eugene to visit her, and I felt thrilled when he texted to see if he could come over. Sweaty and smiling, he arrived on her bicycle, wearing one of her cute sundresses. He brought desserts to share while he recounted their whole magical story, starting with the night of our canceled date.

Jaco's Perspective

Amy and I had a playful interaction in the very first moments of camp. I was new to this scene. In her presentations, she had appealing straightforwardness with sweetness and compassion. She made a good Processwork tour guide. Intrigued, I asked for a date.

We had lunch and then were eventually nude together in a hammock. We started moving together and rocking: very arousing. Amy said, "This is really erotic for me." I loved how she just named it.

We planned an overnight date towards the end of the week. But when the time came, Amy didn't want to go to the Temple with me. It was awkward. She wanted to honor her truth, and I wanted to support that, but also felt rejected. Amazingly, Olive and I connected and spent the night together!

If Jaco and I had spent that night together, he and Olive may not have fallen in love. And, on our fateful cancellation night, I had my own special adventure that brought me much closer with someone else.

Date #60: Body Love at Summer Camp
(Told from both perspectives) July 2017

On the first day of Summer Camp, I walked by Warren as he was showering in the stalls, his soapy, muscular chest exposed. Just a few days before, I had noticed that he had visited my OkCupid profile. I peripherally knew Warren's wife, Karen, and because of that, I swiped left. For some time, I had been semi-consciously avoiding Warren. During my monogamous years, I had "polyphobia." Polyamorous men seemed too open. Imagining unbridled, reckless pursuit, I avoided them by using big, fat, city-sized boundaries to prevent challenging interactions. But I was disarmed when Warren called to me through the spray, broadcasting that he had seen me on OkCupid. He flattered me, saying that my profile impressed him. I perked up.

The second morning of camp, Warren sat down next to me at breakfast and we ate together on a cozy couch. He said that he had heard about my dating blog and casually mentioned that he wouldn't mind having his own entry. My body felt good next to him; his compact physicality was comforting and familiar. Warren had kind eyes, a rosy complexion, and short, thick, curly blond hair. He seemed introverted. By the end of our breakfast, he asked if we could have a date sometime. When I asked what kind of date, he shyly said that he would love to cuddle. Excited, I said yes.

That day, we sat together in each of the 120-person, whole-group circles. We leaned into each other flirtatiously, our smiles unrestrained. Our casual touch was easy and comfortable. His warm sweetness, mixed with deep inner strength, was drawing me in. Warren was the first Jewish man I had ever really flirted with. Among all of the other dynamics at Summer Camp, something was definitely brewing between us.

Later that evening was the Temple opening. While I was massaging Theo, I couldn't help tuning in to Warren. He was being sexually playful with a couple on the other side of a thin curtain, the tangle of bodies just a few feet away. They were laughing and having a lot of fun, clearly comfortable together. Then, Warren moved into the center of the room and joined an older, very dynamic, sexual woman. They were suddenly fucking right there in the middle of the room. Warren was athletic and refined, a sexual panther. I repositioned myself for the best view possible. I stared at the Rodin sculpture in motion. It was beautifully artistic. I loved watching him lie back to receive oral sex, his eyes rolling back in pleasure.

I loved imagining him being my lover.

The next morning I told Olive, our mutual friend, that I had a crush on Warren. Wide-eyed, she couldn't contain her excitement. When I asked about her reaction, she wiggled around and said, "Oh, I'll let him tell you!"

I initiated our cuddle date that evening. We went to the Dome and found a quiet place in a sea of pillows and our bodies matched up instantly. He was just the right size for me, only five inches taller, with a muscular, curved body that fit so snugly into mine. Our bodies were innately fluent together. We cycled slowly through cuddling positions, each of them more intoxicating. Lingering timelessly, we moaned with pleasure each time we repositioned, because it felt incredibly amazing. Each new version released a wave of endorphins, leaving me floating in a heightened proprioceptive state. As we talked quietly, laughing, our limbs continued to wind intuitively and sensually around each other. Highly stimulated and yet relaxed, I felt fully embraced.

Eventually it was time to say goodnight. Warren and I stood up and our eyes met, both of us trembling. Even without kissing, there were tangible tectonic shifts in the earth beneath us, like a mountain dreaming itself into formation.

From that point on, I wanted to be near Warren. The next day, we took a siesta in my tent and kissed for the first time. Pressed against his solid body, I felt young and relaxed. His lips had a strange familiarity as I tasted his sweet essence. Our kisses felt like memories of a time of perfect innocence. I felt Warren was welcoming me into his private world, gently inviting me to know him. My fingertips traced his strong arms. Everything was so easy and delicious, each kiss a new morsel. That night, I went to his tent, and we spent the night getting to know each other, through whispering, kissing, and cuddling. The sweet slowness contrasted with Warren's wild Temple persona. Eventually, we floated off into dreams.

The next day was the yoni massage workshop. I really wanted to go, but felt shy about asking Warren; we had only kissed so far. Luckily for me, five minutes before the workshop, Theo told Warren that I didn't have a partner, and like a prince, Warren offered to go with me. It was such a deep, sensitive, and intimate experience to have him meet my yoni with this kind of touch, such a special way to begin a sexual relationship. After watching a demo, all the pairs formed a large circle. I was nervous and excited. He gently removed my clothes and started, like Vaughn had, by massaging my back. His attentive hands moved lithely over my body, melting my tension and warming my heart.

It was eventually time to turn face up, and to open my legs. Warren sat between them. The way he looked at my yoni made my chest lurch, and warmth poured out from my heart center. Nobody had ever looked at me that way before. I felt incredibly loved and nurtured. When he palmed me firmly, a rush of tears poured from my eyes. I had never experienced that kind of present touch with a lover. Slowly, as Warren began the massage, he studied my yoni with wonder, as if examining the petals of a rose. I flooded with oxytocin and gratitude.

(If you are a woman and have never experienced a yoni massage, run, don't walk, to find someone who can provide this service. Or if you are interested in sexual healing with women, run, don't walk, to learn! A yoni massage can make a woman feel sexually safer than ever. It is a profoundly healing experience).

Once my pants came off, there was no turning back. The next night I cancelled my date with Jaco; I didn't want sex with him, but instead, romance with Warren. I left Jaco and found Warren and broke my year-long celibacy by battery-powered candlelight in Warren's tent.

Our days of tender kissing and cuddling were the foreplay. Now, with abandon, we opened into each other, and spent all of the remaining Summer Camp nights together. Everything between us felt perfect. We planned to continue exploring our connection in Eugene, though we weren't sure how things would go when Karen, his wife, returned in a few weeks.

Warren's Perspective: "The Date That Won't End"

Before she left the country for the whole summer, Karen, my beloved wife, told me I should go after Amy Palatnick.
"Who?" I replied.
"We went to her birthday party a few months ago," she said.

I remembered her house, and that I was surprised by how few people I knew at the party, but I couldn't come up with an image of the host, though her name had been getting tossed around my community for the past year or so.

I had been looking for a lover for some time, but I thought I couldn't offer what most people want from relationships: romance. I'm happily married, I'm busy with my work, and there's also a lot of stuff to read. What did I have to offer, but a quick wit and stiff prick? I thought I just wanted to have occasional sex with some of my friends. Plus, I'm prejudiced against romance; I must be too susceptible to it!

I saw somebody on OkDuped a few days before Summer Camp began. I didn't quite recognize her. She looked cute, she did stuff I do, or at least stuff that my friends do. I thought, *I must know this person*. Then, I recognized a woodstove in a picture taken in her house, Amy's house! I tapped and swiped her profile pic a bunch of times, or whatever I thought you're supposed to do to denote enthusiastic interest.

On the first day of Camp, I'm taking an outdoor shower when she walks by. I flirt something about having seen her recently on OkStupid. At Summer Camp, I am bold in ways I am not in the rest of my life. There is no more likely place on this planet that a happily married man's flirtations are likely to result in a sexual connection. That's one of the main reasons people go to Camp: we're old enough to realize that even though we're married, we still want to get laid with someone new every once in a while, and don't want to beat around the bush too much to accomplish that most natural human goal.

That night, during the facilitated seven-minute dates, I pick Amy for one. We're instructed to stroke each other's faces, or something like that. Did I say I love this Camp? I never know how I'm supposed to touch women I haven't had sex with; I'm sorta shy. The next day, I tell her I want to have a date with her. She asks, "What kind?" Directness inspires me. Honestly, I want to cuddle and feel the measure of each other's bodies. I say something like that. It's a deal. I really like this woman. I really feel a strong attraction that isn't even emerging directly from my dick.

That evening, Aphrodite's Temple ceremoniously opens. We're both in the facility. I'm on a date with my dearest, extremely sex-positive friends, performing all manner of sexual acts behind a thin, gauzy curtain while the priestess speaks the invocations. When I stick my head out of the cubicle to come up for air and to see what's going on, Amy's head is about two feet from mine, chastely stroking somebody. Christ, I feel kinda over exposed. But, whatever. Before I met Amy, I assumed I was going to spend many a Summer Camp night engaging in an abundance of exhibitionistic sex in said Temple. It's the only place I know where that side of me runs wild.

I'm just about to leave the Temple, when I run into a woman I haven't seen here in several years. We've never been together in this sacred venue without rapidly engaging in enthusiastic sex in the center of the room. Amy is still sitting in the corner while I perform what I am compelled to perform. What am I doing: showing off, sabotaging the imminent cuddle date with Amy, just being myself? Probably all three.

The next morning, I'm eager to find Amy. I'm afraid that my sexual exhibition may have negatively affected her impression of me. At breakfast, I confess to Olive both my new crush and my new fear. She asks me if I've talked to Amy yet. It's like eight o'clock in the morning, no. I will. Before I even see Amy at morning circle, Olive gets back to me with intel. "No problem," she says, "Amy shares your crush, and she said she wants some of that sex energy she saw in her life." I love Olive, even though she doesn't have sex with me. Did I say I love this Camp?

Next evening, Amy and I have our planned date among the pillows in the back of the Dome. We talk, and we engage in a form of sexual energy sharing I call "power cuddling." The die is cast.

So now I'm in love. Against all odds. This date won't end. Let this date not end. I haven't really described our date. Tough luck. It's not really describable.

... to be continued ...

I stepped out of Summer Camp with a whole new heart, a whole new body, a whole new me. I had my first polyamorous-feeling experiences, practiced boundary setting and radical honesty, and initiated the path to becoming a sexual healer. I was elated about Warren. My long-desired sexual and personal revolution was finally under way, and Summer Camp was an enormous rite of passage.

10

WALKING THE WALK

Date #61: Amy the Ripper *October 2017*

I loved Gerald's writing style but couldn't get a read off his OkCupid pictures. I like people who shape-shift and prefer a variety of profile pictures showing different angles and aspects over a single photo or a bunch of similar ones. In Gerald's case, the display was confusing; I only felt drawn to one picture. Instead of scheduling a coffee date, I opted for a FaceTime call, to sense the chemistry.

I'd had many undocumented "super short" video dates—they had all stretched out to painful conversations lasting an hour or more. I often struggled to end the call.

When I saw Gerald, I knew we weren't a match. I wasn't disappointed; the clarity was refreshing. I stood at a familiar threshold: *Am I about to get stuck in a who-knows-how-long conversation, faking or searching for interest?*

Before either of us had a chance to say anything beyond "hi," my awareness moved me to go over my edge. I blurted out, "I'm just going to be totally honest. I can tell that we're not a match." *I did that!* His shoulders slumped and his head dropped, but when he looked up, he smiled and thanked me for being direct. Earnestly, I wished him luck and said goodbye.

A rush of relief moved me to dance around my bedroom, celebrating my success. *I had graduated!* I saved us both time. My integrity was fortified. And, I spared him the pain from the crash of high hopes that result from my predisposition to fake being nice—which, in fact, is not very nice.

And it all happened within 30 seconds!

Date #62: Going Beyond Walkward *October 2017*

For most of the fall, I spent one night a week with Warren, and continued dating. But when I opened OkCupid on my computer, there were only two pictures of possible matches. *App changes. Grrrr.* One of them was cute, so I clicked "Like" and adrenaline rushed through me when the "You like each other!" screen popped up. I messaged him to let him know that OkCupid thought "he was the only one for me." He playfully said that he agreed with the app. We fell into animated messaging, and spontaneously decided to meet up right away.

Coincidentally, he was at a friend's house, in my neighborhood, and offered to swing by. I knew better than to invite him over. "Let's go for a walk," I said. "If things go well, maybe I'll invite you in for dinner. Let's see how it goes."

Russell arrived. He had a surfer look: blond hair brushed to the side, fair skin, and blue eyes. His was a standard type of cuteness, but I didn't feel attracted. We figured out quickly that we'd both had booths at the Saturday Market, and traded a mug for a hat fifteen years ago. *I still had that hat!*

But our conversation was stilted. We sometimes physically bumped into each other, and our sentences clashed at awkward angles. I chose a short loop back around to my house. When he asked if I was going to invite him in for dinner, I smiled and said "No," without elaborating. I wanted to see how it would feel to just say "No." He had a slight reaction, but quickly recovered, and we hugged goodbye. After he left, feeling slightly remorseful, I texted him.

> **Amy:** Hey, Russell! That felt like an abrupt ending to our date. Let me know if you want to debrief.

Russell: Debrief? Sure.

Amy: Great. We never talked about what each of us is looking for. I noticed in your profile that you said you were monogamous. I have a lover and should have told you about him from the beginning. But I wanted to check things out with you first, because I wonder if falling head over heels with somebody would change my polyamorous lens. The feeling I had with you was more of a friend vibe than a romantic attraction. What did you think?

Russell: I thought you were fun and cute, but I felt you weren't interested in me at all. You're right about me not looking for an open relationship, but I'm curious as to what that would look like.

Amy: I hope I wasn't hurtful.

Russell: Not at all. Just not interested.

Amy: I felt that there was something missing between us in the chemistry realm. But thank you for saying I'm cute; I think you're cute too!

Russell: Ha ha! You're totally cute. I hope everything works out well for you. :)

Amy: You too, Russell. 🩶

When I said, "No," I could have explained more, but he also could have asked. I felt satisfied with our communication.

∽

Many "successful" one-off dates and experiences were not written up, because they were so short, and I was able to be honest.

I started using Marco Polo regularly for vetting. Video messaging (as opposed to live video chatting), was a game changer! I would set the tone: "Let's just send one or two short messages and see what we think. I'm happy to send the first message." Most people were not a good match, and I was able to say so directly, clearly, and kindly. Profiles can lie; videos can't. I had many short, "no thanks, but good luck, nice to meet you!" exchanges that went well more often than not. Often, I would mention that I was a natural matchmaker, and would keep them in mind as I continued on my dating quest. People seemed relieved and grateful to have a positive-feeling online connection.

A few times, I tried those in person, ten-minute-dates that my friend Stacy had suggested. Once, over a quick tea, I told a skinny, googly-eyed guy, "You seem giddy about connecting. It's very sweet but I'm not in the same space. I can tell this isn't a romantic fit for me." I was almost able to keep it to ten minutes.

Once, during a Processwork retreat, I was sitting at a large dinner table with a bunch of students and faculty members. One of the teachers teasingly asked about my dating life. I joked that dating was like a choir of "no, no, no, no thanks, no ..." with only a few treasures surfacing from time to time. Stuart, one of the men at the table, said, "I received one of those 'no's last year! The way you let me down was impressive."

"I did? It was?" I remembered that Stuart had approached me on the street, and that I was taken aback. But I didn't remember any details.

"Yes!" he said. "I actually told the story to my sister recently when she was struggling with how to reject people nicely."

"That's amazing! What did I say?"

"I invited you to coffee, and without skipping a beat, you asked if my interest was romantic. No beating around the bush with you! I was disarmed, and admitted that it was, and you smiled and said you were flattered but weren't available for that. It was so gentle, and I walked away thinking that was the best rejection I'd ever gotten. I felt happy, even though you said no. It was actually relieving."

More and more, I unapologetically knew what I was looking for, and Russell wasn't it. I wanted to feel desirous, hungry, and activated. I would much rather be at home alone, working, than out on a "meh" date—or stuck with "meh" in my own house.

Date #63: A Man With a Sloth *October 2017*

How could I not like Robert, whose OkCupid picture showed him cradling a sloth? (Now, that's a little manipulative, isn't it? I mean, who wouldn't like a man with a sloth?)

We chatted smoothly through text, discovering similar interests such as higher consciousness, altered states, and writing. He was exactly my age, within a week. Based on our commonalities and the plant medicine Facebook friends we had in common, I didn't need a preliminary video date.

We met at Hideaway Bakery. The first thing I noticed about him —and liked—was that he didn't smile. At all. I was curious. We ordered food and lattes at the counter and found a table by the fireplace.

Robert actually resembled a sloth, with a round, balding head and round glasses that sat heavily on his downward-tipped face. Glancing up at me from time to time, he focused mostly on the table as we spoke. Early on, looking disturbed, he said, "I had an accident. It's been a fuck of a long healing process." I appreciated his connection to himself, his no-bones directness, and his vulnerability.

Every once in a while, his face would break into an out-of-nowhere, sunshiny smile, and I got a glimpse of pre-accident Robert. It was engaging to witness his kaleidoscopic experience. He was emotionally transparent, his inner disturbance or momentary spark reflected in his mutable posture, face, and words.

We spoke frankly. Polyamory wasn't attractive to Robert, and I was not planning on ending my connection with Warren. He wanted to settle down with someone, traditional-style, but seemed curious about me anyway.

I was intrigued, but I didn't think we had chemistry. I wondered, *Do men attune more to sexual attraction, where women tend to look for nuanced romantic potential?* When I feel attracted to someone, it is multi-leveled. My body says yes. My heart opens. I come spiritually alive. Robert felt like a brother.

At the end of our date, I used the Walk Away test. I texted him soon to appreciate the tenderness I felt in our meeting. We agreed to get in touch if either of us felt an inspiration. The date quickly faded.

Too bad, because I really do like a man with a sloth.

Date #64: Above the Belt *November 2017*

After a largely internal, wound-licking year following my heartbreak with Soren (the Wizard), I was out of my shell. My next-level experience at Summer Camp motivated me to find a second lover who was more romantically available than Warren.

I branched out and started using the Tinder and Bumble dating apps to reach new populations. My OkCupid profile bordered on being a novella; the other apps had a 45-word maximum and were simpler, faster, and more intuitive. Tinder felt like a video game, and as a friend said, "Dating apps are just judging local strangers from the comfort of your own toilet." I swiped for fun, swiped like crazy. Dating seemed to be a numbers game: keep going until you find the great ones. Whether yes or no, left or right, I loved to swipe!

On Tinder, I saw a profile that was so wacky and over-the-top that I had to swipe right. "Günther" was 51, a nightclub owner from Sweden with a mustache, a mullet, and glossy lips. He looked like a rocker from 1980. His profile said, "I am a dirty Swedish sex beast. Let me be your pleasureman. Let's sexualize the world, yeah." The whole thing was so hilarious that I took screenshots to preserve it.

In addition to using new dating apps, I began going out more to music concerts, dance classes, and social gatherings. At a few of the events, one extremely magnetic being caught my eye and made me feel shy in an instant-crush way. Light brown wavy hair was casually but sophisticatedly pulled over to one side in classic-movie-style perfection. Their sultry, sensuous dresses were draped softly over milky sweet skin. They oozed a unique, sensual feminine beauty, though they didn't seem cis-female. But at the events, they were always surrounded by friends, and I was too shy to initiate contact.

One day, Flora appeared on Tinder. I held my breath. A short profile described their life as an artist and requested "they/them" pronouns. I had never flirted with a trans/gender diverse person before; it was unfamiliar and exciting. Holding my breath, I swiped right. That magical thing happened where our pictures slid in from either side and bumped in the middle, and the celebratory "They Like You Back!" banner fell down and bounced above our profile pictures. I messaged right away and Flora responded immediately, wanting to meet up soon. But neither of us was alpha with our decision-making; setting a time and place felt clumsy.

We went to Sundial, a cute vegan cafe I had been wanting to try. As we sat down together, I quickly mentioned that I was open to talking about gender. With poise, Flora responded carefully, "Why don't we return to that topic later."

After a while, there was more ease between us. At one point, Flora told me about a unique instrument they owned and casually said, "I'll show it to you one day," which made me smile. "So, how is Tinder going for you?" Flora asked me, and I laughed and showed them my screenshots of Günther. Flora broke into unguarded laughter and started searching for something on their phone. I couldn't believe it when they showed me "Ding Dong Song (Touch My Tralala)," a video by Günther that looked like European porn from the 1980s. *Was Günther really in Eugene, or was it a fake profile?* We agreed it was probably fake but had fun dancing in our seats to the catchy "tra la la, ding ding dong" of his video. The atmosphere between us relaxed and by the end of our meal, Flora told me about taking hormones, wishing to learn how to apply makeup properly, and the ups and downs of their transition so far. I felt honored to hear this more personal information.

Flirting with someone beyond traditional gender constructs was edgy. I was in a tumble, with many wires crossing. But at the same time, it felt simple: I found Flora smart, sensitive, and sexy. And they seemed to like me too.

It had started pouring, so I drove Flora home, just a few blocks away, and parked. Hoping to kiss, I moved my jacket lapel away from my face. I smiled shyly, but didn't voice my typical bold offer, "How would you feel about kissing?" Instead, Flora said "Bye" and stepped gracefully out of the car. I drove away feeling giddy. Soon after we parted, we texted each other and admitted our mutual interest.

Over the next week we flirted through text, sending pictures and videos. Flora sent me a link to porn they liked, which I also enjoyed: a scene with a cis-woman, a trans woman and a big dildo. Then, we met up at Flora's house. We hung out on their bed. Flora was opening up to me, expressing their joy and awkwardness about transitioning into a more female body. I learned that their transition was relatively fresh, including recently beginning to take estrogen. Pulling the neck of their low-cut shirt down just a bit, Flora proudly showed me brand new cleavage from a push-up bra, and also some sexy selfies they took for Instagram. I felt excited about Flora's desire to radiate femininity.

First we held hands, then we touched each other's soft arms and talked about what we might do together. I was nervous about Flora's unwanted penis, and I wasn't sure how it might come into play, until Flora suggested that we could connect "above the belt," keeping all physical contact confined to the upper body. I felt thrilled about that simple concept. We left our bras and pants on and agreed that all exposed flesh was OK to touch unless a boundary was expressed.

Flora's smooth skin, lithe movements, and lipstick were accompanied by a uniquely spicy masculine scent and unrelenting stubble that lightly scratched my face. I loved Flora's fine line between man and woman. Discovering them through this confined touch practice felt kinky and gentle. As we rolled around, playfully kissing and sucking at each other, I wound up accidentally giving them a hickey on the neck. It was fun, but awkwardness arose at times and we would shift, stop, or slow down. We went back and forth from cuddling and talking to making out and tumbling around.

There was mutual curiosity, but when we kissed, it felt like we were *trying* to kiss. Something subtle in our chemistry didn't click. We checked in about it the next day:

Flora: How are you today?

Amy: Are you saying, "How did you feel about our time together last night?"

Flora: Hmm, I don't know if I was actually asking that. I may have been.

Amy: In some moments, I felt more strongly engaged, and others felt more ... mundane? By the end, I felt a slight disappointment that it wasn't hotter or more compelling, but that's just a chemistry thing. I have a basic belief that things always work out as they should, and that true chemistry is always mutual. I feel like you can't force a relationship to happen if it isn't meant to happen, and you can't stop a relationship from happening if it is meant to happen. In any case, I'm still open to hanging out.

Flora: I think I picked up on the same thing you did. Parts of it felt fun but not particularly passionate. I'm also of the mind that whatever should happen will happen if we let it. I still feel open, but not urgent.

Amy: Perfect. Jinx!

We became social media friends and communicated a bit through text but didn't get together romantically again. Both of us were looking for sexy connections. A few months after our date, Flora asked me for some coaching, to get support to put themselves out in public. We met for a few sessions. They wanted to be in films, do camming (livestream sexy videos for money) and to possibly become an escort. I liked supporting Flora to fully express the alluring beauty I recognized in them. I really hope for the best for Flora. I can easily see them becoming a star!

Date #65: Toastmaster Flash *November 2017*

In the fall of 2017, I joined Toastmasters, an international public speaking club. Although I didn't join in order to find dates, I developed a crush on Tony. He was tall and red-headed, with the kindest demeanor. From the first time I met him, at a local speech competition, he felt familiar. He was one of the event's organizers, and we made eye contact many times. That day, I won first place. We continued to see each other at meetings and gatherings, and my warm feelings towards him endured. During one impromptu speech, I mentioned my naked body, and my eyes shyly flickered to his.

Curiosity about him swept me to Facebook, where I initiated messaging. I was the membership vice president of the Eugene Lunch Bunch Toastmasters club and used that role as an excuse to connect with him. We messaged back and forth for a few hours and found lots of common interests, including studying dreams and inventing things.

We indulged freely in spirited, flirty communication over the next few days. When I learned that Tony was leaving town for a few weeks, I asked if he wanted to meet up before he left. We met that afternoon at Ume Grill, a Japanese food cart next to Sundance Natural Foods.

The gregarious owner filled our paper boats with miso butter salmon and sweet potato onigiri. We settled down on a picnic bench, and our conversation began with abundant praises of gratitude for the tasty food. Looking up, I noticed—and remarked on—the absence of lines around Tony's eyes, where crow's feet had landed on my face decades ago. He was *sixteen years* younger than me!

I felt uncharacteristically nervous as we ate and talked. His questions were stimulating and thought-provoking, and I felt suddenly manic, with so much to say. Despite my awkwardness, the warmth between us endured. After we ate, Tony suggested a walk into the light mist. We sauntered to University Park and paused next to the swingset, facing each other. He was significantly taller than me. Gazing down into my eyes, he said that he liked my directness, and wondered how I felt. I looked up at him, smiling, and said, "You mean, about us?" He nodded.

I said, "Well, I was drawn to you from the first time I saw you at the speech competition and have enjoyed all of the interactions we've had so far. Our messaging has been fun, and I'm feeling good right now." Standing in a globe of mist, he bent down and our lips met. Something deep in me smiled. I could have kept kissing him for a long time.

When I kiss someone, I like to feel the person through their lips—their presence and sensitive feedback. I want to sense their hunger. As we kissed, his pelvis pressed his arousal into me, which was magically unexpected.

Walking back to our cars in the mist, holding hands, I mentioned that I was blogging about my dating experiences, and that I was polyamorous. He recoiled, "Oh, that gives me pause. I have avoided polyamory because of the increased STI risk."

Interestingly, that myth is not true. Ethically polyamorous people tend to be much more responsible about STI testing and transparent communication than other demographics. I didn't say that to Tony. As he pulled back, I realized I too was losing interest. I continued:

"Warren, my lover, has a vasectomy, and we don't use condoms. We're 'fluid-bonded.' " Tony's eyes started to bulge. Then, he said he was going on vacation with a woman. It was still misty, but the fog between us gave way to sober inquiry: were we each what the other was looking for? Even though our kissing felt special, our compatibility was increasingly questionable. I wasn't wedded to the idea of only manifesting Person Right, but I do love to find people who could potentially fit into that fairy tale category. I could feel that this was not going to be the relationship to end all others.

When Tony returned from his trip, I invited him to dinner at my house. We ate. We cuddled. We made out. Something was off. I didn't know what it was but a door in me had closed. We didn't have the unmistakable electricity that I crave. I applied the Summer Camp rule of thumb: if it's not a "fuck yes," it's a "no." Unfortunately, "fuck yes" was starting to feel like an endangered species. Oh, how I longed for the fuck yesses to come my way!

Date #60, Warren Continued: A Rocky Fall *Autumn 2017*

Once home from Summer Camp, Warren and I spent time together as much as we thought we could without upsetting the balance of his marriage. Karen was still away for a few more weeks. We indulged in hours-long delicious lovemaking a few times a week, giving our developing intimacy plenty of room to unfold.

As lovers, we moved like water dancers, every shift, every touch, every kiss divinely choreographed. My whole body opened. He touched me with such presence and care that at times I would burst into ecstatic, grateful tears. After several hours of drinking each other in, as we built towards orgasm, I could feel our souls knitting together. At the threshold of mutual climax, Warren's eyes bored into mine, transporting me into an unknown sexual cosmos. Layers of trauma released effortlessly. Before and during our dates, whenever I looked in the mirror, I felt truly beautiful. Because of his adoration, I didn't have to be anything other than my natural self.

But as Karen's return neared, Warren was nervous about the integration of our relationship with his marriage. *Would we all get along?* I felt hesitant too. I had never known what to make of Karen, who was in my social circle but not a personal friend. I had seen her and Warren many times at gatherings and had always intuitively kept my distance. More recently, however, Karen had made several friendly gestures towards me, including showing up to my birthday party with a thoughtful gift.

After Summer Camp, Warren told Karen about our connection. She wanted to talk to me. One day while he and I were in bed, she happened to call from Europe. "I'm at Amy's. Hold on." He looked up and pointed the phone at me with raised eyebrows, to see if I wanted to talk. Nodding, I nervously wrapped myself in a sheet, took the phone, and left him in bed.

Pacing barefoot around my backyard, I listened as she asked me about the nature of our relationship: specifically, if we were falling in love. I replied honestly that it didn't feel like we were falling in love —*how could we be? It had just been a few weeks*. With a shaky voice, I added that I didn't want to create any disturbance in their marriage. Karen said that she had no problem with us being sexual, but if we were falling in love, that would be a different story. When we hung up, I asked Warren about her question. He laughed, like it was obvious, and said that he was pretty sure we were falling in love. I liked that he felt that way, but I wasn't ready to call it that, yet.

This was my first real polyamorous situation, and I was scared. I had been under the assumption that by definition, polyamorous people fell in love with multiple people. But Warren explained that he wasn't supposed to fall in love with someone who wasn't going to become a mutual third in their relationship. They'd been hoping to find someone they could both fall in love with, but I had never felt any romantic sparks with Karen.

Warren and I didn't know what our relationship would look like when she returned. We talked about spending one or two nights a week together, possibly building up to more time in the future.

Soon after Karen returned, she invited me to lunch, just the two of us. We drank margaritas, and I suggested that we could imagine our drinks were truth serum. She took a sip and locked eyes with me. "What are your intentions with my husband?"

I was on the spot, scared. Her eyes penetrated into mine, challenging me, pushing me backwards. Taking my sip, I said, "One or two nights together a week would be great, and three would be amazing. But I honestly don't want more than that." She said that one overnight a week would be a lot, two would be a sacrifice she couldn't imagine, and three would never work for her.

As she spoke, I energetically retreated, and said that I was happy for whatever time I could have with him. OK, one night a week it was. I felt trapped. "And maybe a coffee date or a dinner at our house sometimes," she offered. The margarita helped me say, "It seems like you don't trust me," and she agreed, adding that it wasn't personal; she didn't trust most people. As we parted, I was sweating and shaking, but invited her total honesty as we moved forward. Ominously, she laughed and said, "I don't think you know what you are asking for." Walking away from that lunch, I felt terrible, but also solid in my conviction of desiring transparency.

In the months after our margarita talk, Karen called me on the phone every couple weeks. I appreciated and admired her initiative, as my instinct was to avoid contact. Our talks usually centered on her suspicious questions. Karen was convinced that I had secret designs around Warren, hidden maybe even from myself. Although he and I were ideal lovers, our communication outside the bedroom was jerky. He felt foreign to me: his nose was in *The New York Times* by 6 a.m. and he incessantly talked about politics, economics, and other stressful topics. I preferred to talk about our inner worlds, what we learned about ourselves, and magical things that happened in our days. I often struggled to understand and care about the things that were important to him. He was very intellectual, and although I'm sapiosexual, I am more of a feeler, and like at least a splash of poetry in my conversation style. Because of these differences, I couldn't imagine us ever being primary partners and didn't see myself as a threat to their marriage. But Karen was convinced that we would eventually grow on each other.

Although I was disappointed about having only one overnight a week, I didn't push for more. Instead, we dove into our precious weekly dates all the way, soaking up every moment we had together. Warren would show up like clockwork on Tuesdays at 4:10, we'd have an early dinner, in or out, and then we would ascend into our otherworldly lovemaking sessions. Sometimes we would make love two or three times by the break of morning. It didn't take me long to realize that we were definitely falling in love.

Despite Karen's fears and resistance, she often invited me over to have a meal and spend time with the two of them. The first time I went to their house, Warren answered the door, and seemed rigid. He went to kiss me on the lips, but I didn't want to upset Karen. Nervous about her seeing our intimacy, I turned my head, and his kiss landed awkwardly on my cheek. Over that dinner and the next few, we tried to have open conversations, talking about our feelings and fears, but it was never easy. One time when we went out for dinner, Karen suggested that we not speak directly about our interpersonal dynamics. Her intention was positive—for us to get to know each other as people—but as we talked about things like movies we had recently seen, I felt stunted and uncomfortable. When I mentioned that I wasn't enjoying the experiment, it created defensiveness and added stress. The three of us had a hard time finding a relaxing groove.

The tension in their marriage was apparent, but Warren was protective of Karen's vulnerability. He functioned like an emotional barrier between us: no personal information passed through him. I could only infer that our developing relationship was difficult for her.

It wasn't that I expected us to be best friends, but I did hope to be accepted. After all, Karen was—strangely and mythically—the one who suggested that Warren should "go after me" in the first place. He had been depressed and hoping to find a new lover for quite a while, and because I was in no way scheming to take him away from her, in my view, the situation couldn't have been better. But the intensity of our chemistry, and the fact that we were falling in love, must have been threatening to her.

∽

When I was in college, I lived with and deeply admired Kathleen: a small, powerful woman who taught me the "Sisterhood Code." She started a romance with a man who was visiting town and discovered that he was in another relationship. When she broke it off, I was confused; they seemed like such a good match. I asked Kathleen about it, and she said these words that never left me: "I would never do that to a sister." Even though she didn't know the other woman, she thought of the stranger—on the other side of the country—as a sister. That blew me away. I had definitely broken the Sisterhood Code in the past, and I signed up right then for this level of integrity.

∽

Worried that our relationship would make Karen unhappy, I wondered, *what if she can't take it?* If I could do something to alleviate her suffering, I thought I should. One night, when I suggested to Warren that maybe we should break up because Karen seemed miserable, he countered, "But if you broke up with *me*, then *I* would suffer." I liked his clever answer. Our love felt like a train that neither of us wanted to stop.

One fall day, while I was out and about, Warren called and invited me to coffee. Excited for the spontaneous opportunity, I detoured and met him at Tailored coffee shop. We sat down with our drinks, and his leg was shaking as though an army of ants was going to burst out of it. As we held hands, I asked about his nervousness, and he revealed that he was meeting me secretly. He said that Karen had asked him a while ago to not get together with me beyond our scheduled overnights. I had no idea we weren't supposed to meet and didn't want to be going behind her back. I felt terrible.

"What?!" I asked. "Why didn't you just tell her? And *why can't we have coffee?!*" He said that she was on the third day of a migraine and he didn't want to add stress by asking her, but that he missed me and selfishly wanted to see me.

Leaving the coffee shop, I felt upset to be harboring a secret. Then, on my drive home, Karen called. In a soft voice, she said, "Are you available to come over for dinner tonight? I know Warren would love the time with you. I'm not feeling well but want to surprise him." *Oh, boy.* I either had to lie and not mention coffee or expose his transgression. *Fuck. He should tell her himself!* I was stuck. "Umm, I would love to come over, but ... there's something Warren should tell you."

"What's going on?" She sounded stressed.

"You should really ask him."

Her voice got louder when she said, "No, you tell me! What is going on!" I told her about our coffee and how I was upset about it too. Understandably angry, she hung up. I quickly dialed Warren to fill him in. *Pregnant silence.* He was in trouble. But lying to her would have been the sure end to any hope of peace between Karen and me. It sucked that to do the right thing, I had to throw Warren under the bus.

Everything changed after that incident. Karen felt distrustful of Warren. One overnight a week. No mid-week dates. No more trio dinners. But Karen continued to call me sometimes, to process. It was never easy. In one phone call, she joked about a fantasy of putting my head in a blender. I froze. Violent images involving kitchen appliances began to haunt me. *Was this situation healthy?*

... to be continued ...

11

ANGELS, GHOSTS, AND THE SCUM OF THE EARTH

Date #66: "Can I Be Honest With You?" January 2018

Lee and I connected on Tinder and messaged hungrily with silky smooth communication. He was responsive and witty, and I felt a touch of magic. We met at Party Downtown: one of Eugene's more metropolitan spots, serving craft cocktails and local, organic food. I was happily surprised that he was even more handsome than in his photos. Lee had curly hair, fair features, and a strong face. Right away I said, "You're really attractive!"

However, when I sat down across the table from him, he turned his chair 90°, facing sideways. *How strange.* To talk to me, he had to glance over his shoulder. I asked a few questions to get the conversation moving, but then he just kept going. And going. And going. He talked about himself, with a mixture of eye-rolling weariness and strangely biting negativity, for over an hour. At one point, he came around with a sigh, asking in an exasperated tone, "OK, so what about you?" But then he quickly cut me off with ... more about him! Lee's total self-absorption hadn't been apparent during our texting banter.

Why did I stay? Why didn't I mention his odd choice of seating? When he asked if I'd like to go to a nearby bar, after an uncomfortable hour at the restaurant, *Why did I go?* Because I was being ... *nice.* My inner coach knew that I could have said one of many things:

- "I'm not feeling inspired by our date. Are you?"
- "Do you think it will be more of the same?"
- "What about this date do you want to continue?"
- "Let me think about that. Do I want to go to another place?"
- "Um, no."
- "No."
- "Not really."
- "No thanks."
- "Not at all."
- *"Can I be honest with you?"*

But since I didn't woman up, things just kept getting worse. At the Starlight Lounge, Lee asked where I would like to sit, and I chose the couch, thinking that I could at least look away from him while he was looking away from me. We sat next to each other, staring out into space. I sipped a glass of water. The evening proceeded with complaints about "the scum of the earth": the people he worked with, the person who just texted him. Lawyers. Lee said that he became a lawyer because he hated lawyers. He was motivated by hate.

I wish I had said the things I was thinking and feeling. Instead, I became a wallflower, just existing, shifting uncomfortably in the fumes of his derogatory monologue. If I had felt more open, what could I have said?

- "It is interesting how you don't face me."
- "I notice I am losing interest."
- "You talk about yourself a lot."
- "You don't seem to like your work much."
- "You seem miserable."
- "I think we approach life very differently."
- *"Can I be honest with you?"*

Any of those would have worked. But instead, I suffered. Luckily, bodies tell the truth, and when I started to yawn, neither of us could ignore it. As we made our way out of the bar, I finally opened my mouth and said, "I had no idea I would be learning so much about the scum of the earth on our date tonight." Lee's awkward pause was the highlight of my night. *Thank god I found my voice.*

We stood next to my car and he looked directly at me, the first time all night. I could feel him wondering, *are we going to kiss? Have sex?* And I was thinking, *do you even know my name?* A huge weight was lifting as the date came to a close. Looking off into the distance, he asked if I might want to get together again, and I smiled and shook my head. "No, probably not. But thanks. I'll get in touch if I change my mind." He looked confused.

I made a commitment to myself to use these words when communication felt off: "Can I be honest with you?" And to trust that the rest would follow.

Date #67: The Tortoise and the Hawk *January 2018*

When I was teaching a personal mythology course—*The Do What You Love Project*—in Baja, Mexico, I met an older Italian man. We were both staying at Señor Mañana's, a colorful hostel in the heart of San José del Cabo. I was drawn to the short, bald extrovert who turned his head to smile hugely at me each time he walked past in the courtyard. He knew zero English but was completely comfortable speaking dramatically and rapidly in Italian without any interest in translation. Attempting to communicate with him was joyful and exhilarating. I engaged with him using my beginner's Spanish, mixed in a little French, and added a bunch of *i*'s, *o*'s and *issimo*'s to the ends of words, trying for an Italian accent. Somehow in the mishmash, I learned that his name was Falco. Despite our limited comprehension, we were both having fun, with an obvious kinship of spirit.

The next day, Falco—which means "hawk" in Italian—swooped in and asked me to have some *"vino"* that evening. When the time came, we met in the hostel's courtyard and shared dinner and wine with his sons, who were my age. They spoke English, helped translate, and joked about Falco's big personality, "He always has to be in charge of *everything*." I felt much more comfortable with them there; Falco's eyes on me were penetrating and too hungry. Pretty soon, the boys went to bed and Falco and I continued, pressing hard through another bottle of strong shiraz.

The more wine I drank, the more languages I seemed to be able to weave together freely. Any given sentence had English, Spanish, French, Italian, and Russian mixed in—though I was only proficient in French.

I thought I learned quite a bit about him. He was 66, lived in northern Italy and spent half of each year in Mexico. Then, something like, "Come meet me in Oaxaca, at a very nice place called Shapala. A huge nudist celebration will last many months." Falco explained, "Everything will cost half in Oaxaca from San José, twice as long for your winter *vacanze* in the sun."

We laughed a lot as we tried to understand each other. I liked the passion in Falco's voice when he said, with expressive fists high in the air, something like, "We only have one life; live it now!" Eventually, he sidled around to my side of the table and dove into kissing me, too aggressively. But in the spirit of vacation, freedom, and fun, I decided that his tongue pushing into my wine-soaked mouth was OK.

I didn't feel threatened, just a little annoyed that he was putting me in the familiar position of having to slow a man down. I tried my best with mixed languages to explain to him: "*Soy tortuga*," which I thought meant "I am a tortoise." He didn't understand. I pointed at him and said "Falco," then swooped my hand down strongly to show the speed of a hawk and then pointed to myself and walked my fingers slowly on the table to show a slow tortuga.

But then he kissed me again. His determined tongue filled my mouth and his hand was quickly on my breast. *Grrr. Why can't he move more slowly?* Disappointed, I shut down. Because he ignored (or didn't understand) my tortuga plea, I decided to say goodnight. I wish men—the fast ones—would learn this one skill about romancing:

Sense a woman's feedback. Don't overwhelm her.

It would make them so much sexier! I washed our wine glasses. Falco kissed me one more time, and I said goodnight, thinking,

Maybe I'm done with Falco. I like to be romanced and seduced, not captured and cornered.

The next evening, Falco asked about my plans, and I said I was going on the Art Walk. He asked to join me, and too quickly, I said, "OK." *Instant regret.* Really, I longed to head out on the town alone, open to whatever, or whomever, I might run into, but off we went into the warm evening. The moment we hit the street, he put his arm around me. I squirmed away. He grabbed my hand. Clearly, this was a date in his mind, but each push made me less interested. As several attractive men passed us in the street, I wished I'd just said no to Falco when he invited himself.

I should have listened to my feet.

After the previous evening's wine-soaked date with Falco, in the middle of the night, I realized that I was shredding my feet in a half-asleep state. It's not a glamorous topic, but I have athlete's foot. Ever since high school, I have had itchy feet, and I developed a semi-masochistic and strangely satisfying habit of impulsively scratching and peeling them, often to the point of drawing blood. Sometimes, I pull chunks of skin off and I have to hobble for a day.

In Processwork, body symptoms are considered to be dreamings of the body. The subconscious mind symbolically expresses specific information through the physical body. Like recurring dreams, chronic symptoms reflect vital internal conflicts, blocks to our personal growth. *Why do I have athlete's foot?* There must be a reason, a lesson, but it can be challenging to be open to the message of a chronic body symptom because we have a big "edge," or mythic block, to its lesson. It's like quitting an addiction: a part of us doesn't want to change. We get comfortable with our patterns, even when they are unhealthy.

Curious about the meaning of my athlete's foot, I started tracking it. *When did it get aggravated?* On my video date with Bjorn, I felt trapped and was semi-consciously digging into my feet. On the call with big-bearded Eric, I felt stressed and bloodied my toes. And once when Warren and I were struggling, I lay awake while he slept, obsessively peeling the skin between my toes. The pattern was consistent: whenever I was itching, I was stressed about a relationship issue.

One Processwork method of exploring the message of a body symptom is to focus on it and wait for a simple, dreamlike picture to appear. So when I caught myself scratching during the night, after my first date with Falco, I decided to listen more deeply. I had worked on unfolding the meaning of my athlete's foot in the past but hadn't ever taken my inner work deep enough.

Relaxing, I tuned in to the sensation between my toes and thought about words that described my sensory experience: "sharp, pointy, hot, and screaming." Eventually, a picture formed that looked something like this:

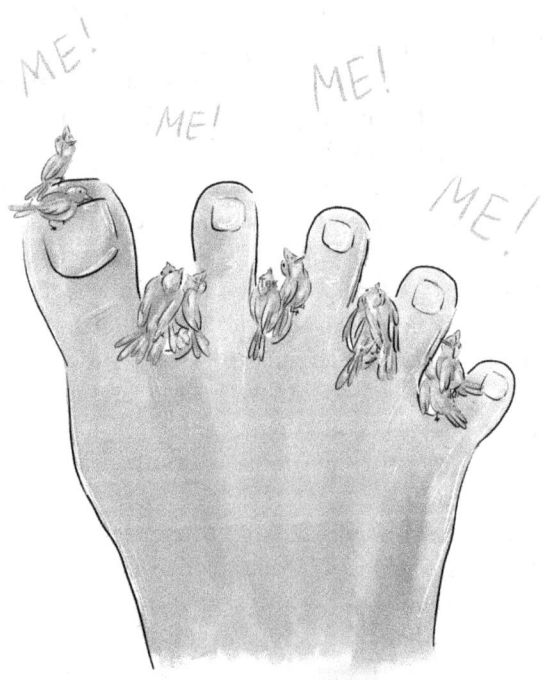

ANGELS, GHOSTS, AND THE SCUM OF THE EARTH

An enormous foot had wide spaces between each toe. In each gap were baby birds, their sharp, black claws digging in—tons of baby birds, with hungry orange beaks pointed upwards. They were all screaming "ME! ME! ME!" in a very high-pitched tone.

The image hit me like an anvil: "ME! ME! ME!" was the missing piece! After this epiphany, my feet calmed and the itching disappeared. It was Processwork magic. In the morning, the skin that should have been peeled and raw had dried out and was mostly healed up. It made no sense, but it happened. I told the story—and showed my feet—to my students, who were there to learn Processwork.

Those baby birds naturally did what I had not been able to do: they asked for what they wanted, freely. They screamed for what they wanted!

∽

On the Art Walk date with Falco, the baby bird realization supported me to say what I wanted. When he reached for my hand, I smiled and shook my head. It was time to make "ME" choices. I wanted ice cream and I bought some. I wanted to check out the art galleries, so I just walked in, and Falco followed behind me. When he asked if I wanted to go for a glass of wine, I said "No, let's go back to the hostel." I let my desires—and feet—lead the way.

We sat in the hostel's courtyard where colorful murals of happy suns, flowers, and butterflies surrounded us. The trees smelled like fruit. Children were using their long-hanging pods as musical instruments. A Pisces like me, Falco was wonderfully open and light. We finally realized that instead of ridiculously weaving unknown languages together, I could just speak in French, and he could kind of understand.

Predictably, he soon suggested that we go to his room: "No sex, of course" he said, in Spanish. I said *"Non. Merci, mais non."* He looked confused, though this French was as basic as could be. *"No me gusta,"* I tried in Spanish. Dancing around flirtatiously, he mixed Italian and Spanish and charades: "Just cuddling, so nice!"

"Mais non, pas pour moi. Soy una tortuga," I tried again.

"*Porque?*"

"*No sé! Soy una tortuga. Tortuguissimo!*" Did I have to know why I didn't want to be more physical with him?

He kept at it. "You fear of me?"

"*Non, je n'ai pas peur. Me gusta solamente solo.*"

"*Cinco minutos? Dos minutos?*" He wasn't taking "no" for an answer.

Eventually I grabbed his arms, leaned towards him, and said emphatically, in French, "Falco! You push and push and push! You're not listening to me. I said *no!*" His face turned sad, like a little boy's. I hugged him goodnight.

Falco was harmless, but amazingly persistent: the perfect boundary-setting practice partner. Even in our last hug, he tried to worm his tongue into my mouth. He was so good at being the baby bird. I am grateful to him—and the birds—for helping me access my "ME! ME! ME!"

The Sexual Healers' Tribe: 2017-2018

Since Summer Camp 2017, I had been actively focusing on my sexuality. I indulged in weekly cosmic erotic journeys with Warren and had regular sessions with Vaughn, my mentor, who lived in California. Several other women were doing therapeutic work with Vaughn, and we became a cohort. Most of them were working on their own sexuality, whereas my goal was to start a sexual healing practice of my own.

Because Vaughn saw only female clients and I wanted to work with all genders, he recommended getting a subscription to www.eroticmassage.com, where I learned genital massage techniques from certified sexological bodywork teachers. Craving one-on-one guidance from a woman, I searched tantra sites online and messaged a sexual healer in Portland named Ellen. She called me immediately. After a short, enthusiastic video chat, she invited me to her home for lunch.

Ellen was an awesome combination of motherly warmth and badass Buddhist sex goddess. I felt at ease as she walked me through her earthy but sparkling clean, tastefully decorated house. It was blessed with an abundance of plants, crystal bowls, a meditation room, altars, and sacred-feeling wall hangings and statues. Her backyard Zen garden had a fountain. The healing room where she saw clients was regally wrapped in golds and rich, sensual burgundy and featured a very impressive, double-wide massage table.

After we ate lunch, with a twinkle in her eye, Ellen said, "Would you like to take a bath together?" I smiled and nodded, excited and curious about what it would be like to bathe together. Her bathroom had a huge, majestic tub that sat in a sun-filled nook surrounded by vibrant jungle plants.

Luxuriating in her massive bathtub-palace, we talked and laughed together like ancient friends. It was playful and sexy, though not sexual. We didn't touch; the feeling between and around us was more of radiance and beauty. I embraced the experience as a sacred initiation ritual.

During our bath, Ellen's face lit up when a call came in from a favorite client wanting a session that afternoon. As they talked, she looked at me with excitement and asked him if he'd enjoy an extra pair of hands in his session. "Great!" she exclaimed. "We'll see you soon!" She hung up and grinned widely at me. "He'll be here in a few hours. I knew he would say yes!" Elated, she continued, "Hassan is the perfect first erotic massage client for you! What a synchronicity that he would call right now. I haven't heard from him in months." We got out of the bath and dressed, feeling happy and excited, like teenage girlfriends.

Hassan was a young, tall, Syrian storybook prince, with the longest, thickest eyelashes and the biggest, roundest eyes. *Wowza*. As we checked in, sitting in chairs and sipping tea, I energetically leaned towards him, wanting to be absorbed into his rich, masculine aura. Ellen asked about how sex was going with his wife, and he complained that recently he had been coming too quickly.

After the intention to extend arousal was established, Hassan undressed completely and climbed up onto the massage table. Ellen chose a favorite playlist, and ethereal music filled the room. Then she took her clothes off; so I dropped mine too. She stepped close to me and said in a deep and serious tone, "Every time I put my hands on a client, it is with great devotion. I fill with the awareness that this could be the last body I ever touch, or the last time my client is ever touched."

I definitely found the right mentor.

The handsome prince lay face-down, his body a sensuous landscape. Ellen placed one hand along the valley between his perfect, round cheeks and reached the other up between his thighs, gently cupping his penis from underneath. She said that was how she usually started with her male clients, because it was very calming. Then, she climbed up and draped her body softly over his, her head resting between his shoulder blades. It looked so sensual and relaxed, and he released a loud sigh. After a long minute, she slid off him and we moved into a four-handed massage. I shifted my weight down through my hands, rocking his broad shoulders as Ellen worked circles in Hassan's beautiful buttocks. Then, like a dance, we began slowly circling the table, both of us touching him everywhere, gliding oily hands and arms along his muscular curves. Watching her cues for timing and location, I moved with intuition, attuned to my inner melody. Hassan moaned gratefully. Ellen smiled steadily. I was ecstatic.

After some time, she invited him to roll over. He was erect, and I felt drawn to touch his penis. Ellen gave me a smiling nod. I placed one hand on his cock and the other on his heart, connecting his "love muscles," as I had learned on the erotic massage website. Then, I moved both of my hands to his penis to "open the gates," another one of my new moves, using my thumbs to make circles on his frenulum. He looked suddenly fearful and said, "That will make me come!"

Whoops! I stopped, pulled my hands firmly down his thighs, and he got softer. *Phew!* I returned to his cock, this time moving more slowly. Touching his smooth body was delicious, and I felt excited for the chance to practice the techniques that I had learned from the erotic massage videos. I slipped into a groove, tenderly pouring love into his cock while Ellen made long strokes up and down his body. At one point, I slowed my hands, cupped his testicles and with the other hand, held his erection firmly. Hassan's eyes met mine and the world paused. I was hypnotized and wanted to kiss him and to be touched by him. I hadn't expected to feel desire, and I didn't know the rules. *Was touch only one-way? How far did Ellen go with clients? How did her pleasure fit in?*

The prince and I gazed at each other for an extended moment and my heart burst open with love. Hassan's face softened and he asked gently if he could have my breast in his mouth. I looked to Ellen and felt relieved by her loving nod. I stepped closer to offer him my breast. His big lips buried into the flesh around my nipple, where he kissed, sucked, and moaned. Completely turned on, squirming, and barely able to stand on the ground, I said out loud, "Whose massage is this?" But soon, Ellen noticed the time and whispered into the air that we needed to start wrapping up. Hassan's big eyes looked troubled, and he said, "Can we do just one more thing?" He looked at me. "Can you make me come?"

Enthusiastically, I replied, "I can try!" I moved my oiled, loose fists, hand over hand, from the tip down the full length of the shaft, doing a move called "Perpetual Penetration." In just a few moments he came, a lot, all over both of us. It was glorious. We spent one final moment looking into each other's eyes. Then, he closed his eyes and Ellen covered him with blankets. I skipped away, laughing and feeling sexy, to wash my hands—and arms!

Unlike my mentorship with Vaughn, Ellen and I never had direct sexual contact with each other. We spent long, sensual afternoons lounging around and eating delicious food while she shared lesson-filled stories about her experiences as a sexual healer. She often scheduled clients when I came to visit, and I loved working with her.

I was being initiated into a very special tribe of undercover sexual healers. It seemed like the most important job in the world.

Meanwhile, I met with Vaughn weekly via video chat and we visited each other a few times—either he drove nine hours to see me (plus a few other local clients of his), or I took a short plane ride to visit him. He had a list of topics for us to cover at any pace, in any order. Our video sessions were a combination of reviewing the curriculum, receiving coaching on my relationships and my sexuality, and eventually getting Vaughn's supervision for my own sexual healing practice. When we were in person, the focus was on sexual bodywork, which we couldn't do at a distance.

I had orgasm goals: bigger, longer, deeper, and juicier orgasms. Normally too sensitive to be touched after orgasm, I wanted to be able to tolerate post-orgasm stimulation. One day, after my climax, Vaughn adjusted his touch in a way that I could handle it. That orgasm lasted for several minutes, during which time I was laughing loudly and freely, both from the new sensation and from sheer joy. We later referred to it as "the laughgasm."

Vaughn and I always checked in before bodywork: about what I wanted to focus on, and anything that needed to be asked or spoken before starting. I often recorded the coaching part of our sessions on my phone, and had forgotten to stop the recording when we went into the bodywork that led to the laughgasm. And so it was eternally preserved, and at the time, the clip of me laughing was shared freely among a small group of trusted friends.

A profound part of my work with Vaughn was finding my voice in intimate situations and feeling more sexual in my everyday skin. Once, during a yoni massage, Vaughn took a picture of my engorged vulva and had it printed and framed as a gift for me. For the first time ever, I found my yoni beautiful. I hung the picture in a discreet place on my bedroom wall.

Vaughn was wonderfully supportive. He continued declaring, "I'm in love with you," but I knew he asserted this to all of the women in our cohort. He didn't ask for anything other than thinking of us as his "girlfriends," though none of us would have called him our "boyfriend." I was willing to be a player in his harem fantasy. He gave me so much.

My most unforgettable time in my entire mentorship with Vaughn was receiving a Taoist erotic massage. He first explained the sequence of the session, including the different guided breathing patterns and how the session would conclude.

We started, as usual, with a full body massage, but this time Vaughn cued me to breathe deeply, and because of that sustained focus, I was soon buzzing from head to toe. When I rolled over, he touched my whole front body, then focused on my yoni. Using a vibrator plus his quickly moving, lubricated hands, he brought me to an unknown state of extreme stimulation. I didn't orgasm, but my sensations were so intense, I thought I might faint. Mixing deep breathing with sexual stimulation was acutely altering, and I was starting to go numb in places.

When Vaughn said, "You may lose sensation in your hands and feet," I told him I already had. "Then, it's time for the transition breath," he said. Putting the vibrator down, he came close to hold my eye contact as he guided me in a series of three specific breath patterns he had shown me earlier. I felt like I was in labor again. On the very last breath, I gulped a lungful and held it in while lifting my upper body and legs, clenching every muscle in my body. After holding the contraction and my breath as long as possible, I slowly released and lay back.

Vaughn wrapped me in a sheet and whispered, "I'll be sitting just over there until you feel complete."

I soared into a sexually-induced spiritual experience. This was very different from the momentary rise and fall of a more familiar climax. The high, unknown euphoria had me up in the clouds for a very long time, feeling extreme peace and joy. I could feel—and almost see—angels, all around me. As I floated in sustained bliss, I was convinced that Taoist erotic massage had the power to eradicate negativity and stop wars, and I prayed that it would one day be offered to prisoners, drug and alcohol rehab patients, and world leaders. And everyone.

Vaughn's Sexual Healing Curriculum

Over the year of my sexual healing mentorship with Vaughn, we referred to this list during our weekly sessions. He wanted me to be comfortable in all of these areas:
- Intention Setting
- Guided Meditation
- Self-Empowerment, Boundaries, No & Stop
- Safe Sex/Condom Use
- Agreements & Taboos
- Withholds
- Daily Practice

- Self-Pleasuring
- Finding Your Partner
- The Transition from New Relationship Energy to Long-Term
- Alternative Relationships
- Navigating Polyamory and/or Jealousy
- The Five Love Languages
- Tantra
- Eye Gazing
- Breathwork
- Core Erotic Theme
- Gross, Subtle & Causal Bodies
- The Sexual Matrix
- Sexual Healing
- Betty Martin's Wheel of Consent
- Orgasm vs. Ejaculation
- Energy Play & Circuits
- Mixed Chakra Connections
- Subtle Body Play
- Fantasy/Role Play
- Baths
- Four-Hand Massage
- Vulva Anatomy & Mapping
- Vulva Massage
- Sacred Spot & AFE (Anterior Fornix Erogenous) Zone Massage
- Breast Massage
- Anal Massage
- Buttocks Massage
- Taoist Erotic Massage
- Penis Massage
- Prostate Massage
- Altered States & Transcendence
- Assertiveness & Receptivity
- Letting Go of Control
- Technique vs. Flow
- Music & Dance
- Pleasure Scale Exploration
- No Movement Until Request, Then Back to Stillness

After many months of training, my mentors and I agreed I was ready to start working with people on my own. I sent an email to Summer Campers, and a handful of volunteers became my practice clients. Grateful that they trusted me, I offered them each a series of three sessions. I set up my space with a massage table, curtains, chairs, a heater, oils, gloves, sex toys, and music. Several special experiences ensued.

One client complained about erectile dysfunction. I suggested that he reframe it as "erectile inconsistency," a less stigmatizing term that I learned from Ellen. Through a Processwork lens, I wonder if a soft penis might be a message that a man needs his softness and vulnerability to be seen and "touched." Our session was very gentle, not pushing for an orgasm, just being present with his soft nature. I encouraged him to relax, to be expressive and free, and to move and make sounds as I touched him. Together we moaned, hummed, and laughed. It shocked us both when, towards the end of our session, he ejaculated, semen spilling from his soft penis like a long flow of tears. I had never heard of or imagined an erectionless orgasm.

Another session was with a woman who bravely wanted to address sexual trauma. We started in chairs, and she told me about her experience. She said that after being entered repeatedly when she wasn't ready, it was hard for her to feel anything, vaginally. I invited her to share her boundaries, fears, and desires regarding the session. At her request, I would wear gloves. She undressed and lay down on the massage table. After a brief full-body massage, I covered her, and asked "Are you ready for me to touch your yoni?" Her eyes were closed and she nodded. I reached underneath the sheet, placed my hand firmly over her yoni, and stated out loud that our intention was healing. Crying, she re-told the details of the earliest experience she could remember, how she had frozen and lost her voice. I asked, "What do you wish you had done?" and looking up at me sadly, she replied, "I wish I had just said something. Anything." We decided to re-do the original experience, using whatever words and emotions she wanted.

When she felt ready, she asked me to put two fingers inside of her. She squeezed her eyes closed, clamped down, and told me to "Get out!" I slowly removed my fingers. Enjoying this power, she wanted to explore it further, so we did it several times. Each time, her voice grew stronger and louder, until the final time, when she looked right at me, and yelled "GET OUT!" fiercely and loudly. Then she cried and cried. I cried too. She was in a very innocent, tender space and we spoke softly for a while. Once she felt complete, we shared a deep hug goodbye.

The next day, I received this email: "Since our session, I have some noticings. I'm really loving my belly. I have a tight dress on today and I just think it's so cute. This is new. Also, I feel quite powerful. I notice that I'm not triggered, or afraid to ask for what I want. I've been feeling strangely calm and clear-headed. Could this all be from just one session? I'm really feeling a shift! Thank you!" Receiving her unsolicited communication, I was filled with hope. I wanted to help people heal. This felt like the deepest way possible.

Sexual trauma is usually invisible; we learn to live with it, and most people don't even know they could benefit from sexual healing. The number of people who have been sexually abused, plus those of us who have had negative sexual experiences, is staggering. Even though the mind does its best to protect us, bodies hold memories until they feel safe again. We are all affected by culturally repressive messages about sex. Societal traumas become personal and live silently in our tissues, in the most vulnerable areas of our bodies. Genital wounds—both physical and psychological—are incredibly common and rarely acknowledged.

Receiving present, loving sexual touch can be profoundly healing. I wish there was accredited training for sex and intimacy professionals, that sex-positive education was standard in public schools, and that basic insurance plans covered sexual healing. But unfortunately, there is almost nowhere to formally learn about pleasure-based touch.

We should all *always* be treated with the utmost care for our sexuality, by ourselves and others, but most people don't even know (much less know how to ask for) what kind of touch they like. Unfortunately, almost every adult has experienced giving or receiving nonconsensual sexual touch.

So many of us get our first sex lessons through objectifying pornography. As an adult, I have found more beautiful forms of erotica, but I've had to search. We all need sexually loving models. Violence in the world would lessen if we only had access to loving sex.

Some people find safe, mature lovers and experience sexual healing within a committed relationship. Most of us aren't so lucky. In relationships, imbalances of attention—who gets more, who gives more—are rarely mentioned and processed. I wish everyone had access to one-way, non-romantic sexual touch, where it is easier to have clear boundaries, no strings attached, and an opportunity to heal. Anyone who tends to be a giver should have the opportunity to receive purely.

When I had seen a variety of clients and was ready to start charging for my services, Ellen and I met. We talked about websites where I could advertise, and she told me to avoid mentioning sexuality explicitly. She laid out the risks: by law, the combination of sexual touch and money is considered prostitution. Therefore, if I ever felt unsafe with a client, I wouldn't be able to seek legal support. Ellen and I had spoken about legality before but standing at the threshold of investing in advertising and putting myself out publicly, I considered it more seriously. Also, I had only practiced with a handful of people I already knew. *Who would show up if I had a web presence? Could I handle any situation?* Our conversation scared me. After putting in so much time and energy, it was a heartbreaking shift. But the dangers, and needing to lie and hide, felt overwhelming. I stopped seeing practice clients.

Ellen and Vaughn modeled so beautifully the integration of healing and sexuality. Seeing clients was a deep blessing; I felt honored to be present with people's deepest sexual issues. I long for the day when hands-on sexual therapeutic touch is condoned, decriminalized, and normalized. I was strongly drawn to work with people in a sexually therapeutic way, but it also felt right to let it go.

Date #68: Tin-derrrrrr! *February 2018*

Peter from Portland showed up on Tinder and from the start, I felt both pushed and pulled. He was a professional inventor, ten years older than me. His main profile picture had a Ted Talks banner in the background. But in his write-up, he said, "If we hang out, that doesn't mean I'm into you. If we have a second date, that still doesn't mean I'm into you. We might go out a third time—don't make any assumptions about *that*." Despite (or, because of?) his snarky detachment, there was something very attractive about him, so I reached out.

He sent links to his Ted Talks. Watching Peter move and hearing him speak confirmed my attraction: he was handsome and comfortable in his body. What moved me most was his enchantingly deep, resonant baritone voice. I sent my YouTube channel link, and he responded with overwhelming enthusiasm, showering me with compliments and questions. After watching a handful of my videos, Peter asked if he could drive to Eugene and pick me up to go on a road trip right away. *Whoa.* I enjoyed the flattery but wasn't ready to skip town with him just yet.

We mostly communicated via Marco Polo. Peter had a great personality; he was super charismatic and refreshingly upfront. After a few days, he reported having sexual fantasies about me, whereas I was more dreaming of his deliciously deep and sensual voice reading me to sleep. Not that I don't love sex, but, *that voice!*

Excitedly, we made a plan for a visit the following week. He promised to arrive with flowers. The week seemed long as we messaged frequently through Marco Polo videos and text, getting to know each other. But on day five, I recoiled when he said in a video message that he was in love with me. The next day he sent a long series of overly sexual selfies, cross-dressed with terrible makeup, looking like the Joker. Suddenly, red flags seemed to be stacking up quickly; I went to Facebook to research him further.

We had several Facebook friends in common, and one of them

was Ellen. I messaged her to say that Peter and I were moving in a romantic direction, and I was curious about her impression of him. Her instant reply: "Oh, my. Clearly, he's getting around. I had a date with him on Tuesday." Of the million people in Portland, the one person he happened to be seeing was my mentor?!

Frozen, I was unsure how to proceed. I messaged Peter to let him know about this strange new complication. He panicked and started barraging me with messages. His normally cool, deep romantic voice turned sour and desperate as he tried to convince me that there wasn't a problem because he "wasn't interested in Ellen at all." As a gesture of his commitment to me, he sent her a quick message and cut things off abruptly. *What an ass.*

That was the *last thing* I wanted him to do.

I called Ellen. With total equanimity and grace, she encouraged me to check things out with him. She said that she would never want to get in the way of that, and that she was curious if he would "use the same lines and put the same moves" on me. Hesitantly, she told me that they'd had sex for the first time that week (he brought flowers), and she wondered if he was too good to be true, too charismatic to be trusted. I felt sad. She had complained about how hard it was for her to find an intelligent and attractive man anywhere close to her age, and I think that before my call, her hopes about him were high.

I felt relieved after speaking with Ellen; my relationship with her was way more important to me than Mr. I'm-In-Love-With-You, and her response of authentic encouragement created the best of both worlds. It had been a long twenty-four hours of Peter sending stressed video messages, pleading with me to stick with him and not think of the situation with Ellen as a big deal. With reverence and gratitude for Ellen's poise, I messaged Peter to say that we had her blessing, though I wasn't sure where we stood with each other anymore. What followed was so strange.

Peter reported distantly that the experience had been too emotionally exhausting for him. Fading off, he said that he didn't have the "bandwidth." Peter was evidently so done that not only did he stop responding to my messages, but he also blocked me on text and Facebook. Later, when I asked Ellen about him, she said that she never heard from him again.

He loved me ... not. It wasn't love, but obsession—or an attempt at manipulation. I wish he had just ended it with clarity instead of disappearance, drama, and media blocks. I honestly didn't even know adults did that to each other.

Date #69: An Angel at My Table *April 2018*

Gabriel seemed very old; he moved like a cloud-walker. We met at my house when he came to pick up some mugs for his daughter, who was one of my pottery customers. In my driveway, passing colorful mugs back and forth, I was inside the deep world of his dancing, wise eyes and flowery heart. He must have been in his late 60's, with long white hair and a beard, an ethereal version of Gandalf from Lord of the Rings. When I spoke, his head tipped like a curious dog's. I didn't want him to leave. A little later, I sent him a text to say that I was touched by his gentle spirit and asked if he would like to meet for tea. He said he "still felt my eyes long after we had parted." *Was Gabriel a prospective lover?* It would be so out of the box for me to be with someone so much older. He seemed otherworldly. *Sex with an angel?*

We met for breakfast the next morning in the Whit, at New Day Bakery. Across the table, I took him in. He was physically striking; his body was strong, and I imagined his muscles were formed during angelic projects like rearranging galaxies.

Experiencing undeniable attraction, I celebrated that my ageism had clearly transformed. But as we spoke, many emotional needs rose to the surface. Gabriel was surprisingly frank, divulging deeply intimate and difficult personal accounts of addiction, loss, and poverty. Along with his beauty and spirituality, an unmistakable vein of anguish surfaced. He struggled both emotionally and financially, and admitted that he felt lost. Knowing that I didn't want to get romantically involved with someone in a low state, my heart closed off. By the time our food was finished, we had spent the whole hour talking about him. I tried to interject and share personally a few times, but my efforts didn't catch. As we were parting, he shared the sentiment that our meeting was way too short. It was sweet of him to say, but I was ready to go, and relinquished my hopes for sex with an "angel."

A few days after our date, I sent a text, *just because*, but the human Gabriel never responded.

All the Beautiful Girls: 2017-2018

For a bisexual woman, this is a very heterosexual dating memoir. Out of my long-term relationship with Samantha, I was ready to celebrate and explore the male-female polarity. I treasure the ease and familiarity that I find in my intimacy with women, but I love—and craved—the mystery, chemistry, and challenge of men.

My profile was always open to both women and men, and I had many conversations with women. Several women reached out as sisters asking, "So how's this whole dating app thing going for you?" I had a handful of semi-promising actual in-person dates. None stuck, but as a card-carrying bisexual, I must mention them.

There was Elizabeth, the goat farmer and Waldorf school teacher from Pennsylvania. Shy in her messaging, she said she was just considering dating women. We shuffled our schedules to make time for tea at Friendly Street Market, our mutual neighborhood grocery store cafe. Elizabeth was short like me, but smaller, and mousy, and super cute. We had similar interests: writing, gardening, and wildcrafting medicinal plants. We would have made perfect friends, but we were both busy people. "Who needs more friends?" was our shared attitude. Hopefully, we will reconnect in a future, more friend-seeking, time.

Then I met Tatiana, a gorgeous Russian woman in an open marriage. She had tons of curly black hair and a round face. We walked our dogs together at Amazon dog park. Our moms had both died in the last few years, and Tatiana became paralyzed by depression. Recently, she found that microdosing on psilocybin mushrooms was a perfect antidepressant for her. I had heard of microdosing, but hadn't ever talked to anyone about it, and really enjoyed her openness and revelations. She was sweet, beautiful, and lovely, but I felt no romantic or sexual pull.

Gina was a local smokejumper. I'd noticed her from afar during my twenty-plus years in Eugene. She was tomboyish and cool, with loose blond locks and the face of a Taurus: solid and pretty, with a soft strength. I was happy when we matched on OkCupid. We walked our dogs at the Wayne Morse Ranch dog park, and our conversation was animated. I would have liked to kiss. But when we met for tea the next week, I learned she had just bought a piece of property out of town and would be moving soon. We joked about whether or not she would be in my dating blog and parted sweetly.

Sheela was a local badass I'd admired for decades. After matching on OkCupid, we met at the Bier Stein. I was thrilled to be on a date with her and was nervous beforehand. Sheela was a wild-eyed, radical anarchist and well-known local artist. She wore ripped jeans and a leather jacket; jagged black hair sprung in every direction out of her ponytail. I discovered over drinks that Sheela was too rough around the edges for me to be a romantic fit, but her huge heart and passion touched me. We seemed to genuinely like each other's minds and hearts. After ciders, she came across the street with me to try the Tuesday night bachata open dance. I put on my heels; Sheela danced in combat boots. I loved her wonderfully awkward but joyful engagement. After our date, we messaged a few times. She invited me to an event, but I didn't go.

I eventually had a noteworthy connection develop with an amazingly beautiful, talented, artistic, intelligent, all-around-impressive woman, but that comes a little later.

Date #18, Jonah Continued: A Ghost in the Flesh *May 2018*

In 2018, things with Jonah, my ephemeral ghost, shifted. I had gotten used to our distance and accepted the ebb and flow of our connection. I felt satisfied with Warren, but was still looking for a second lover, and doubted that would ever be Jonah. One day, he reached out and uncharacteristically asked me to meet up. (That request had always come from me before.) We met the next day at Monteith Riverpark in Albany, halfway between us. On the drive, I felt settled and grounded, with no expectations. When he opened his car door, Jonah was shaking. *Was he afraid?* As we hugged hello, he was sweaty and I felt his deep tremble. I had never witnessed his vulnerability in person. Feeling maternal, I took his hand. He relaxed into the moment with me.

We wandered along a winding trail, identifying the forest plants. I felt romantic and light as a butterfly. We found a perfect spot on the riverbank and laid a blanket down. It was the first time we were ever in private, with full physical access to each other. Settling in, we shared relaxed, emotional eye contact. His questioning eyes looked back and forth between mine. Holding each other's faces, the moment deepened and we laughed and cried. Other emotions arose as we rolled around and grew primal, sweating and writhing as one under the piercing hot sun. We grabbed and bit at each other with a hunger that had been building between us for three excruciating years. Our kissing went from dynamic to sweet and back again; we lingered in the playful exploration for a long while. Reaching down to touch each other's sex through our clothes felt edgy enough; we didn't venture underneath. So little had manifested between us before, and I hadn't fully believed that our feelings were mutual until that mythic day. The power between us finally took form. When it was time to go, we twirled woozily back to our cars, and had one final magically hungry kiss to conclude the exquisite rendezvous. As we drove off, Jonah texted, "Driving away from you, my heart feels cracked open and tender. I feel raw and vulnerable in the best way." Lots of heart emojis followed.

The next night, Jonah and I lingered on the phone, late into the night, and talked about him moving to Eugene. A few weeks later, he came to visit me, mid-day. At first, we lay quietly together in my bedroom, clothed, cuddling deliciously, soaking in the surreality. We talked about how we were feeling and what we would like: our boundaries, fears, and desires. I said that I was open to having intercourse, but he wasn't, saying it felt too fast. His boundary provided clarity, invited creativity, and supported me to set limits myself. Once "no intercourse" was agreed upon, the atmosphere between us relaxed. There was a playful fire in his eyes; it was time to get more physical.

Our primal selves engaged and we wrestled hard, activating each other's strength. I loved feeling our full power. When we slowed down, breathless, we let our hands explore each other freely, touching everywhere that felt good. I felt transparent, and very alive.

Carefully, we removed each other's clothing, piece by piece, savoring every moment, unwrapping our special gifts. There he was, the man I'd spent years longing for, naked in my bed. He seemed so vulnerable, and I poured all of my bottled-up love through my hands into his body. I loved touching sweet, emotional Jonah, and felt the deep blessing of being in a sexual space with him. When his penis softened, I bent to kiss it, to love it in its gentle form. Soon, he started moaning and writhing. We danced together as my hands and his body found their rhythm. When the moment silenced, I could tell he was about to climax. Witnessing Jonah's orgasm was nothing less than sacred.

And then, as the afternoon turned to evening, the clock ticked us back to reality. It was time for him to go. I made him a bowl of brown rice and steamed kale. I loved watching him eat out of a bowl I'd made. We sat pensively together in my kitchen. *Jonah in the flesh, in my home?* When a ghost visits, the real can feel like a dream.

He left, and things predictably trailed off. My human heart deflated as the wires went dead again. It felt exquisite when things were "on" between us. I had to build resilience again, to not get my hopes up, to find a way to be fine, and to completely accept Jonah for who and how he was.

... to be continued ...

12

LOVE IN A BOX

Date #60, Warren Continued: Heart in a Blender
Winter 2017–Spring 2018

Despite a rough fall, Warren and I kept getting closer during our weekly overnights. We had stopped our mid-week dates in November after he initiated coffee behind Karen's back. She checked in with me every few weeks on the phone, and we met in person a few times.

One day, Karen came over while I was working in my garden. We sat in the grass together and she shared her deeper feelings about how challenging my relationship with Warren was for her. Her vulnerability helped me feel more open to her; we were almost becoming friends. I relaxed with her when she was in that soft space.

Meanwhile, our mutual friend, Olive, and I had been flirting lightly since before Summer Camp. For years, there had been an amorous feeling between us. A year ago, before Warren, Olive and I had a flirtatious evening of tea on her couch, and she hinted that we could have a sleepover sometime. When I asked what kind of sleepover, she glanced away, smiling, and said that she wasn't sure. It was very rare for me to feel a strong, lasting attraction to a woman—or to anyone, for that matter—but I had always had a romantic leaning towards Olive. We didn't have the sleepover. I was too shy.

At Summer Camp, Jaco and Olive had gotten together when I awkwardly canceled with Jaco. In the late winter, Jaco came to Eugene to visit Olive (as he did from time to time), and they invited me over for dinner. With wonder, I looked forward to that evening. There was a karmic feeling among the three of us. I loved them both.

Olive and Jaco greeted me at the door. Bubbly and giggling, they suggested right away that we share some intimacy. After dinner, we moved to Olive's bedroom and had the standard Summer Camp "boundaries, fears, and desires" conversation. We agreed to not have any kind of penetration. Olive set a boundary of not having her yoni touched. We decided to structure turns, shifting who was "in the middle," getting attention, as long as everyone consented along the way. We went through several rounds, each of us asking for what we wanted. Jaco cooed in delight the entire time. For a long, juicy while, we cycled through kissing, touching, spanking, and role playing. They were exceptionally playful together, and I treasured being invited into their amorous connection.

A few weeks later, Olive and I were drinking tea on my couch. We confessed our mutual desire to explore more intimately with each other. I was excited to have an authentic, reciprocal attraction. My dating life was mostly barren, and Olive was one in a zillion. We were the same age. She was smart, artistic, deep, and all-around impressive. Dark, curly locks sprung out from beneath cute, colorful hats. Her large collection of bright, flower-print dresses flattered her very sensual, curvy body. I loved how her enduring smile wrinkled up her eyes. In motion, she had the artistic beauty of a classic flapper.

I think everyone was in love with Olive. The only catch was that she was Karen's best friend, and we were both nervous about that. Hoping it might be a fertile time, I asked Olive to talk with Karen—who wanted me to find another lover—about the possibility. Over the winter, whenever I had a hopeful date, I texted Karen to reassure her that I was looking. Sometimes, I felt like I needed a second lover more for Karen than for me! Once, she and I joked about going out together to practice flirting. I wished that she would find another relationship, both to have the yummy feelings that she envied between Warren and me, and to focus less on her feeling of loss. I was full of hope, and impatient to dive in with Olive, and prayed Karen would be supportive. I pressed Olive several times to broach the topic, but she was hesitant.

In the early spring, I awoke one day to a text from Olive. She had finally asked. Karen was upset. *Shoot.* I sulked but trusted it would work out. I was blindsided later that morning when Karen called on the phone and berated me: "How could you even *think* that you could have both my husband and my best friend?" She was livid, her voice harsh. *Why was she so angry? I was the one not getting what I wanted.* Accusing me of wanting to take both Warren and Olive away from her, Karen's words were razors in my gut. I said, "It feels like you are trying to hurt me," and she replied "Yes, I do want you to feel the pain I feel."

I froze. As a child, my grandfather made me promise that I would never allow myself to be abused. Extremely stressed, I fretted, *what will happen with me and Warren if I stand up to Karen? Was there a way for me to protect myself and keep my beautiful romance?*

I hung up and frantically texted Olive. She called right away. We agreed, regretfully, to put on the brakes. The next time she and I ran into each other, we had our strongest hug ever. Olive held me tight, shaking. I could feel her deep care. We broke away and she looked at me with tear-filled eyes. Sailing her hand through space, she said, "Our relationship has a *long* arc." I felt sad and heavy, but her long-term vision was soothing.

A few days later, Karen sent an apology email, asking to talk in person. We planned to meet at a cafe. When the day came, she messaged to suggest that Warren could facilitate our discussion at their house instead. Hesitantly, I agreed. *Could he be impartial with the two of us?*

When I arrived at their house, sweating and trembling, Warren met me at the door and handed me a large, round river rock to hold, " ... for grounding." I appreciated the intention and noticed they were both holding big rocks too. They sat together in chairs, leaving me the couch.

Knowing I can easily lose my center in emotional situations, I had emailed them earlier to ask if I could audio-record our conversation, as a kind of witnessing. I never heard back, and brought it up.

Reluctantly, they agreed. Using mostly "we" language, they formed a solid front; it already felt like two against one. I had a strong urge to leave. *There was no way this could go well.*

Karen began by apologizing again for lashing out. I could tell that she felt bad, but it wasn't enough. *How could I trust her?* She seemed offended; her voice seethed with anger. Looking straight into my eyes, she spoke sharp, measured words that were delivered in a strained attempt at a "calm" voice: "How could you have thought it was OK to ask for a sexual relationship with Olive?"

"I am sorry that you are upset by it, but I don't agree. I should stifle my desires because you might not like them? I hoped you might be happy that I'd found someone besides Warren, or at the very least, appreciate that we checked in with you. It feels like you hold the destiny of my sex life in your hands."

She replied, "I *do not* hold your sex life in my hands. You and Olive can do whatever you want."

Yeah, right. I was defensive, angry, and righteous. So much of my personal work was to not be silent, to stand for myself, to access anger and my voice. In my Processwork studies, I consciously worked on developing my "inner dominatrix." I had to speak my truth, I just had to.

The worst part was that Warren was siding with her, against me. He kept saying defensive, angry things to me like "that's not true" or "that's not what she's saying."

Facilitator, ha! He couldn't possibly be neutral.

Why had I walked into this situation? I could have held my own with Karen much more easily without Warren there. *This three-way conversation was sabotage.* I felt manipulated, my relationship suddenly threatened.

Though clearly seething inside, Karen held her anger down with what seemed like indomitable strength. The tension underneath her carefully enunciated words started to make me feel crazy. I said, "Right now, I want to throw this rock through the window," and in an attempt at humor, Warren said, "That's not what it's for."

I freaked out. Jumping up on their sofa for effect, I said, "This is how your energy feels to me." I pointed down at her, exaggerating the way I was perceiving her, to illustrate the condescension, control, and hatred I felt coming towards me.

With me up on the couch, Warren said, "We're not getting anywhere. I think you should leave." Noticing his clenched fist and body, I rigidly plummeted off the couch. Shaking, embarrassed, I walked out wordlessly. My legs were numb; I couldn't feel the ground beneath my feet.

What just happened?

The next day, Warren called, stressed, and suggested an outside facilitator at a neutral location. When the three of us met with the facilitator later that week (at Olive's house, of all places, while she was away), I was sweating and shaking from the moment I arrived and couldn't calm down. Gratefully, I accepted a pile of fuzzy blankets from Karen and wrapped them around me, trying to feel safe. I relaxed a little when the facilitator started speaking. She was strong and solid, with a clear and effective system of active listening. We were to simply listen and repeat back what we had heard.

As the evening progressed, Karen surprised me when she interrupted Warren—more than once—exposing his coldness towards me. Her equanimity was impressive. Even though she seemed to hold a lot against me, she also had an amazing ability to be fair. Wrapping up, we all agreed that Warren and I would continue. I felt partially relieved that our relationship wasn't over, but felt far away from him, hurt by the way he had treated me in both conversations. Nervous about returning to our relationship, I wondered, *Who were we to each other now?*

On our next overnight date, he laid it out: if I couldn't find a way to get along with Karen, our relationship had to be "in a box"—limitlessly deep when we were together, but strictly limited otherwise. Over the next few months, we tried to ease back into our connection, but whereas we used to text, talk, and email in between our weekly deep dives, mid-week communications disappeared completely. When I asked about his radio silence, he said, aloofly, that it didn't bother him; he didn't miss me because I was "always in his heart." *Aargh*. I was in pain.

When Warren and I were sexual, we were fiercely, impossibly close. Life fell away, and we entered a dreamy tantric dimension. But in between dates, I was raw and moody. Each week, I fell in love with him on Tuesday and then had to break up with him on Wednesday, to let him go. Our relationship seemed obviously destined to be a glorious cherry tree but it was potted in a planter, stuck in the shade. After a few months of "the box," I was torn apart and exhausted. In May, 2018, I ended the relationship.

The night I broke up with Warren, I fell asleep in distress, hoping for clarity. I awoke in the morning from this dream:

I am with Warren and Karen at their house. They are lying down on cots, completely out of it. They have taken some kind of drug and I am an outsider, not invited into their experience. Their house is very dark and has low ceilings. I feel uncomfortable and unsafe.

Then I am with a different couple. They warmly invite me into their kitchen, which is a solarium, abundantly overflowing with huge, bright green houseplants, bursting with light and life. I feel incredibly happy, everything perfectly balanced. My heart feels full. Suddenly, the man opens his eyes wide, grabs his beard and takes it off, revealing that it was actually a mask! When I see his bare face, I realize that I am really attracted to him, and also to the super-cute, blonde, friendly woman. I find them both so beautiful. They are bubbling over with affection for me, and I feel supremely light and joyous just being there with them.

I carried this dream symbol forward as a gift, hoping that if I connected with another couple, it would be a "solarium" relationship.

... to be continued ...

Date #70: Like a Virgin *May 2018*

OkCupid was still showing me only a few matches at a time. The app was constantly apologizing: they were sorry, there just wasn't anyone out there for me. *What happened to my hundreds of possibilities?*

Logan must have been new on the scene, because he popped up as one of my only hopes. We had a high match percentage, and he was cute, with messy blond hair and deer eyes. From his profile, I imagined him to be peaceful and sensitive. We messaged enthusiastically and then met for breakfast. Everything was simple, easy, and … bland. I thought, "There aren't sparks between us, but I can enjoy breakfast with this nice person." Because of that conscious choice, I was more engaged than usual on an uninspired date. After we finished and paid—separately—for our meals, we stood on the street corner to say goodbye. I was surprised when he said, with gusto, that he definitely wanted to get together again. His bold statement made me reconsider my assessment. I suggested, "Let's walk away and see if we are drawn back together."

As I walked away, Logan's affection touched my loneliness. I liked the feeling of being liked. I felt strangely bouncy and happy, and quickly messaged him to let him know that yes, I would be happy to meet up again. *Why not?*

Logan lived out of town and was excellent about being in touch that following week. He sent lots of texts and pictures. The next weekend, we met again, this time for cider at 16 Tons Cafe. I was a little bored, still, but decided that I liked him enough to kiss him: sure, why not? *Why not? Because people get attached and get their feelings hurt.* Although I wasn't a "fuck yes" to this experience, I went along with it in lukewarm ambivalence.

At Summer Camp, I had learned that a good question to ask is "What will it mean to you if we ____ (kiss, cuddle, have sex, etc.)?" Most people assume reciprocity: if I'm casual, they are too; or if I'm romantic, they are too. So it is good to bring the "meaning" conversation out into the open, early on. I didn't do this with Logan. It pairs well with the "boundaries, fears, and desires" conversation which I also should have had with him.

We went for a short walk when we were done with our drinks.

Instead of employing any of these clarity-enhancing integrity practices, I basically just went ahead and kissed him, standing on the sidewalk, the old-fashioned, semi-uncommunicative way. At first, our kissing felt good. But when we broke apart, Logan looked at me with wild eyes and breathlessly said that I was the first person he had kissed, other than his now-separated wife, in *twenty years*! His hunger was on the surface. I needed to be clear with him. As we walked to my car, I told him that I wasn't monogamous, and he stopped in his tracks and looked confused.

Logan spent the next week wondering if he could be polyamorous, reading and researching it and lots of other things about me. It was flattering, but way out of balance; meanwhile, my relationship with Warren was in tatters. I was crying all week. Logan enthusiastically tried to be supportive. But I felt overwhelmed.

In an attempt to move on from my Warren heartbreak, because he lived an hour away, I foolishly invited Logan to stay overnight. He said he was open to sleeping on the couch. Predictably, everything about our sleepover was perfectly wrong. I was too in my mind and break-up pain. Logan was testosterony-eager. To slow things down and establish some boundaries, I taught him some simple communication games I'd learned at Summer Camp. Transparent relating blew his mind. But I wasn't looking for a student; I wanted a lover.

He was energized; I was exhausted. I suggested we go to bed, kiss and cuddle, and see how things felt. As soon as we settled into bed and started kissing, I knew it wasn't right. Logan was in a completely different space, ramping up with twenty years' worth of bottled excitement, but I stopped it before we started. Apologizing, I told him that I needed to sleep. Logan's eyes were wild as he lay on his back trying to manage his disappointment. Half-dressed, we slept and cuddled on and off through the night. I rested pretty well; he didn't sleep at all.

We spent the next morning together. As planned, he came to my Nia class and then we went for a walk and talked. He was puzzling over the experience, trying to understand what had gone wrong. As we were parting, I told him that I was nearly certain that ours wasn't going to be a sexual relationship. *Ouch*. I'm glad I didn't nurture his optimism, and hoped that I communicated with him gently, as I didn't want to be like the Wizard.

Meanwhile, random people were responding to my dating blog, messaging me to see if they could be my next entry. I yearned to manifest my two perfect lovers so I could be done with my quest. Online dating, where the only interesting prospects seemed to be a hundred miles away, at times felt exhausting.

Date #52, Raphael Continued: Return of the Shaman *May 2018*

After our wild dancing experience almost two years earlier, I moved my Nia classes to Salseros, the dance studio Rafael and I had gone to. His laughing spirit still lingered there. Now he was back in the States on his workshop-teaching circuit again, and called to ask, "Can I come stay a few nights with you?"

"I'm not sure," I answered, "I'm definitely excited to see you again, but can we play your lodging by ear?"

Confident and happy, he sang, "Of course!"

When he arrived, within our first few moments, our connection felt more poignant. I was suddenly enthusiastic about having him stay at my house. After a delicious night of cuddling, kissing, touching, and surfing the dreamworld together, I wanted him to stay all four nights. In bed, our bodies intertwined perfectly, and each day, while he was busy teaching, I looked forward to his return for our nightly sexploration. His kisses were soft and gentle, without the electric-shock intensity of our first kiss. His warm, silky skin against mine was intoxicating.

On the second night, as we were playfully kissing and touching each other in bed, he whispered into my ear that he would love to be inside me. He had a very large cock, which I loved to play with and kiss, but I wasn't ready for penetration. It wasn't easy to say no to the beautiful shaman, but I did. I told him that even though I felt so much affection for him, it didn't feel right to me, yet. He grew heavy in my arms. We cuddled and Rafael sighed, expressing his vulnerability around sexual rejection. My heart softened, touched by his honesty. He whispered, "Over the last few years, I've been working on taming my primal nature."

"When we kissed the first time you visited, I was surprised and overwhelmed by the intensity I felt. I thought your sexual energy might be too powerful for me, and I could have sworn I felt a snake spirit trying to jump out of you."

Rafael laughed, raised his eyes to mine and nodded his head, barely whispering "Yes." The transparency of our conversation felt invigorating, and our intimacy deepened. Over our four days together, Rafael's big, bright, smiling eyes bathed and nourished me. The space between us was a new, but ancient, home.

My dream is that we will continue to meet whenever he passes through, maybe even into our old age. One day, I hope to say "yes" to that mysterious snake.

Date #71: Sex Without Love *June 2018*

Antonio smiled like the horizon in every one of his Tinder pictures. You can't fake that kind of smile. We connected quickly and he seemed eager, initiating copious daily messages and instantly responding to each of mine, no matter the time of day. He was syrupy sweet. But our dialogue was just a bunch of "how are you today" and "glad to hear it." I was open to meeting, and we decided to go to 16 Tons for evening tea. As he walked up, I saw he was tall. *Oh well.* Then, as we hugged, a thick blanket of cologne pushed me backwards. I wondered: *could I ask a man to not wear cologne, or would I just have to get used to it?*

We sat at an outside table under the darkening sky and settled into a groove. Antonio grew up in Cuba in extreme poverty. His mother had recently lost everything in a tropical storm. The more he talked, the more I liked him. He seemed natural and honest. The biggest con, besides the cologne, however, was his "selfing." The few times I tried to interject something personal, Antonio suddenly had to go to the bathroom, or quickly changed the conversation back to himself. *Hmpf.*

After a while, we started speaking more directly about our romantic agendas. I told him that I found him attractive. He said that he was very interested in a sexual connection but nothing more—*no wonder he didn't want to know anything about me*. I said I wasn't looking for casual sex but was open to sharing a kiss. Suddenly, his big-lipped, sloppy wet mouth was mopping over my entire face.

I was partly relieved; if the kiss had been great, it might have confused me. My mind was clear: "I don't want to be sexual with someone if there isn't a potential for a relationship," but my body might have argued, "I feel good with him, why not try it?" Luckily, my mind and body were aligned. But unlike me, Antonio was turned on, and came up like a horse puffing hot breath, anxious for more. With a shiny, wet face, I told him that although I was polyamorous, I wasn't interested in sex without the possibility of love. He reiterated that he wasn't looking for anything serious.

We said goodbye and released each other: no harm, no foul. Our "peace out" transition felt effortless and without rejection. It was easy for us to be honest with each other.

Date #72: What About That Raw Juice Diet? *June 2018*

In his pictures, Chuck matched my core erotic theme, with emerald eyes, a boyish look, and cuteness that melted me. In his description, he was sensitive, poetic, and on a raw juice diet. I projected all over his pictures and profile. Chuck was the one for me—except that he was just passing through town and had some vague and questionable income source. But, *those eyes!*

We messaged immediately and he wanted to meet, NOW! He said that he was strongly attracted to me, and felt "scared of me." I was touched, and perplexed. I mean, Chuck was drop-dead gorgeous in his pictures. Why would he be scared of *me*?

Our messaging was strange; he was pushy and persistent, wanting to take me out here and there, for this and that, *as soon as possible.* But then he suddenly disappeared, and reappeared hours later. This cycle repeated a few times, and I started to feel wary about his spewing enthusiasm, but made a plan to meet him for a drink. I asked Jess, my best friend, to stay in touch with me throughout the date. Something seemed off. On my way to the date, I messaged him to say that I wasn't a hundred percent sure I even wanted to get together.

But I drove downtown anyway. From first glance, Chuck was

frumpy and slumped, 6'2" and graceless. Everything about him, from head to toe, was sloppy. He moved around in a bobbly, bouncing way: when we met, I realized he was already drunk. This was beyond a red flag. It was the perfect moment for my "*Can I be honest with you?*" line. Although I didn't use the actual phrase, it became the theme of the entire evening.

I was in the communication dojo. This was a test.

He started the date by asking if he could get me drunk. I said no, but that he could get me one margarita. We went into the nearest bar and he came back to the table with two beers. I said, "I don't drink beer, I don't like it." He slapped his head drunkenly, and then insisted that I should drink it anyway.

"Chuck! I don't *like* beer! This isn't going to work out between us. Hey, maybe I can help you find some cute girl and you can give this beer to *her!*" He didn't like that suggestion and wanted me to *please* give him a shot. I sighed, smiled, and gently said, "Chuck, this is not a match for me. Nothing is going to happen between us. But I'm happy to stay and talk a little." I wanted to help him if I could.

Chuck was negative, about me and about people. He thought I, like all women, was viciously judgmental. I said I didn't think I judged him; I simply knew what I was looking for. I think he believed me. I said, "Tell me something totally honest."

"I can't."

"Just try, any little thing."

"Honestly, I can't."

"Are you really on a raw juice diet?"

"No, I lied. I just said that for fun."

"At least you're honest about that."

During our time together, I kept having the urge to arm wrestle with him. Every once in a while we would make eye contact and hold hands for a moment across the table. Once, our hands wound up in the arm wrestle position. I grabbed the opportunity and clenched. Chuck engaged, and I flattened his arm down to the table. He looked at me, shocked, and said, "You're Chinese!" and I said, "Yep!" I didn't know what he meant, but I received it as a compliment. For some reason, I've long imagined that in a past life I was a hardy, wrinkled, old, smiley-faced Asian fisherwoman.

"You know, Chuck, people are mostly beautiful, smart, creative, and loving if you give them a chance." He kept shaking his head, maybe to get rid of his dark thoughts. I felt parental and told him, "Maybe if you start letting people in, you won't be so lonely." I suggested that maybe he could try to soften his heart whenever he noticed he was shaking his head, which was still tightly grinding "no." I don't think he heard me.

We did our best, me and Chuck. We navigated some tough communication territory, and I left after forty-five minutes. I had never communicated more fearlessly on a first date: I was clear, direct, and not caretake-y. I didn't compromise any boundaries. The wrestling moment was my highlight.

Date #73: Undercover Husband *June 2018*

In the summer of 2018, I discovered a new passion: salsa dancing. Social dancing felt very "poly" to me: enjoying different chemistries with people of various ages, ethnicities, genders, and dancing abilities. We invited each other to dance and sometimes said no. I was using the same skills I had been building through dating, but communicating mostly without words. Partner dancing was a great arena for setting boundaries, practicing flirting, and learning a fun, new skill.

Each week, I attended a beginner's lesson that was followed by social dancing. One night, as we switched partners during the lesson —a great time to scope out people one might want to dance with later—I met Hector, who clearly wasn't a beginner. He was a bit older, and not too tall. Each time I rotated into place to partner with him, his face lit up with unbridled joy. It seemed clear that he was interested in me, and I liked his fiery dancing style.

Hector grabbed my wrist during the open dancing and we were instantly moving wildly, fast and furious. Our dancing was like a pressure cooker. Unfortunately, I didn't know very many moves yet, and didn't recognize most of his. Following was a subtle art, a sensitive somatic language, but his Tasmanian devil salsa style left me no room to listen. I appreciated his enthusiastic spirit but was lost.

I'm not sure how it happened, but as I was trying to keep up with his unpredictable movements, suddenly, I was balancing on one high heel while my other shoe was dangling from my ankle strap. I had danced right out of my shoe! A few women—including the studio owner—covered their gaping mouths on the sidelines. I hobbled on my one heel off the dance floor. Hector felt terrible, but I laughed, fixed it, and we tried again. He corralled his fancy footwork, and we found a more balanced groove.

After an hour of social dancing with various partners, I changed out of my dancing shoes and gathered my belongings. Hector saw that I was leaving and dashed to catch me, breathlessly attempting to slow my departure with, "But I've barely gotten to know you," and "I feel like I've just found the most amazing book but I can only see the cover." I felt flattered, and I liked his transparency. I handed him my *Amy the Potter* business card, then floated down the fairy-tale staircase and slipped, smiling, out into the night. *Ah, salsa!*

Later that night, I received a slew of notifications that he was "liking" and commenting on Facebook posts of mine from years ago. I enjoyed the attention. We messaged late that night and made a plan to get together a few days later for dinner and then dancing. I had been looking for someone to practice dancing with during the week, and he said that he used to teach salsa. We were flirting—until I checked his Facebook page, where I discovered that he seemed to have a wife. I messaged him,

> **Amy:** Hector, are you *married*?
>
> **Hector:** There is a ring on my finger. It's complicated.
>
> **Amy:** Well, I guess we'll have plenty to talk about over dinner.

When we sat down together at the restaurant, despite my initial physical attraction to him, we lacked in many other areas of chemistry. I knew right away that I was not interested romantically. Hector moved nervously when he talked, and his self-esteem was much lower than it had been on the dance floor. I did have compassion for him. His tone was resentful and deflated when he said, "I snuck out to dance because my wife is out of the country. She doesn't let me go to salsa." When I asked why he would stay in a miserable marriage, he said he was a Christian, and committed.

After dinner, we went to my house to dance. Hector was nervous and fluttery. I could tell from his oogly facial expressions and body gestures that he was fantasizing about wild, adulterous sex. His younger, vibrant spirit was straining to resurface through a leathery shell. Positive sexual feelings were bringing him back to life—but we were emotionally diverging. I was an appreciative student learning some new dance moves; he was a man unleashed. Throughout the night, I kept it real with him, constantly deflecting his dreaminess around me. I let Hector know that I absolutely would not be adulterous with him, and suggested to him that maybe I *represented* the things he longed for: freedom, aliveness, and passion. When I asked him how his wife (my "sister") would feel about our dinner and dancing, he said that she would probably divorce him on the spot. I ended the dance lesson.

From my post-monogamous perspective, I wondered why cheating was a viable option. Why would anyone choose to have a secret affair rather than communicate about their evolving desires? Every seven years, all of our cells regenerate, and biologically, we are a completely new person. Shouldn't we also renegotiate and update all contracts at least every seven years?

I felt relieved when Hector left. His fantasizing was so distracting that I could barely focus on the dance moves. Afterwards, he messaged me on various apps daily. About a third of the time, I responded. We saw each other at the next Friday night social dance. When he invited me to dance, I said yes, but it took energy for me to hold emotional boundaries. He was clearly still deep in a fantasy, and his wife was still away. The third time he asked me to dance that night, I said no. The next week, he stopped coming to salsa, and I guessed that his wife must have returned. Wary, I faded out of communication with Hector.

About a month later, he showed up again at salsa—with his wife! We didn't interact that night, but when I messaged him about it the next day, he said he just came out and asked her and she was excited to go! They danced together that entire night, choosing not to switch partners. She seemed drunk, but happy. They continued to show up together for a month and something had obviously lightened up in both of them. She was a big and bold dancer, able to follow his dancing much better than I ever could. I felt really happy to see them in their new groove.

Part IV

SPIRALING TOWARDS SOMETHING DIVINE

13

ECSTASY AND AGONY

Date #74: Liquid Skin *July 2018*

In 2018, I was invited to teach at both Summer Camp East in West Virginia and Summer Camp West in Oregon. Although I was suffering because of the end of my relationship with Warren, I felt hopeful about whatever the back-to-back camps had in store for me.

I landed in D.C. at 10 p.m. and a volunteer from the camp picked me up. We drove three hours to a campground deep in the Appalachian Mountains. Stepping out of the car, I heard a rushing river. Unlike Oregon's dry summers, the air here was thick with humidity. A friendly but tired camp host met me for a short tour. We ducked into the Lodge, a community space with bathrooms, a kitchen, and a large den where several campers were lazily milling about. A man who was standing near the coffee pot paused his conversation and turned to face me with a subtle grin. He had freckled, rich, mocha skin, and his familiar, hazel eyes tapped my center like a tuning fork. Looking straight into my soul, he tipped his head and asked, "Don't I know you?"

Woozy, I said, "I don't think so, but you are strangely familiar." He smiled, nodded, and held out his hand.

As my fingers touched his palm, he said his name, "Jameson." My insides were vibrating. As I made my way through the dark woods to my tent, I dreamily imagined more contact with Jameson.

I experienced a great freedom at the Summer Camps, where it felt easy to initiate from my heart. One exercise we did at every camp was "Unsaids and Withholds," the radical honesty practice where we cleared the air with each other. This could be something positive, like an appreciation, something difficult to bring up, like "It really bothered me yesterday when you ..." or something edgy, like revealing attraction. We did that exercise my first morning in the Dome. Noticing Jameson sitting quietly, looking pensively at the ground while the rest of the campers were occupied in pairs, I plopped down in front of him, looked directly into those magical eyes, and said that I was drawn to him and would love to spend time together. His eyes danced between mine as he broke into a smile, and said he felt the same. We agreed to find time to connect.

The next day, I realized that Jameson was there with a woman and their child. I mostly saw him from afar, and he seemed distressed; I assumed that he and his partner were in a relationship struggle. We collided one afternoon when Jameson and I were the only people taking showers. I said over the water spray, "I would still love to hang out if you do."

Apologizing for disappearing, he said, "I've been in a difficult space, but yes, it would be nice to connect." We agreed to take a walk later that evening.

At twilight, we set out on the winding, rocky path. The hemlocks felt like grandparents, their wide, low-hanging boughs inviting us into the magical forest. The pungent humidity enveloped us and became part of our bodies with each breath. Jameson's voice was strained as we navigated the uneven terrain. I learned that he was a passionate man who had chosen a safe job and a mainstream life. As he spoke, he punctuated the gravity of his message—his pain—by pausing his steps and looking deeply into my eyes. He was grappling with something. But when he smiled, his whole face softened and opened. The path guided us forward, like a gentle river.

About a quarter mile from camp, we came upon a firepit surrounded by rustic carved-log benches. We decided to sit there and talk as the sun was disappearing. I had no idea where this date was going and asked how he envisioned the rest of our evening. A rush of warmth moved through me when he suggested discussing our boundaries, fears, and desires relating to a potential sexual connection. His only boundary was to not have intercourse. That felt perfect. My main fear was upsetting his partner. *Please, no more Warren and Karen situations for me.* Jameson said that although things were rocky between him and his partner, Dee, he felt confident that she would be thrilled to hear he was finally exploring a new connection. He explained that he didn't identify as poly, whereas Dee was "truly polyamorous," and had remained actively non-monogamous for their entire sixteen-year relationship. Evidently, she'd always been troubled about the imbalance.

We both desired to feel connected to ourselves and each other, both during and after our experience. When I expressed my desire to touch him, he told me to caress him in whatever way I like to be touched. Appreciating the simplicity of his direction, I straddled his lap and started exploring. My hands were drawn to his strong arms, and the silky feeling of his skin was a psychedelic revelation. I was intoxicated. Slowly, I moved my cheeks, inner arms, and hands over his smooth, muscular landscape. My fingers climbed up and sunk into his thick hair, hungry to touch his center. Soon, we found lips, and I was swirling, absorbed in his delicious physicality.

Suddenly, a loud chorus of bright voices was roaring towards us. It was the band of camp children; one of them was his daughter! We frantically put our clothes back in place, shifting into innocent side-by-side formation as inquisitive flashlights beamed straight at us. *Busted!* Were we suddenly going to be hanging out with a bunch of kids? *Oh no.*

Thankfully, he didn't slip into SuperDad mode. Instead, we escaped to my tent and crawled in. Everything at that West Virginia camp was damp, which took the sexiness down a notch. He set the mood by playing some R&B on his phone. We rolled around in the small, uncomfortable tent, kissing hungrily and playfully, and then took off layers to have more access to each other, exploring freely, using our hands and mouths.

As much as I'm into dating, and desire relationships, love and sex, it is rare that I go beyond kissing. After casual sex, I would inevitably have a backlash both in my vagina and my nervous system. I didn't want people inside my body unless I felt some level of love and emotional trust. Ever since my romantic—but never fully "consummated"—jolt with Soren the Wizard, I'd had intercourse only with two people, Oliver and Warren, and both were connections from Summer Camp. Many people can have multiple sexual relationships of varying depths but being sexually "sporty" didn't work for me. I realized that I am demisexual: I need an emotional bond in order to be sexual with someone. I felt that rare, strong potential with Jameson.

Our energy was building. Kissing, sucking, licking—everything felt good, until Jameson's words surprised me: "I want to change my boundary."

My entire being contorted. I responded, "What? You can't! That's what they are for!" Vaughn had taught me that we absolutely do not cross agreed-upon boundaries during a session. Then again, Jameson wasn't a client. I objected, but he countered that it was his boundary to shift.

Confused, I didn't take the time to consider if it was really right for *me*. If I had named a boundary, it would have been the same: "no intercourse," but I didn't, because he did. In that juiced-up moment, I felt hungry and ignored my annoying inner conflict.

Right away, Jameson felt far away, bumping into me. *Why is intercourse so often more detached than foreplay?* He blurred and was suddenly just some guy having sex with me. Twisted up inside, I croaked out, "I have to stop." Jameson stopped and rolled off me. I felt deflated.

He held me, whispering soothingly. "I think it takes three sexual experiences to really feel out a new relationship." Petting me gently, he said, "I do not have one night stands. I see our connection lasting into the future."

I felt shut down, but was comforted by his tone and words. "That sounds nice. Hopefully, we can have a more spacious and relaxed experience sometime. Thank you for your sweetness, Jameson. I think I need to go to sleep." I felt low and needed space.

The next morning, I looked around but didn't see Jameson in the opening circle, until he and his family came in late. I was shocked when the organizers asked if anyone would be leaving that day: the three of them stood in the center for the early departure ritual. *He was leaving?* With their backs to each other, they rotated slowly, making eye contact with us. Jameson seemed reserved. As he turned past me, his eye contact was slippery. *Were they leaving because of what had happened between us last night?* I hoped that we would at least say goodbye, but I was busy all day teaching workshops. I didn't see him again.

Wow. He was the first person I'd had sex with, besides Warren, in the last two years—and he left without saying a word to me. I felt disturbed. A week later, back at home, I found him on Facebook and saw his most recent post.

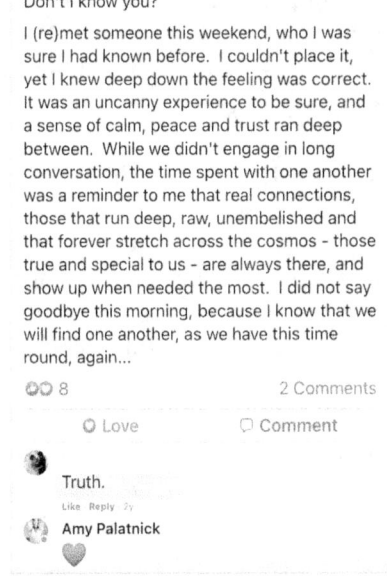

Reading it gave me the chills. Feeling much better, I messaged him:

Amy: Hey, you. It was such a surprise when you left camp without saying goodbye. I had no idea that we wouldn't speak again after our time together. I was relieved to read your Facebook post, as I wasn't sure what to make of you not connecting with me after our evening together. As a woman, that kind of thing can be traumatizing. I could have really been thrown off. I stopped letting myself believe that our connection was as special as I'd thought. Hearing that you did care lets me re-embrace it.

Jameson: I wondered how that might have affected you, but in my experience, our parting the night before was perfect and fulfilling. It validated something special for me, and in my mind, there's only more to share.

Amy: It was very special to me. I wished more of our time had been where I could see you. It was such a dark night and you are so beautiful. I believed you when you said you wanted more; at the time, I did trust the things you said. You disappearing was just jarring.

Jameson: I'm sorry. Truly.

His apology was heartfelt and genuine, and we were able to move on. We have stayed in loose contact since then, communicating in satisfying fits and starts. I do think we will meet in person again, one day. His wife, Dee, sent me this message a few weeks after camp.

Dee: Hello, Amy. I am writing because I felt it would be a nice sister connection to reach out to you. As even a momentary metamour, I feel connected to you. I have longed to share Jameson with others because his soulful medicine has been an elixir of personal and spiritual growth for me for a long time. He has directed the intensity of his being and his loving body towards me exclusively for over a decade. I know his somatic wisdom will always listen to my body and respond to its needs. Thank you for being a contributing author in our story. I appreciate your holding and loving the tender being called Jameson. Much love and luck to you!

Amy: It is touching to hear from you, and I too feel a sister connection to you. I can feel your depth and aliveness and I feel blessed to be crossing paths with you. I was honored to get the chance to dip in briefly with Jameson, and your reaching out with such tenderness and openness touches my heart.

Date #75: What Happens at Summer Camp Stays at Summer Camp *July 2018*

On my first day at Summer Camp East, I noticed an extremely cute young man with shoulder-length hair, a perpetual smile, and bright, warm eyes. He seemed light in his body, and reminded me of a delicate fern. *But so young.*

Just about everyone at Summer Camp is open to breaking most norms, which was refreshing. The dating scientist in me believed that if attraction was real, it was mutual, but I also felt like I was thirteen, wondering, *why would he like me?* I had arrived a couple days after camp was underway. I noticed Nate from afar, on kitchen duty and participating in group activities. After I taught my first Processwork session, he joined my lunch table with eager eyes and a tumble of questions. Suddenly all of that cuteness was looking right at me, and I came uniquely alive.

The rest of that day, Nate and I continually caught each other's gazes. During a break, I walked straight up to him and said I would love to spend time together. He wanted that too! We planned to connect later that night; I was leaving the next day. When evening descended, we found a comfy couch in the lodge den. He paused at my simplest questions. I was hypnotized. Eventually, I was sitting cozily in his lap. We kissed playfully while ambient campers milled about nearby.

Everything felt effortless. We decided to spend the night together and made our way through the dark woods to his cabin. On the walk, I got nervous about potential expectations. I felt knocked off center from my experience with Jameson the night before, and I was grieving Warren. *Sex with Nate would be too much.* I laid it out, "I can't have intercourse with you tonight." I felt relieved when Nate welcomed my boundary with a big nod. Once boundaries were established, I asked about his camp girlfriend, and just as he said her name, she appeared on the path. She was much younger than Nate and was on her way to the Temple with a much older man. (You wouldn't believe it, and it's a longer story, but that man was Karezza Man Scott).

The four of us stood on the path awkwardly together. Nate told her gently that I would be staying in the cabin that night, and I sensed her discomfort. They shared a sweet hug, and Nate and I walked on. When I asked if everything was OK, he nodded and smiled, "Nothing to worry about." It was fun to move on to our desires: we both wanted our precious time together to feel light and easy, like a sleepover party.

Inside the cabin, Nate's soft spirit seemed to have permeated the cedar walls. We got mostly undressed and slipped under the sheets. It felt sexy to be in our underwear together. We talked easily about what we did and didn't like, touch-wise, and did some relaxed, educational body exploration. I showed him how I love to be touched gently, through my underwear. I guided him to cup me with his hand. Then he gave me an introduction to his penis, which was very sensitive. I love slow, present touch, and have found that men who appreciate delicate touch are more sensitive when they touch me.

We were affectionate, kissing and snuggling, gently touching and massaging each other. We spoke softly. Nate adorably set several alarms leading up to the time when we would finally have to go to sleep. It felt good—mature—to prioritize self-care together and go to sleep early. When the final alarm rang, we closed our eyes. In the morning, we were both surprised at having slept so soundly.

Our night felt strangely easy and familiar. I loved sliding back into bed after peeing outside, and then getting dressed together in the morning. It was nurturing to feel simply domestic. As we walked to breakfast, he slipped his fingers into mine, stabilizing me as we navigated up the muddy trail towards camp. I was enamored and thrilled about our sweet and simple intimacy. I disappeared into the contact between our hands, and imagined him as a future boyfriend, my heart free and hopeful.

Before interacting with anyone else, we stopped on the trail, looked into each other's eyes, and expressed gratitude for the beautiful night. With sincerity, he asked to connect again before I left. I wished we could have spent every moment together, but I was teaching that whole day. We planned to meet up later to share a few final moments before I left.

In the evening, Nate found me and led me to a hammock, where we cuddled, kissed, and talked. Shyly, I asked if we could take a selfie. He grabbed my phone and we posed and kissed while he clicked away. I felt an extreme affinity, but was also aware that Nate echoed my "cute boy" core erotic theme. Lying in the hammock, I said, "I could fall in love with you." Googly-eyed, looking between his eyes and the patch of sky above, I said, "It would be amazing to have you come visit me," and we fantasized out loud about him making a trip, although I feared that our brief time together wasn't enough to inspire an enduring connection. I put my hand on his heart, looked away, and said, sadly, "No thick root can grow in such a short time." But then I thought, *who died and made me Botanist?*

We had a sweet hug, and I skipped off from camp feeling optimistic. With Nate, I desired to bond. It gave me hope. Once home, I reached out. After a few days of radio silence, I sunk, disappointed. A week later, he sent an enthusiastic email, letting me know that he had been without Wi-Fi since camp and was excited to reconnect. We talked about the idea I'd blurted out about a visit, but coming across the country wasn't a small thing for Nate. Due to a congenital blood clotting issue, he needed to lie down every few hours and so could only travel by train. *What had I promised? How long would he stay? Where would he sleep? What if it didn't feel right? What about my other love interests?*

It was so easy to feel "in love" at Summer Camp, but now, fantasy and reality crashed. I liked the idea of a slow process and told him that a shorter visit would be better for me than diving into something long and undefined.

Within a month, I went from falling in love with him and fantasizing about a life with him, to waffling hesitation. Everything looked different through my real-life lens. In the end, I was relieved that his trip idea and the connection fizzled. But for a camp mini-romance, it was perfect.

Date #76: Wrestling With a Champion *August 2018*

After Summer Camp East, I flew back home and prepared to go to Summer Camp West in Southern Oregon. Warren and I had separated in May. He and Karen were also going, and I couldn't imagine how it would feel to be there, but not *with* him. I hoped to connect with some shiny new person right away.

During the get-to-know-you exercise on the first night, I moved through the group, feeling lackluster. I wasn't attracted to anyone, but then I caught eyes with a new camper. He was boyishly handsome, with a buff body, dark hair, and piercing eyes. We nodded, agreeing to sit with each other for a seven-minute "date."

Horatio was young and artistic, but our time was more casual than flirtatious. He seemed vulnerable in that big body, and I know that it can be overwhelming to arrive at Summer Camp for the first time. I didn't want to scare him off. After our seven minutes, I rotated to find another "date." My heart felt cauterized. Over the first few days at camp, I spent a lot of time looking down at my feet. Sometimes, I would stare at someone, head tilted, wondering, *could I be with them?* But I felt no spark anywhere.

I had been feeling anxious in the months leading up to Summer Camp West. I missed Warren terribly. Right before Summer Camp, he and I had one of our monthly post-break-up, platonic drinks at Sam Bond's Garage, a rootsy, bohemian neighborhood pub in the Whit. One moment, we were saying goodbye in his living room (Karen wasn't home), and the next, he guided me onto his ottoman, pulled up my skirt, and we were suddenly fucking. It was nothing like our previous cosmic explorations. The experience didn't last long, and I walked away feeling disturbed and confused. Trying to split up, and then having sex when there were so many complex feelings between us, was heartbreaking, especially with Summer Camp coming up. I had no idea how it would be with us, and I felt scared.

Once at camp, I was hypervigilant about Karen and Warren. *Where were they? What were they doing?* I was too distracted by the situation and feared I wouldn't be able to teach when the time came. My solution was to work openly on my emotions at the daily community forum in the Dome, with the whole camp witnessing.

I walked around the middle of the circle telling our story, releasing my held-in emotions to the large group, most of whom knew all three of us. When the facilitators urged me to express my anger, I screamed (referring to Karen), "Trying to hurt someone, wanting them to feel pain, is ABUSE!" That public accusation was another nail in the relationship casket. The year before, Warren and I couldn't get enough of each other. *How had things changed so drastically?*

The tension among the three of us was incredibly high. I missed Warren and thought he would schedule at least one overnight with me, but he said he "couldn't." Karen was one of the leaders at camp, so she was very visible, and we were often all in the same space. It seemed like Warren and Karen were always walking off together, or Warren's eyes were bulging with his tongue hanging out as he chased after a buxom woman who was new to camp. I felt like he was avoiding me; our only interactions were accidental run-ins on the path. When we did see each other, he approached me stiffly, as though his whole body was saying no, or sorry, or both.

One morning, Karen announced to the group that we were going to do something new: 24 hours of no words. Instrumental music and guttural sounds were encouraged, but the agreement was to not speak unless necessary. During that time, camp would be mostly unstructured, to give everyone a break from the workshops and offerings. As soon as I heard about this, I felt eased internally around the Warren/Karen melodrama. I love not speaking, and a part of me wished we could be silent forever.

The period of no speaking began ceremoniously, on Wednesday night, with a contact improvisation-inspired dance experience. The guidance, explained beforehand, was to experiment with touch, share weight, and move intuitively. Music filled the Dome, and people began to move through the space. I grabbed a blindfold out of a pile and put it in my pocket. At first, I connected with two adorable male friends. One of them was very tall, strong, and lanky, and the other was stout with big pouty lips; they both loved to flirt with me. The three of us gripped wrists and ankles tightly and tumbled athletically through the crowd in a rolling ball. Our triple, uneven body weight powered the human tumbling knot, each of us diving up and over the ball, head first, when we were in the proper position. I felt a huge rush from this wild, physical creativity. Eventually, we tired out, the knot melted into a puddle of joy, and I soon separated, put my blindfold on, and slithered away on my own.

Crawling around curiously, I paused when I felt like I was in the very center of the Dome. Someone else was prone, right next to me; our hands began a palm-to-palm conversation. I felt activated by our contact, inspired into a state of heightened sensitivity. I had a very sensual "fuck yes" response, and my hands started exploring any skin I could find, gently caressing a large landscape. *Who could this be?* Huge muscles burst with aliveness; their vibration transferred into my palms. Moving together intuitively, like soft underwater creatures, our fingers became sensory tentacles. His skin was liquid, mercurial, and ... otherworldly. *Could iridescent be a texture?* I felt intoxicated.

I had found a prize, a secret that had been at camp the whole time. As the two of us moved in ultra-slow motion, bodies climbed and slithered around us. Needing to know who had this psychedelic physicality, I peeked out beyond my blindfold ... it was Horatio!

He pulled his blindfold off. We had been bodies in the dark, but now, we had identities. Since he was twenty years younger, I hadn't even considered a connection. We smiled, looking from eye to eye, and relaxed into a profound moment of consent beyond the blindfold. Our slow, sensual dance spiraled snake-like, for a long time. My whole body was filled with swirling, ecstatic surprise.

We separated wordlessly. Later in the evening, I walked up to the outdoor Lounge where large, illuminated jellyfish sculptures hung from the surrounding trees. A musician sat nearby, plucking harmonic guitar sounds. When I spotted Horatio lying on a sofa, I jumped in next to him, unbridled. He wrapped me up in his arms, pulled a comforter over us and we cuddled. At some point, he woke up, kissed me on the forehead, and disappeared into the darkness toward his tent.

The next day, as the period of silence continued, I was drawn into the Dome by earthy, percussive beats. Sylvan (my first ever

Summer Camp fling) and his new girlfriend were joyfully playing hand drums. I enthusiastically bounded in and joined one other stray mover. In the huge, mostly empty tent, there were two people drumming and two of us dancing. Way on the other side of the Dome, two people were on their hands and knees, focusing on a large-scale collage project, and I realized that one of those bent-over artists was Horatio.

Leaving the other dancer, I ventured across the Dome to finally touch Horatio again. I signed hand gestures, "You, me, OK?" checking to make sure nothing was weird between us. His eyes softened. Then he quickly grabbed me and pulled me down to the ground where we were once again body to body. We rolled around for a bit, giggling, and soon parted. Like a young king, Horatio bowed with a large dramatic flourish and exited the Dome. I returned to my primal dance party of two.

That evening, when the day of silence concluded, Horatio and I decided to spend the evening together. We headed to the big meadow and lay down on a blanket, under the stars. The whole world was quiet, and the air smelled of grass. I told him that I was leaving the next day and that I felt open to intimacy with him. We had the "boundaries, fears, and desires" conversation. Horatio didn't want to kiss or have any genital contact. Our voices stayed soft as we whispered. I heard the wind move through the Douglas firs. We talked about space, time, existence, and the people who had made the biggest impacts in our lives. Looking up at the Milky Way, we asked questions like children and answered them like sages. Horatio was spectacularly intelligent. I liked the me that came out with him. It felt *a lot like me!*

Yearning to deepen, I initiated wrestling on our blanket. It was ridiculous to think I could really wrestle Horatio. I wanted to be wily and outmaneuver him. He was amused, and called me "feisty." Imagine how hard I laughed when, a week later, he texted me the link to a professional YouTube video of him defending his MMA (Mixed Martial Arts) Heavyweight Champion title!

My futile wrestling efforts left me sweaty and chilly, so we migrated to the Dome where there were cozy nooks. Strangely, at 11 p.m. it was empty. We cuddled up in a pile of warmth, fully clothed, and gently massaged each other. But Horatio "pulled a Jameson" on me and wanted to shift his boundary, to have genital contact. It was OK with me. He unzipped his pants and I stroked his cock, making eye contact with him. Before long, he said, "OK, better stop, thank you," and we returned to cuddling. *Was Horatio working on sexual self-discipline?* Starting to drift into sleep, exhausted, we caught ourselves and migrated towards the outdoor sinks to brush our teeth together, and then had a long hug under the moon. I hoped he would initiate a sleepover, but he didn't, and I was too shy to ask. It was romantic and beautiful, though I felt sad strolling back to my tent alone.

The next morning was my last; I would leave after lunch. In the wee hours, I heard the sound of my tent zipper. It was Warren, climbing into my tent! My heart burst open. I had been suffering, witnessing him enjoying his time with everyone but me.

When he lay down next to me, I thought, *is he here to apologize, to beg me to reconsider? Were we finally going to have a sweet moment of connection after such a long, hard week?* But instead of cuddling up and whispering about our eternal love, Warren lay on his back, looking up at the top of the tent. A million miles away, he said with neutral curiosity, "You being here at camp didn't affect me much." Warren is beautifully honest, but this was a knife to my heart. *Did he come to my tent just to tell me he was unmoved by my presence? Thank god I was leaving camp early.* I felt sick.

At breakfast, Warren was eating with a group of friends in the corner and didn't seem to notice me. When Horatio approached me with a huge smile and handed me a flower, I forgot about Warren for a moment. When Horatio kissed my forehead, tears flowed. And when he asked if he could help me load my car after lunch, I fell into his arms and gratefully accepted.

After the morning session, Horatio and I ate lunch together. He wanted to wait for me while I left to pack and say my goodbyes. When I was finally ready to leave, I returned to the picnic table, and found him surrounded by art supplies, smiling up at me, holding a beautiful, colorful painting. He handed me this:

Wow! I wrapped the gift carefully. We grabbed the rest of my stuff. As we walked past the Temple, I mentioned that I would love to have one last touching experience with him. But he had never been in the Temple and was hesitant. Not everyone at camp feels comfortable there; it's always been edgy for me to go in. Once my car was loaded, we had a nurturing goodbye. I didn't see us as partners, but when we spoke about what we each wanted, and when his skin was so freaking amazing, and it was all so easy between us, I wasn't completely sure. When we were together, there was no age. It was just the two of us, balancing our hearts on a big rock screaming at 70,000 miles per hour through space.

When I got home, Horatio texted right away. We initiated connections through multiple communication channels: text, Marco Polo, Instagram, and Messenger. Our digital communications flowed easily.

He lived a few hours away, close enough to see each other again. A week after Summer Camp, Horatio came to visit me for two nights. Before he arrived, I felt nervous. I treasure my personal space. When people visit, I'm not always sure what to do with them, and can get ungrounded. But our time together was easy. We cooked, picked blueberries, and took my dogs Sasha and Delilah for a swim in the McKenzie River. In bed, we massaged each other, and were cuddly and tender. He kept his boundary against kissing, and I had a boundary against penetration. What was left between us was pure sweetness. Horatio was so much younger, but more nurturing and emotionally present than most men I had dated.

After that visit, we stayed in touch, had some video sex, and then planned another visit soon. But a few months later, Horatio moved away. We kept our hearts open, to life and each other. Every once in a while, we send a loving message. When I think of Horatio, my heart blooms like his painted sun.

Date #77: Don't Go Partner Dancing on the First Date
(Told from both perspectives) Summer 2018

Earlier in the summer, before the Summer Camps, I met Amir on Bumble, an app where only women could initiate conversations. He was a very attractive thirty-something chemistry professor who used endearing emojis in his profile to describe his diverse interests. Amir was open to using Marco Polo and we found a smooth groove communicating there. We made a plan to meet for dinner, and sent lots of flirty, get-to-know-you video messages on the days leading up to our date.

Arriving at The Bier Stein, we each "appeared on the set" at the same exact moment, from opposite directions. My heart swelled: he was wearing a white, short-sleeved linen shirt. *So handsome.* It complemented his olive skin. Soft and confident, Amir's huge smile beamed at me. He wasn't too tall, and our strong, warm hug hello felt just right. *Ahhh.* I was instantly relaxed and happy.

Filing into line, we stood side by side to look through the extensive menu. We chose to share the artichoke parmesan dip and my favorite, the Mona Lisa (grilled chicken panini), then found a comfy place to sit. Amir was funny: he jumped right into talking about sex. Like, right away. Because I say in my profile that I am interested in high-consciousness sexuality, many men assume I'm a nymphomaniac.

ECSTASY AND AGONY • 249

When Amir mentioned the girth of his cock, I stayed as present and direct as I could and let him know I thought he was cute but had no preference regarding penis size. Soon after, he asked to put his hand on my leg. "Yes, sure!" A moment that could have been uncomfortable was just funny and fine. Amir seemed free, open, and up for anything. I felt at ease with him, and our conversation wove together effortlessly.

After our lovely dinner, I invited him to go dancing. But doing salsa together was mucho awkward, and I instantly regretted it. I was in a new phase of excitedly learning to partner dance, and treasured the weekly Friday night experience, but Amir was a beginner, and didn't know how to lead. Dancing with him was funny; he bounced around playfully, making smiley eye contact and moving absurdly to the music. He was so sweet, but the Type A part of me couldn't stand not doing the moves right.

I felt caught between being on a date with Amir and wanting to practice my salsa moves with stronger dancers. Even though Amir completely understood and made space for my desire to rotate mostly among better dancers, my inner struggle was exhausting. *Note to self: inviting a newbie to salsa is not a good idea for a first date.* Amir waited for me as I spun from one person to the next. We checked in between songs and danced together several times. When he asked if I had plans the next morning, I said I did. He wasn't invited to come home with me, but I did want to check out the kiss.

We gathered our things, stepped out into the dark night, and paused on the lawn in front of the Vet's Club. It was just the two of us again. He looked into my eyes and very slowly brought his big lips towards mine. When our lips eventually touched, I felt suddenly weak and softened into Amir, completely absorbed in the sensual moment. The kiss ended as slowly as it started, like the final, lingering note of a song. I smiled up at him, managed to say "Wow," and wobbled away. The kiss continued to spiral inside me.

In the wake of our date, my romantic interest waned. I thought Amir was probably too immature and only looking for sex. But he continued to message me, and I said that I would love to hang out as friends and see what might build from there. We had the same favorite Mexican breakfast restaurant by the University of Oregon campus. I hadn't eaten at Cafe Siena in years, and met him there with great anticipation, but a sign on the door said it was closed. Slightly disappointed, we settled for Greek food next door.

After Amir paid for us, he walked me to my bike and gently offered to help me adjust my helmet. Tightening the strap snugly under my chin, he encouraged me to get a new one, because "helmets have expiration dates." *Who knew?* There was a deeply warm, caring flair to this simple act, and I soaked it up.

As we continued to message on Marco Polo, my heart continuously opened towards him. We had a profound affinity. Soon, we planned a dinner date at my house. I felt enthusiastic, but also hesitant. Although Amir was casual and respectful on our lunch date, he also seemed sexually ambitious. I imagined that once there was an opportunity to touch, he would move too fast for me, so I prepared to set boundaries.

When Amir arrived, we shared a warm hug, enjoyed dinner and wine, and then sat on my big sofa together. I suggested that we play a touching game: Betty Martin's *Wheel of Consent: the 3-Minute Game,* which I had learned from Vaughn (and played on the sleepover with Logan). The practice is intended to increase clarity and awareness in touch communication. I was thrilled that Amir was open to playing. I explained the four different touching roles—Serving, Accepting, Taking, and Allowing.

Amir was puppy-dog eager for physical contact, and the feeling between us was light and playful, although my boundary muscles were at the ready. We started off simply, non-sexually, touching arms and hands, to get the rules and format clear.

Setting three-minute timers on my phone, we went around the wheel and debriefed between each type of touch. "Let's start with a round using only hands and arms. I will 'serve' you first; you will be 'accepting.' How would you like your arms to be touched?" Amir wanted massage, especially on his wrists and hands. Communicating as we went, I encouraged him to be specific so he could have the best possible three-minute experience. Then it was my turn to accept, and

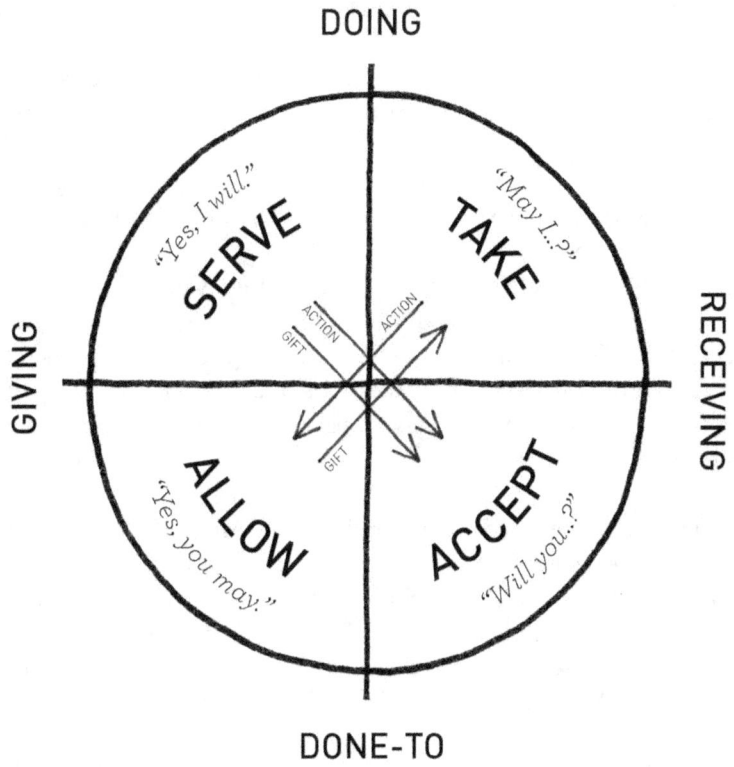

"The Wheel of Consent" from The Art of Receiving and Giving ©2021, Betty Martin

his to serve. I asked for long, slow squeezes up and down my arm, going extra slowly on my triceps. Amir's quality of touch was very sensitive. He was able to tune in and listen to my words and my body. Those two turns were easy for us.

Then I suggested that I do the "taking" role first. I asked, "May I use your arm for my pleasure?" and he nodded, eyes wide, smiling broadly. Amused by his eagerness, I thought, *Slow down, soldier!* I love my arms to be tickled, so I ran my arm up and down his. The sensation of his arm hair on the inside of my arm, especially the inner elbow, made me shiver. Then, the ultra-smooth feeling of gliding my inner forearm along his inner arm gave me a wonderful rush of pleasure.

But when Amir tried to "take," he confused serving and taking. I could tell he was trying to give me pleasure, and I reminded him, "This is for your own pleasure."

Shaking his head, he countered, "But I do feel pleasure." I encouraged him to use the back of his hand, but he reverted quickly to massaging me.

We debriefed and I tried to explain taking. Amir loved allowing but didn't seem to understand the difference between taking and serving. We played another round. Everything felt good between us so far, and I suggested that we could integrate more body parts. Adding cuddling and kissing, we became more sensual. I felt good with him, so when Amir suggested going upstairs to my bedroom, I said yes.

The next time I was in the "serving" role, Amir asked, "Touch me all over, everywhere, anywhere, however you want." I moved my hands up and down his soft clothes and skin until my hands rested on his chest. My whole being was vibrating. Then, I put one hand on his heart and reached down with the other to cup his erection through his black Calvin Klein boxer briefs and looked up into his eyes.

We ditched the timer, and the distinction of the touching roles, but continued exploring, retaining the consent principles of the game. Amir had a wonderfully playful nature. I loved teasing his receptive, strong body. When we slowed down, in the places where our skin touched, there was a delicious warm tingle. His hands were sensitive as they traced my curves. But he easily sped up, so the game functioned as a foundation to help me keep him corralled and to say "no" any time he suggested something I wasn't 100% on board with.

Sometimes, I asked him to touch me differently. When I didn't feel like he was hearing my request, we paused. I said no when he asked for a blowjob. I had grown and changed over the last year. Even though I was turned on, keeping things slow helped me stay attuned to my body and desires. Amir was non-defensive, graceful, and receptive. "How about just hands?" he asked lightheartedly, gesturing to the bulge in his boxer briefs. He was enjoying the freedom to ask for anything; I was relishing setting boundaries.

At that point, we had both taken some layers off and I responded, "Let's keep our underwear on today, but I'm happy to touch you through them." He felt happy about that, and after some erotic massage-style stroking, we wound up making out and grinding. Everything felt alive between us as he moved on top of me slowly, still with our underwear on.

"I think I'm going to come, is that OK?" he said.

I smiled, "Of course!" and used my hands to nurture the orgasm. We lay together and whispered about the experience. I told him, "Setting boundaries with you was strangely effortless, and even fun, for me. I feel amazing." I wondered, *was there something special about Amir that made our sexual communication so easy? Or was he just willing to do anything for sex?*

"How would you feel about me sleeping over?" he asked. I wasn't ready for that, and we decided to cuddle instead. Amir spooned me from behind, and our bodies softened so perfectly into each other. After we lingered awhile, I walked Amir to the door. We shared a lazy, long goodnight embrace. Our night of clear communication was a fresh salve on my weary dating spirit.

We continued meeting up, before, between, and after the Summer Camps. Amir had such an accessible personality, and I always enjoyed our sexy dates. We filmed many of our first sexual experiences, and I experimented with editing them into artful erotica using music and effects. In bed, Amir was no longer the silly, bouncy boy from salsa. His sexuality was primal. His hands and mouth were extremely present and gentle. Highly intuitive, he knew exactly how and where to touch me.

Our sexual atmosphere was a place of wonder, where new things could happen. In one early experience, I accessed my dominant side, straddling Amir in a state of abandon and unpredictability I had only imagined. As we made genital contact through our underwear, an amazing, thick wave of sensation flowed like a sparkly river straight up my spine. For a few moments, my body gyrated spontaneously, flooded with joy. *Was this a new kind of orgasm?*

But that summer, I felt shy and protective; I struggled in my breakup with Warren, then had the ungrounding intercourse-then-disappear sexual experience with Jameson. With Amir, I enjoyed our developing sexy friendship, but I didn't feel a deeper romantic connection and wasn't ready to have intercourse with him. Emotionally, he seemed distant. When I asked Joanne about him, she said that Amir "wasn't able to take in the entire landscape of Amy." That resonated with me. *Sigh. Were my standards too high?* I had recently picked up a book called *Marry Mr. Good Enough*. At first, I felt angry about the title, believing that we should all hold out for the absolute best relationships, but then I had to agree that high standards can also be limiting. The book helped me stay open to my developing connection with Amir.

At the end of the summer, Vaughn visited for a weekend of sexual bodywork, and at that point, Amir and I had gotten closer. He was smart, stable, and very funny. I felt genuinely *good* when I was around him. After Vaughn's visit, I felt juicy and open, and for the first time, I had an authentic hunger to have sex with Amir. But when we finally did have sex, I felt emotionally disconnected from him. We were just fucking. My heart hurt with disappointment. Our previous explorations were creative and sensual. I had felt so connected to him, and to myself. After we had sex, I told him that I felt disconnected, but he didn't understand what I meant.

We kept trying, and I did my best to groove with his style. It was hard for me to talk about what I wanted once we started having intercourse. One night, as we were kissing, getting ready to be sexual, he asked me, "Know what you could help me with? I'm still not over one of my ex-girlfriends. I obsess about her and it eats at me. Maybe Processwork could help?" *Ugh.* He had mentioned her before, but never in bed. As he began to speak about it, I shut down. Jealousy spiked my gut. After some miserably awkward communication, we slept on opposite sides of the bed. Over the next week, I didn't communicate as much. I felt embarrassed about desiring him. He sweetly sent several apologetic texts and voicemails.

The following week, we met for dinner at Noodle Bowl, our favorite Korean restaurant. He looked at me with round eyes and a sad, apologetic mouth. The space between us felt tender. I longed for him, but he didn't seem that interested in me. I leaned towards him and said, "I don't want to be the girl who is interested and available. I want to be longed for and obsessed about."

I told him about Esther Perel's book, *Mating in Captivity*. She believes that in modern relationships, we want both security and passion, but the two are usually mutually exclusive. Tension, the opposite of security, inspires passion. I felt happy to see Amir so emotionally present, and said, "Maybe I pulled away to draw you in?" He nodded his head slowly, curious. A deeper interest in our relationship seemed to have awakened in him.

I was afraid to say it, especially after feeling rejected by him, but I admitted that I wanted to get closer. Holding my hands and looking at me, he acknowledged the special feeling between us, but also admitted his conflict: "Since I'm monogamous, and you're not, what can we be? I don't want to use you and just drop you as soon as another woman comes along. That doesn't feel right."

I responded, "For me, getting closer, even for a while, is worth the pain. We can transition to friends later; I know I could handle that. Who knows? Maybe you'll find someone who would accept our connection." Amir seemed skeptical.

Amir's Perspective

My adult life was a long-term pattern of relationships that didn't work out. I had gotten a divorce five years before I met Amy. I was trying to meet people online but also working on building confidence by going out more and meeting women in person. None of it was working, and I was becoming hopeless about finding a partner in Eugene. Even though I had a good teaching career, I was considering moving to a place like Portland or the Bay Area to find a partner. I hate to say it, but Eugene is very white, and as a brown-skinned man, it wasn't easy to get dates there. I knew what I was looking for, but it felt unlikely to find it all in one person; I wanted to find someone who was intelligent, attractive, laid back, liberal, a homebody, not wanting to have children, and not financially dependent on me. I met people who checked some of the boxes, but nobody who filled even a majority of them. I would start dating someone and it would be good for a little while, but for a long-term partner I wanted someone who was stable and mature, but also dynamic and fun.

Amy and I liked each other right away. It was obvious from her profile that she was a very sexual person. I felt like I had to be open and forward to match her energy. I appreciated it when she asked to talk on video. I don't want to text for hours; I much prefer a real time connection. In the first week, we sent several video messages back and forth. Amy seemed both chill and inspired and would video message me late at night when she was naked in the bathtub. Seeing her from her submerged shoulders up was flirty and she was easy to talk to. She wanted to go dancing, which sounded great. I liked the idea that we would mingle and dance with other people.

Even though Amy sounded fun, I didn't think this was going to be what I was looking for, so the stakes were low. We met on a beautiful warm day. I rode my bike. When we showed up at the restaurant, even from far away, I could tell she had good energy. Wearing a polka dot dress, she looked super sweet. She was fun-size, really cute. Her short hair had a slight tomboy effect—I liked that. When we stepped up to the register, she was friendly to the people who worked there, and that impressed me; how people treat others means a lot to me.

Because of her profile, I felt like I had to be bold. I didn't think that I was very impressive. I'm not that good looking, and I'm not that good of a dancer. During our messaging over the previous week, Amy had told me about a temple sex party and I thought, "This girl needs to hear about the big cock." So I mentioned it almost right away when we sat down, just to put something out there, to capture her attention. When she didn't flirt back, I instantly regretted it.

I didn't feel like Amy wanted a timid guy; she wanted a man who was ready to play! In an attempt to practice consent while still being forward, I asked if I could put my hand on her leg. That went over pretty well; she was warm and seemed amused. Even though I may have put my foot in my mouth by talking about my penis right away, she was a good sport and we had a good time. Our conversation was dynamic. When it was time to go, Amy had barely touched her cider, and she sneakily emptied her water bottle and poured the cider in. I appreciated that she cared about not wasting things, and it was questionably legal in a fun way, kind of "Bonnie and Clyde Lite." With a wink, she said we could share the cider at the dance event.

I couldn't keep up with her at salsa, and the "beginner's" lesson was way beyond my level. Even though I felt self-conscious because I couldn't shine on the dance floor, I gave it my all and did the best I could. Amy danced with me every few songs. The scene was great and I thought, "What a great way to meet people."

After a while, we decided to leave. It was beautiful out. I would have loved to go back to Amy's for a hot tub, but she didn't seem open to it. She suggested kissing, and I had one more chance to make an impression. I felt happy when I noticed the skip in Amy's step as she walked away.

We kept getting together about once a week. I was dating a little and busy with projects at home. I didn't think we had long-term potential. Amy traveled a lot and went to two Summer Camps. She was wild. I called her style "the ride."

I am kind of anxious, and I'm a homebody; I like to improve my home and work in my garden. My life was pretty simple, while Amy seemed to juggle twenty projects, including other lovers, which was all a lot for me. She had two dogs, one of them a puppy. Amy's world was big and busy, dancing every day, always buzzing around, excited about something new, with so many friends and so many different ways of making money. It was all fun, and I even got involved: we started writing *Brail's: The Hangover Musical,* about an iconic Eugene restaurant that has a famous hangover breakfast. We even did an interview with the owner, but due to some roadblocks, the project lost steam.

Her house and car felt chaotic to me, as though the bolts were all a little loose. She would barely sleep, waking up early and going to bed late, the exact opposite of me. I'm a pretty boring person: work, go to the gym, eat, sleep, repeat. But I loved all the things she did. I loved going to the Nia dance classes she led: she shined even brighter in her element, and I felt welcomed by her free-spirited, loving community of students. I started to get used to, and maybe even enjoy, the ride.

... to be continued ...

Date #78: Just Don't Make Me Eye Gaze *July 2018*

From his profile, Syd seemed "out of my league." Standing 6'4", he was model-gorgeous, highly intelligent, wild, polyamorous, and all-around impressive. On Tinder, he stated, "I'm wondering what kind of trouble I might be able to get myself into this summer in Middle-of-Nowhere, Oregon." At first, I suspected it was a fake profile.

Our initial messages were flirty. We video chatted right away; he was real and staying about an hour away from Eugene. I assumed we wouldn't ever meet in person, mostly because of his height, but when Syd gushed over my smallness, calling it "terrific and adorable," I yielded.

We were quickly sending texts, photos, and videos. Whenever I messaged, his response came fast and furious. He asked for more of my silly home project videos. I liked how using the time-lapse function made my construction and demolition projects—building my swinging bed, stacking firewood, or pruning a tree—seem more impressive. Almost every morning, I awoke to a sweet video of him welcoming me to the day. I felt excited, yet overwhelmed. He wanted to make the drive to visit me, to do intimate things like eye gazing, cuddling, and hand holding. But I don't eye gaze with just anyone!

Though I was authentically drawn to him, Syd's hunger pushed me away. I like to move towards people, to reach for them, to hope and long, at least a little. His desire created pressure and the expectation that I would need to set boundaries. We made plans a few times, but I kept canceling, nervous about in-person connection. Syd accepted my resistance spaciously, and masterfully, patiently quelled my fears. "We don't *have* to eye gaze," he joked.

When I mentioned my stress about the long drive, he said, "But I *love* to drive!" Syd seemed so BIG in his body, mind, and desire. When he suggested that we meet for breakfast in a few weeks, on his way back to California, I became excited. That was waaaaay less pressure than the original epic plan of dinner, cuddling, and the dreaded eye gazing! A casual breakfast on the road out of Dodge felt way better than moonlight walks and who knows what else.

We met at Hideaway Bakery *aaaand* ... he was gorgeous. With a lumberjack body, eyes that watered, and emotion that shook his voice, Syd spoke about things that were important to him. A polyamorous social studies teacher, he was passionate about relationships and education, and had recently quit his teaching job to become a lobbyist for educational reform.

On dates, I often had lots of distracting body symptoms and needed to stretch or reposition for comfort. But with Syd, I felt completely at ease, as if he were an old friend. Our conversation had the relaxed pace of a horse's canter. I was joyfully surprised at our kinship and similar idealism about polyamory. Syd had an expanded view of love and relationships, and he used the same lingo I had been learning in my self-educating polyamory pursuit: words like *metamour, compersion, primary partner, demisexual, and relationship anarchy.*

Why had I guarded myself from this exceptional human being? I was grateful that Syd had stayed amorous despite my walls. He had a long drive home, so we didn't linger; he playfully took my hand and led me to the edge of the parking lot, where he placed me on a big railroad tie so I would be closer to his chest than his belly. Up on my tiptoes on the ledge, I reached upwards and we shared a long, warm hug, my head on his heart. Then off we went, leftovers in hand; he, heading south and I, circling back to my life. When I looked at my phone, he had already texted:

Syd: I hope we'll try again next year!

I felt light and fluttery, and an effervescent rush passed through my core. Laughing out loud, I texted back:

Amy: I'll probably be open to some eye gazing by then. ;)

14

FROM CHEMISTRY TO CUDDLINGUS

Date #60, Warren Continued: Chemistry is Chemistry *Fall 2018*

In the fall of 2018, Warren asked if we could spend a day together. I missed him terribly, and texted back yes. But I wasn't sure how I wanted it to go. Although I felt nervous about spending extended time together, the idea of seeing him again was soothing.

When he arrived at my door, we were both awkward, like a first date, though our passionate and painful history surrounded us. I felt strange riding in his Honda again, heading towards the coast together like we used to. As the drive began, his leg was shaking and I felt his stress, which I assumed was from his desire to get back together. Warren's forlorn smiles, as he glanced sideways at me, tugged at my heart. We stopped to get coffee and he paid for mine, shyly leaning into me. My heart softened. Back in the car, listening to Hank Williams, I couldn't help opening back up to our magical chemistry, the matter-of-fact in-loveness between us.

We drove almost to the coast and up a windy mountain road to the lush Sweet Creek Falls trailhead. The pungent fir forest felt like a place of newness and beginnings. The trail went along a river, up to the falls. As we climbed, the true nature of our magnetic connection was undeniable. Warren reached for my hand, which slipped easily into his. He told me about *Sing, Unburied, Sing*, the book he'd been reading, stopping in his tracks to relate the poignant parts, looking straight into my eyes. Trembling, he recounted the heartbreaking narrative of hope and struggle, impossible love, prison, and addiction. We were the addicts. Everything between us hurt so beautifully.

At times, we stepped off the trail to walk on the flat rocks that lined the sides of the river, away from the other hikers. Pausing to find stillness, with the water rushing by, Warren pulled me into his arms. We buried our faces in each other's necks, finally smelling each other again. We kissed and laughed and cried and held each other. It was painful, and it was beautiful.

In the evening, on our drive back to town, we spoke about what might be between us, what we each wanted. He pleaded with me to "own my side," so we could continue. Karen felt that I didn't take responsibility for my part, and Warren had promised her that he wouldn't get back together with me unless I had "done my work." But I honestly didn't regret my behavior. When I asked him to clarify what they wanted me to own, he couldn't.

It was time to finally ask for what I wanted. I straightened up and stated some new boundaries. "I don't want to attempt to make nice with Karen anymore. If we're going to be in a box, I want it to be just about us. I don't want to talk about Karen on our dates anymore." I added that I didn't want to go back to our old, weekly date schedule, where the intensity of yoyo-ing from a fourteen-hour cosmic bond to a week of his silence was purgatory.

At my request, we started meeting once a month for an overnight date and met for a meal or a walk in the weeks between. I felt a shift in Warren. He was softer, more vulnerable, and maintained unprecedented contact with me during the in-between times, sending lots of loving texts, photos from his long walks, and poetic emails. Our new configuration took hold. After a few sweet months of reconnection, I wanted more, and was open to sleepovers twice a month. After a few more months, things between us felt better than ever, and we went back to our weekly overnight dates.

Date #79: Three Beautiful Pairs *September 2018*

I had known Zelda and Marco superficially for over a decade. Envious of their beautiful relationship, I'd always longed to know them. They were both musicians and often invited people over to play and sing around a campfire. Marco was a beloved middle school teacher and Zelda was like an adult Shirley Temple, with a headful of golden ringlets that gave her a girlish charm. She owned and managed a thriving vintage clothing shop.

One day in the spring, Marco messaged me to say that he had discovered—and binge-read—my entire dating blog. He said that he too was writing a lot, and we decided to co-edit each other's poetry online. We became instantly close, and I started calling him my "BFF."

We hadn't seen each other in person in many months. When Marco shared that he and Zelda were going through a rocky phase and that he was suffering, his poems amplified. After a few weeks, he invited me out for a drink, and we started spending quality time together. The lines between us blurred; ostensibly, we were "BFFs," but there was subtle flirtation, and we eventually admitted mutual curiosity about a potential romantic connection. We spoke openly and cautiously. The situation with Zelda and Marco was still unclear, so the ceiling of our physical intimacy was resting my head on his shoulder for a moment while we watched a movie at his house one afternoon.

Their marriage soon re-stabilized, and I didn't hear much from either of them for quite a while. We crossed paths a few times and were always warm, but I had a slight sadness; Marco and I had begun to bond and then quickly lost touch. I wondered how Zelda felt about us having become closer, and if he was pushing me away because she was jealous. I hoped not.

Then, in September, Zelda and I passed each other driving on West 18th in cinematic slow-motion. When we caught eyes, our faces linked up and expanded from their centers out. Zelda was bright and sunshiny beautiful. Her enormous smile was a great relief, since I had been worried about how she felt toward me. My phone started buzzing and buzzing and buzzing as she sent a flurry of texts, revealing with coy ebullience and much beating around the bush that she and Marco were *both* attracted to me. I felt flattered. We hinted at a get together, a time to "go deeper."

Later that day, Marco texted, acknowledging that Zelda had broken the ice. He said they were feeling giddy, hoping the three of us could get together soon. I felt attracted to both of them and was a big "yes" to this—but my mind went into overdrive. So many things have to be just right for *any* relationship to work: so many moving parts and moving hearts. To have chemistry with both people in a couple seemed highly improbable. *But not impossible!*

I wondered about their intentions and assumed that they were looking for a "unicorn." According to the Urban Dictionary, a unicorn is "a magical creature, usually female, who suddenly appears in a couple's bed." *Were they hoping I would join them for sex? A relationship?* I tried not to guess.

Soon, Zelda suggested we all go out to dinner, their treat. We decided on Barre Trattoria, a new Italian place in the Whit. I made the reservation, requesting a private-ish table, and they promised us a dimly lit corner. I felt nervous. *What would we talk about?* Long-term acquaintances suddenly becoming romantic potentials was a strange phenomenon.

Marco and Zelda each texted me separately about date logistics, and although I wondered why we didn't just have a group text, I fell in with their dual-stream flow. I bounced and bubbled along with their effusive enthusiasm.

As I approached the restaurant, I spotted them on the street corner, their hair and clothing billowing in the wind. The way they looked around together, expressively pointing, was like a scene from an old black and white movie. They spotted me and turned. My nervousness dissipated when I saw both their smiles directed at me.

The restaurant was warm and intimate. Sitting across from them, I felt special, chosen, novel. Their eyes danced over me. The often-awkward phase of ordering food flowed easily.

They had both been reading my blog and started by asking me lots of questions about my life. I loved the attention and obliged. *But, what about their intentions?* Eventually, I suggested that we speak more directly, about *us*. They smiled slowly at me and each other, nodding.

Zelda spoke first. She surprised me by boldly stating that she had no interest in a threesome. Instead, she wanted her own thing: a girlfriend or female lover for herself, separate from her marriage. Through her eyes and her words, Zelda kept reiterating that she was attracted to me. I realized that this date was about them wanting to set me up with Zelda! *Ah! Hence the separate texts.*

As she spoke, Marco's subtle smile was continuous. *If this was about me and Zelda, why was he flirting with me so blatantly in our texts?* She spoke more deeply about how she had always felt more attracted to women, but her desire had never manifested. As she spoke, I was lost in her sparkling green eyes.

Digesting Zelda's proposal, I wondered, *would my near-romance with Marco remain unexplored?* Our re-kindled flirtation in the recent flurry of texts had been exciting. Turning to Marco, I asked what he wanted. He started by speaking generally about feeling stifled and not knowing how to find a lover. The #MeToo era made him afraid to do anything that would be perceived as a transgression. Marco added that although he didn't usually feel comfortable being transparent about attractions, he felt very drawn to me, and I seemed perfect for him "in this situation." *Perfect for him? What "situation"?*

Trying to help me wrap my mind around it, Zelda said that they both wanted to date me separately. "It would look like me having a date with you on Wednesday and Marco having a date with you on Thursday!" They were proposing two separate relationships!

Zelda said she would be fine with us all having meals or watching movies, but she wasn't interested in sex together because the one threesome she had tried turned out terribly. *Hmm.* Marco and I both liked the idea of all of us being together, and I silently wondered if there might be a way that it would work for her. I'd only had one threesome, with Olive and Jaco, and our boundaries, fears, and desires conversation had made everything fun and easy. But I admired Zelda's boundary-setting, and once the concept finally settled in, I felt curious about, and open to, this "fork" experiment. I asked them to reach out whenever they were ready to schedule our next date or dates and dashed off to salsa dancing. Later that evening, I had texts from them both, inviting me to dinner at their house a few nights later.

Over the next weeks, the three of us enjoyed long dinners at their house a few times. Each time, I lingered late into the night because none of us wanted our enchanted dates to end. One night when we had been drinking, I decided to leave my car at their house. Zelda waited with me for the Uber in their driveway, and we had a sloppy, wine-soaked, midnight kiss.

After a handful of these dinners, we decided to watch a movie. Zelda messaged me all day about how anticipatory and nervous she was. "Should we sit on the couch? Make a bed on the floor? Who will be in the middle? What will we wear?" She seemed energized but had been clear about not wanting a threesome. *Why did she suggest this intimate "bed" configuration?*

I voted for the bed on the floor, and it was set up when I arrived. We watched *Professor Marston and the Wonder Women*. It was about an actual, racy, high profile, three-way relationship from the 1930's. I nestled between them for the entire movie. At one point, we hit pause so Zelda could go to the bathroom. While she was gone, Marco reached for me, rolled me towards him, and brought his lips to mine. When Zelda came back, he and I were still kissing, and I felt concerned. As she lay back down next to me, I rolled back towards her and asked, "How did it feel to see us kissing?" and with joyful relief she gleamed, "It was *fine!*" We were all excited that it didn't stimulate jealousy. Zelda looked up at me with blinking eyes and shyly asked, "Would you kiss me?" Her innocence cracked me open.

We looked at each other for a long moment, all smiles. Then we found our kiss. The moment our lips touched a wave of desire flushed through my core. Our smiling-while-kissing felt playful and right, and delight seemed to surround us. As we kissed, Marco spooned me, making cooing sounds. Eventually, we paused, and Zelda and I searched each other's eyes. I was silently recognizing the potential of a love relationship and swelled with warmth. Whereas I felt friendship and ease with Marco, in this moment I realized that with Zelda, deeper romance was possible.

It was hard to focus, but we continued to watch the movie, taking kissing breaks. Going from kissing him to kissing her was so sexy. I loved the feeling of our bodies all in contact, even as I was kissing the other one. *So much pleasure!* I had never before experienced anything like it and said that we were "three beautiful pairs." Naysayers—even polyamorous ones—had previously shunned my dream of a "solarium relationship" as overly idealistic.

Between our weekly group dinners, Marco and I would sometimes go out to a bar to shoot pool. It was fun and a little flirtatious. Zelda and I had a hard time scheduling one-on-one time, though I wanted to prioritize connecting with her, sexually and emotionally. Our relationship was more unknown, and I felt a stronger, more natural attraction with her than with Marco. Zelda enthusiastically encouraged me and Marco to spend time together, including sexual exploration. Her attitude was very free and light. One night, a few weeks in, of course with Zelda's knowledge, Marco invited me over while she was at work, and we planned, openly, to go beyond kissing. In a strange way, I felt like we should be sexual *for* Zelda, to help the system progress.

Marco and I touched awkwardly on the couch; chemistry-wise, our bodies didn't fit organically. I think he still enjoyed the novelty of being sexy with someone besides his wife, but our exploration felt forced, and uncomfortable. I didn't stay long.

The next day when I woke up, Marco texted. He apologized profusely and said that during our going-further date, Zelda had a completely unexpected emotional breakdown. She went into a spin, and they needed to pull back and reassess. He felt terrible. I was confused, but not terribly hurt. My parents' divorce prepared me for these kinds of unpredictable shifts.

Sadly, our relationships waned. Zelda initiated a walk once, about a month later, but said she didn't want to talk about anything personal. It felt strange to not address our situation—I'm not good at ignoring things and had no interest in a surfacey relationship. We stopped texting. When Zelda and I ran into each other at the store sometimes, the space between us was thick with confusion. A few times, Marco or I sent a head-scratching, rhetorical message asking, "What the heck happened?" Our three pairs had felt promising and beautiful, but the system fizzled as quickly as it formed.

Moving on, I continued to daydream about a solarium relationship.

Date #80: Perfect Tens? *November 2018*

Lars was married, and poly. His strong, square jawline and staring eyes gave him an intense-seeming presence, and I felt cautious. But once we started messaging on Tinder, I experienced him as gentle-spirited. Lars was willing to brave Marco Polo, and my heart leaned in during our video messaging. I looked forward to our scheduled date significantly more than most others, sensing potential with him.

We met for dinner on a Friday night, just before my weekly salsa class. Dressed in a tight pink and black ruffled dress I rarely wore, I looked like a five-year-old. It had dropped off the hanger when I was wondering what to wear, and I couldn't say no to the jumping-dress kismet.

I was in line when Lars entered the Bier Stein. We caught eyes from across the room and his radiant smile spread across the restaurant. As he approached enthusiastically, I blurted out, "I love your smile!" We hugged eagerly. He was gorgeous, with a big body and a big head, dark hair parted to the side, and piercing, blue eyes. The space around us was bright and sweet. *Who cares if he's tall?* I felt surprisingly attracted.

At the counter, I ordered the grilled chicken ciabatta with pesto and garlic aioli, and a local raspberry cider on tap. Lars chose a spinach salad with pears, spiced pecans, and bleu cheese, and a stout to drink. He insisted on paying. We found a spot in the middle of an ocean of tables. My excitement about this beautiful, brilliant man increased steadily over the hour. I loved how he leaned towards me and tilted his head slightly as though sharing a secret. He reached over to my plate and grabbed some fries without asking. We felt playfully at home, loving every minute.

At one point he told me about being abducted, including details about being on the alien spaceship and a summary of the lecture he heard from its telepathic alien leader. He spoke with conviction about the experience. Who was I to judge? *I love aliens!* Lars just kept getting cuter and was obviously enjoying our time together. Once when I tried to speak, my words twisted up. I said, "It's so interesting that when I'm attracted to someone, I'm suddenly not as grounded as usual."

Between mouthfuls, he said: "There's a word for that."

"There is?" I smiled.

His big, trickstery eyes looked straight at me. "Yeah. *Normal!*"

We laughed. I was beaming uncontrollably, but before long, I had to run to my dance class. As we were bussing our table, I hastily gave him the rundown of my other lovers, their other lovers, and my STI status. With glittering eyes, he joked, "Whoa! Slow down, sexy!"

I countered, "Hey, we still have ten minutes! Where's your car?" Flirting about having a quickie at the end of our first date, so open about our desire, felt wonderfully wild. When my best friend, Jess, texted to see how the date was going, Lars and I posed and sent her a series of selfies we took together. My pheromones radiated in every direction.

He said, "Let's at least kiss." I stepped up onto a curb and he came close to me. Our kisses were playful and passionate. We were both smiling hugely. *This was a dating delicacy!*

After salsa, I checked my phone and had a "Call me!" message from him. We talked on the phone for two hours. He was a prolific poet. I swooned. We talked about our nighttime dreams and planned our next meeting.

Over the next three days, we traded many video messages. At night, we indulged in long, yummy, deep phone calls. Lars was smart, funny, and irreverent. He sent me a batch of his poems. I was blown away and dreamed about us weaving our poems into a book.

During one late-night conversation, Lars told me that after he liked me on Tinder, he had a numinous vision of my face hanging in the dreamy air. When he told me that he sensed we were destined to be together, a chill rushed up my spine. Suddenly mutually afloat in oceanic love feelings, for three days we were in near-constant touch through many different apps. I walked around smiling out of every cell, like a cartoon teenager with hearts circling around my head.

Lars teased that we were doing a little *too much* smiling, that there was a little *too much* happiness going on. He joked and made up "frown therapy" for us, to balance things out. I hadn't felt this swept-away feeling since Soren the Wizard—except with Lars it was mutual. I asked for his birth info and plugged it into my astrology app, Time Passages. I often check for astrological compatibility, and ours was extreme. When I texted this image to him, a spiritual silence enveloped us. It was shocking. I wondered, *could our relationship be too big?* I had never seen this before:

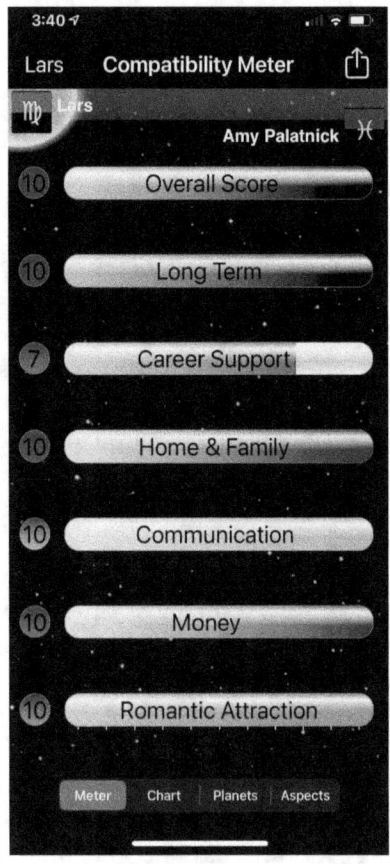

Screenshot from TimePassages® Astrology App (created by Astrograph.com)

Tens, almost across the board! Lars was clear from the beginning that he and Darcy were happily married. He said that she was "more gay than straight," and that he was an anomaly for her. I asked, hopefully, if they were dating together as a couple. Unfortunately, they were dating separately.

He spoke about Darcy with reverence and adoration and called her his "queen." I found her on Facebook and clicked through ten years of her pictures. This woman had a deep feminist strength: a different hair style and color in each picture and multiple tattoos and piercings. Her poses accentuated her badass power. I wistfully looked through the album of their creative wedding ceremony, seven years ago. I felt jealous, and for the first time, I longed for my own fun wedding.

Even though it felt unmistakably like we were falling in love, I was hesitant. It was all very fast, and cosmic, and over-the-top. Also, I was wary because of the difficulties with Warren. Nothing had ever been easy between Karen and me. I would need to have a much different relationship with Lars's wife.

I curbed my impulse to message her and sent Lars a video message to make sure reaching out was appropriate. He responded a few minutes later; his eyes darted around. My stomach contracted from his vocal wobble. Darcy didn't want to get involved. She wanted us to have a good relationship, but she didn't want to meet me or communicate with me. *Oh, no!*

Lars sounded dry and far away. I crumpled inside. Something didn't add up: *why would his happily married, more gay than straight, polyamorous wife not want to know me?*

An ominous feeling gripped me. The "in love" sensation between us was gone. How could I have felt so yummy and sparkly minutes ago, and now, nothing? Desperate to have that special feeling return, I messaged him about it, but he said he didn't think anything was wrong. He was hollow; I couldn't reach him. I was in a *Twilight Zone* episode. The sacred emotional gate between us had closed.

Was I making it up? I tried to steer myself back to the happy place but was overwhelmed with doubt. *Maybe there would be struggles. Maybe I wouldn't be welcome. Maybe I wasn't good enough for him.* "Maybe, maybe, maybe," tumbled like way too much dirty laundry inside me. I tried several times to address my fears with Lars, but he was mostly unresponsive, and I started to feel like I was annoying him.

I went to my friends, my dreams, tarot. I went to Joanne for guidance. She looked up at the sky, swayed slowly, and said, "You and Lars could fall in love many times. The purpose of your connection is to show each other the contours of your souls' growth." That sounded beautiful, but elusive. Then she gravely stated, "Lars's marriage is just about over."

"Oh, no," I assured her, "they are deeply in love. He calls her his 'queen.'"

Tapped in to a different awareness, Joanne said, "Well, that's not how it looks."

On our second date, Lars came to pick me up and asked, "Would you like to go upstairs and lay down naked with me?" We went up to my room. He had long, sensitive fingers, but it often seemed like he was doing "moves." He clearly wanted to please me, in a near-studious way, but he wasn't tuned into my body, and I was too overwhelmed to communicate clearly. He felt far away. After he touched me awhile, we had intercourse, but like a glaze that doesn't fit a clay body perfectly, we were not bonding.

We went out for dinner and then back to my house where he kicked back on my couch, a comfortable stranger, and drank a liter of wine. I didn't bring up the odd feeling and felt relieved when he left. Afterwards, I sent a video message asking him to *please* tell me honestly how he was feeling about our connection. His message back said, "I don't question things that seem evident to me. It's obvious that we click. I think you should soak it up and bask in the sunlight of my affection for you." The words were poetic, but seemed far away. Within a week we "fell in love," had sex, and drifted. Since he still supposedly felt something, I stuck with it, hoping the sweetness might return.

I think the hardest thing for people to say—myself included—is that we feel hurt. I had been training over the last year to simply say "I feel hurt" as soon as I recognized it. When Lars texted to invite me out to a movie for our third date, I was offended that he would suggest something so shallow. Watching a movie seemed like something bored couples did. To me, the message was that he didn't want to spend the precious time digging hungrily into each other's souls.

I made myself call him on FaceTime, and looking into his eyes, I said I was upset. Lars apologized, and laughing in a sweet, maybe patronizing way, he said he loved movies and was just trying to offer a fun suggestion. Instead, we went to a delicious Indian buffet, but when we returned to my house, we had mediocre sex again. I felt empty, zombie-like.

Next, Lars invited me to his house, out in the woods. Their home was artsy and warm, and he said that Darcy finger-shakingly told him to clean it up for me before our date, and to change the sheets. She was away, and she was apparently happy to have me there. I liked looking at her jewelry and body products; I felt curious about this "queen." I thought about her a lot when Lars and I were having our strange sex.

Driving away the next morning, I was filled with *we shouldn't keep meeting up*. Our mythic-level, high romance beginning had completely clouded over with a dry, distant feeling. I didn't feel settled when I was with him. My astrology app only reads potential, not actuality.

We barely messaged the next week, and I felt relieved. Then, he stopped by briefly one day, seeming scattered, and let me know that "things were complicated" and that he needed to pause our connection. Standing in my doorway, he said he'd get back in touch soon. We had a businesslike hug goodbye.

A month later, he texted, crushed and falling apart because Darcy had asked for a divorce. I was shocked. His marriage was crumbling and he didn't know it. Our disconnect was part of a bigger disconnect.

He apologized for being flaky and said that he was leaving town to go on a shapeless spiritual quest. I was relieved for the chapter's ending. Our juice went sour as it was being poured.

We stayed connected through social media. Lars eventually moved back to Eugene with a new girlfriend. Sometimes he and I send each other short messages. Between us remains a funny bone memory about our short, strange trip.

Date #77, Amir Continued: The Boyfriend Proposal *Winter 2019*

As fall turned to winter, Amir and I started spending more time together. He met me in downtown Eugene for Halloween. He was dressed as a "pizza ninja," wearing a hilarious and adorable tight, black, hooded onesie with a pizza slice print. *Crazy guy.* We went for drinks and tapas at the fun, new spot, Party Bar. Then, the next month, I felt happy to be his date at the annual "Friendsgiving" he held at his house, where I really enjoyed his friends.

We had a special date on New Year's Eve. I invited Amir to a soft rock concert. (I knew all of the words to Journey and Air Supply; he knew none.) Some of my heavy hitters were there: first he met Karen, Warren, and Olive. Then, one of my best friends from college stopped in briefly. Marty, an ex-partner of mine, was the DJ, and at one point, he pulled Amir and me onto the dance floor and the three of us danced to "Got To Give it Up" by Marvin Gaye.

One day as we sat together in his kitchen, Amir spoke pensively, "Maybe this *is* the right connection for me." I didn't let myself grab onto his words, but secretly prayed they would marinate. We spoke more openly about our feelings and fears. Once we acknowledged the temporary nature of our relationship—due to my polyamory and his monogamy—it became precious. We were soaking up our time together.

We started pausing as we kissed, with our faces close, and held languorous eye contact. When we lay down to cuddle on a sofa or bed, we synchronized our breathing. Amir said I was the first person to ever breathe with him.

We even started saying "I love you," though I wasn't sure what the words meant to him. My heart was cracking open: capital L-Love was matter-of-factly hanging in the space between us. *What could we be?* One January day, I told him vulnerably that given the chance, I would spend more time with him. "We can talk about that," he mumbled, deflecting. Slightly hurt, I also trusted: whatever was meant to be, would be.

After several years and so many dates, so many near-misses and so few potential partners, I had a fresh appreciation for true love potential; I didn't treat it nearly as lightly as I had when I was younger and a new relationship always seemed to be around every corner. Realizing I was falling in love with Amir, I felt an impulse to make it official. On a blustery February day, I walked the loop at the dog park and dreamed romantically about my developing closeness with Amir. I took a breath and called him. I asked, "Can we talk about our connection? Lately I feel like something is different."

"Yes, we've definitely been getting closer."

"I feel shy about this, but I wonder how you would feel about calling ourselves boyfriend and girlfriend?"

After a pause, Amir responded, "Boyfriend? Uh ... what would that mean?"

"That we are committed in some way?"

Amir took an audible breath. "I don't want to hurt you, and I really love all the time we spend together. But I have to admit that I'm still going out to events, hoping to meet 'the one.' I'm just not sure what that would mean for me to be your boyfriend. I'm sorry."

Crushed, shut down, and heavy, I hung up. *Why had I let my heart get wrapped up in him?* That week, every morning, I did a tarot reading for myself using the Osho Zen Tarot deck. I kept drawing the same card: "Sorrow." The word cut me. *Why sorrow?* Trusting the card, I carved out time to explore sorrow through art, which evoked many tears. I had always avoided sorrow. To reckon with it, I knew that I had to face intimacy. My emotional struggle with Amir triggered this memory:

When I was ten years old, my parents divorced, and my world turned upside down. On my darkest night, I lay in bed alone at my grandparents' house, screaming. *There were so many adults downstairs. Didn't anyone hear my cries?* Realizing I could not trust anyone, I made a big girl decision to never again bond my heart to another person. The inevitable separation was too much suffering to bear. In my mind, I saw a little black box where I could lock up whatever damage and feelings I had at the time. I vowed to go through life emotionally alone, to never need anyone.

The power of connection I had known before that moment was doomed to a silent eternity inside the box. It was finally time to challenge my ten-year-old self and break the vow. I wanted to be able to bond with someone. Intimacy was worth the risk of getting hurt.

Instead of shutting down to protect myself from Amir's rejection, I resolved to stay open and vulnerable.

After a few quiet days, Amir invited me over to talk. We sat close together on his kitchen stools, holding hands, facing each other. Looking into my eyes, he seemed serious when he said, "I need you to know that you are my favorite person on the planet, the person I trust more than anyone. I think about our relationship all the time." I let Amir's words into my heart, and they comforted me, but I wondered, *if I was so important to him, why didn't he want to be my boyfriend?* He mumbled something about his family. There were mysteries about Amir that I didn't understand.

> *Amir's Perspective*
>
> I was holding back from the very beginning because of Amy's non-monogamy. It wasn't that it took time to fall in love with Amy; I had a wall up against letting her in. Her style and everything she did went against all I had imagined in a potential partner. I had been conditioned to find a committed, monogamous relationship. I didn't see long term potential. When we hit the six-month mark, I worried about misleading her. We always had such a good time together, but I couldn't see it working out long term, and I wasn't as forthcoming about my misgivings as I could have been. I wished I could be as open as her, but I have always been a jealous person.
>
> *... to be continued ...*

Date #81: From Baby to Babe *February 2019*

I had known Jamari since he was in diapers. He was a little older than my daughter, and they were in the same playgroup circles. Jamari would always look up at me with his round face and huge, angelic eyes that conveyed *so much love*. He was a sweetheart. As far back as his toddler days, his adoration of me was palpable; his parents remarked on it too.

The kids went to different schools and I didn't see Jamari for several years. One day he knocked on my door. *Fifteen years old, and much taller than me!* Jamari leaned against my doorway, nervous but dreamy-eyed, shifting around and stumbling over his words. His big, pleading eyes were rounder and softer than before. Looking at the floor, he said, "I've been thinking about you a lot lately." I felt nervous and was bracing myself, quickly strategizing. In his strangely deep voice, Jamari said "Football's got me feeling all sore. I was just wondering, do you give massages?"

I told him that I didn't, but that I had friends who were professional massage therapists and I could refer him to them. Jamari bravely and innocently responded that he really was hoping to get a massage from *me*. His childhood crush had matured. And so had he! It was cute, awkward, and very strange. Feeling uncomfortable, I explained that it didn't feel right to do that, but that he should really call one of my friends. Immediately, I texted him a few numbers.

When Jamari was nineteen, he stopped by to let me know that he had moved in with some friends just a block away and asked if we could go for a walk. As we walked through the woods near my house, he told me that he had his first girlfriend and wanted some relationship advice. His sticky eye contact seemed full of attraction. I kept envisioning us running into his parents, and felt a little uncomfortable.

We started to see each other regularly around the neighborhood. He was often outside, working on his car or shooting hoops, and would wave excitedly when he saw me. I would sometimes stop to briefly say hi. His crush was obvious, flattering, and sweet.

Jamari became my always-eager, go-to helper for everything from house projects to taking care of my animals when I traveled.

Our hello and goodbye hugs were extra-long—he wouldn't let go. His hints were transparent. And, I couldn't deny that he was becoming extremely attractive. I had always been matter-of-factly closed to his flirtation. Our connection was multi-layered: we were like family, but now there was a sexual or romantic interest on his part. Jamari's angelic nature and youth made his pursuit seem innocent. I appreciated it for what it was, and let it be.

When he was twenty-one, after helping me set up a swinging bed in my backyard, he stopped me in a narrow walkway for one of our usual ambiguous, long goodbyes. Trapped there, I knew it was time to finally address the elephant:

Amy: Thanks for your help today.

Jamari: You know you're my girl. I'd do anything for my girl.

Amy: Maybe we should talk about our relationship.

Jamari: Really? I'd love that!

Amy: I always feel like you want something, that there is something unspoken.

Jamari: Well, yeah! You're my fantasy girl!

Amy: Oh my gosh. Really?

Jamari: Didn't you know that?

Amy: Maybe I did. I don't know. Oh gosh, it feels complicated.

Jamari: It doesn't have to be complicated. It would be amazing just to cuddle with you. That would be my dream come true.

I thought about it. *Maybe it would be OK.* This was all virgin territory, and a potential minefield, but I had recently begun my training with Vaughn, and wondered if Jamari and I might be able to have a therapeutic, mentor-type connection. We made a plan for a short "cuddle date" in the new swinging bed the next evening.

As soon as we lay down—wow, things *really* started swinging. Testosterone was bursting out of his pores, splashing all over me. "Cuddling," ha! Jamari was all over me, asking "Can I touch your ass," "Can I rub on you?" He climbed on top of me and said, "Can you feel how hard you're making me?"

Fantasy exists in the past or the future, inside someone's head. It's never real. I wanted to be Jamari's wise sexual elder, but he was in a fantasy, not *here,* with *me.* Struggling to stay centered, I needed to stop his fast-moving train.

"Jamari, wait. STOP." I put an end to the "cuddling" and sent him home. When he messaged that night, apologizing, I said that I was open to us having formal, sitting in chairs, coaching sessions where we could focus on his sexual development and growth. He didn't respond. I suggested meeting at a restaurant, and we made plans to go out twice, but he canceled both times. Just like the massage I suggested from one of my friends, that wasn't what he wanted.

The next two years, the few times we saw each other, his waves and hugs were even bigger. He messaged once in a while to tell me I was beautiful, and that I would always be "his girl."

When he was twenty-three, we spoke on the street one day and he seemed different: relaxed and mature. He texted afterwards to say how nice it was to see me again and asked if we could get together.

Jamari: It would be nice to go over there right now and cuddle.

Amy: I am really touched by that, and maybe sometime we could try something in the PG realm. Let's have a meal sometime. I would want to talk a little first, before we engaged physically, even just cuddling.

Jamari: OK, what kind of food do u like?

Amy: How about Angkor Cafe, that Cambodian place near 18th and Chambers? Wednesday?

Jamari: I don't have anything planned. Or you could go to a Halloween party with me on Thursday.

Amy: Ha ha, no. I would go dancing with you sometime, though.

Jamari: You can be my MILF.

Amy: I am NOT going as your MILF!!!! LOL, that is hilarious.

Jamari: Ha ha OK fine. u would get hit on so much.

We didn't go out that week, but Jamari surprised me the following week when he accepted my invitation to come to the Tuesday night bachata lesson. I swung by and picked him up. It was fun! I liked the feeling of our bodies as we danced. He was warm and sensitive; we moved well together. After that, his late-night messages came nightly, and I enjoyed our flirty chatting.

One day in February, my car died in my driveway. I messaged Jamari to see if he could help me jump it. He happened to be across town but dropped whatever he was doing and dashed over with a battery pack. While the car was charging, he asked for some water. We went into my kitchen. He asked for a hug.

Then he asked if it was OK that he was kissing my neck.

It was. Our lips met effortlessly. I held on tight, because it felt so good, and just right ... except for *everything*. Our age difference, the fact that I had known him all of his life. His parents. My daughter.

It took some effort to not think about all that, but our kissing was undeniably delicious. I was surprised to feel comfort as he pulled me into his warm, strong body. Jamari caressed me as we kissed, rubbing my shoulders and running his fingers gently through my hair. *So sensual and affectionate.* He smelled so clean and was maybe wearing a light cologne that actually smelled good to me. I thought, *Jamari, of all people. Cute little three-year old crushy Jamari with those big, round eyes*. And now suddenly we were twenty-three and forty-nine, kissing in my kitchen. He offered to give me a massage, and I smiled and said, "Maybe next time." From our past, I knew that we needed to move slowly.

As Jamari was leaving, he asked, "Why are you afraid to love on me?" It was a good question. Over the next week, I considered: What *was* I afraid of? The more I let myself feel open to it, the more special our connection felt. *Was Jamari a lover from a past life?* I imagined him in the future, at my age, and thought, *what an amazing man he will be.*

After that kiss, my hormones and heart were activated and wanting more. But I felt ashamed. Up until then, I had felt closed to connecting with him sexually. I knew his parents—not well, but we were still friendly. *Would they find out? What would they think?* I decided that they didn't need to know—it wasn't like we were cheating on anyone. *How many people tell their parents the details of their sex life?* For my own conscience, if I framed our relationship as therapeutic, keeping it confidential felt OK.

Amir and Warren were both supportive—excited, even—about my connection with Jamari. Amir said he wished he'd had that opportunity when he was in his early twenties, and he agreed that in an ideal world, teenagers would be ushered into sexuality with someone safe who could respectfully teach them. Jamari and I messaged almost every night.

Jamari: I don't want to get married to someone else before we cuddle. UR on my bucket list

Amy: What exactly do you mean by "cuddle"? Is that a euphemism for having sex? Or is cuddling really the bucket list item?

Jamari: Oh no. Just cuddling

Amy: Mm-hmm.

Jamari: I like to take things slow. I promise, I would be slower this time.

Amy: OK, if you can control yourself, we can do that sometime. I think it would be nice.

Jamari: I know it can't be permanent but we can have fun while we can

Amy: We permanently have a special connection.

Jamari: Yes! UR so sexy

Amy: Ha ha. Thank you.

Jamari: U get my hormones going. U make the boys go crazy.

Amy: Ha ha! Cuddling hormones? 😂😂😂
How old were you when you realized you had a crush on me?

Jamari: 😊 When I was younger, maybe fourteen, I saw you kissing your ex and it was sexy seeing you with another girl. And then I started to notice your curvy body and how loving you were to me. I fantasized about coming over shirtless and having you rub me.

Amy: Blush! I don't know if I could be sexual with you, but I want to find something that feels right between us. I have to move very slowly and be 100% clear about everything, with a lot of awareness.

Jamari: Oh I would be aware.

Amy: Ha ha, not that kind of aware.

Jamari: I know u worry that I might lose control again.

Amy: My role with you feels tender and I need to be very responsible with it, to protect you and to take care of myself.

Jamari: Just don't be afraid to love on me 😊

Amy: OK, I'll try!

Jamari: Would u like it if I picked u up? Would you put ur legs around me?

Amy: Yes, I would like that but I would be conflicted.

Jamari: Because u think I'm going to fall in love with u?

Amy: No, you can feel however you want about me, that is fine.

Jamari: Oh, ok. So you love me?

Amy: Yes, of course.

Jamari: Like romantic love?

Amy: No, I don't know what to call it. I've always felt a unique bond and big warmth between us.

Jamari: Then what's holding you back from loving on me?

Amy: Now that you are older, there is a confusion because I do feel an attraction.

Jamari: Wouldn't you regret not connecting sexually before it's too late?

Amy: I thought you only wanted to cuddle LOL 😂😂😂

Like a horny teenager, I looked for Jamari when I drove past his house, hoping to run into him. I felt excited when he messaged and tingly when I thought about him. After a week of nightly texting, he came over and up to my bedroom. We made out on the bed and touched each other outside of our clothing. I liked the slow pace.
"You're shaking," I said.
"I'm excited, but I'm trying to go slow for you. This has been my fantasy for so long."

"What did you imagine? What was your fantasy?"

"You kissing me all over my chest," Jamari said.

I took his basketball jersey off. He moaned. Smiling wide, his eyes rolled away as he flopped backwards onto my bed. His bare chest was broad and muscular, but baby-soft and hairless. Jamari was the exact combination of child and man. I put my head to his chest and lay there for a moment, listening to his heart. He smelled so good. I took my time as I kissed my way across his chest, riding the contours with my lips, making sure to cover the whole landscape, spending extra time gently kissing his large, soft nipples. He groaned and shook and thanked me.

Then he asked if he could touch me, and I said yes, but that I wanted to leave my clothes on. He was worked up and started rubbing the crotch of my pants hard and fast, porn-style. I physically recoiled and was surprised and relieved when he asked me if I liked the way he was touching me. I said that especially at the beginning, I need gentleness and connection. I offered to show him how I like to be touched the next time, but for now, he could just experiment and I would tell him if there was anything that I didn't like. He slowed down and, like a gentleman, kept asking me how I felt.

The quality of his touch changed completely, from *doing* to *listening*. I liked how he was touching me, and told him so. He was getting super turned on and said that he wanted to have an orgasm with me. He asked if I would touch his penis. I told him, "I'm not sure. Maybe." From our first cuddle date a couple years ago, I knew that he could be pushy, and that it was important to establish boundaries between us. But the next thing I knew, he had wriggled out of his shorts. There was his twenty-three-year-old hard-on, right in front of me. *What were my options?* I saw two: pull his clothes back on, or move forward. I made the *carpe diem* decision to give him an erotic massage.

I was happy to touch him that way: a lingam massage is worlds different from a handjob (lingam is the Sanskrit word for penis, which translates to "wand of light"). I knew about thirty different moves, many of which could be paired for maximum effect. In erotic massage, orgasm isn't the focus. Sexual touch is spread out to connect the rest of the body, and a variety of sensations from using different strokes and techniques creates a much different experience than the single-motion, classic "jerking off."

Jamari said, "I've never even thought about touch like this." As I was doing a stroke called "twist and shout," his eyes were closed and he said, "I have no idea what's going on. Are you using your mouth?" I wasn't. And when he eventually came, he was disoriented and didn't know it was happening. I cleaned him up with a towel, and he lay silent for a few minutes, shaking and squeezing my hand while I sat next to him. Then I lay down with him, we talked sweetly for a while, and off he went. I felt deeply satisfied.

After that experience, our connection was more natural. He didn't message me immediately afterwards, and I was relieved that he didn't press for more every day. Because he wasn't obsessive, we continued easily. I imagined teaching him how to touch me, how to communicate about his desires, and about boundaries and consent.

When I went to Wesleyan for college, I decided to take private guitar lessons and developed a long-term crush on Garrett, a music professor my parents' age. The first time we met in his office on campus, I asked about an instrument that was hanging on his wall. Shyly, he took down the dulcimer and began to pluck it. Hauntingly beautiful sounds filled the space, evoking uncontrollable tears from a place deep in me. He was so kind, and kept playing, smiling softly, even as my emotions ran freely.

Garrett was bright, spunky, handsome, manic, short, and from the South. During my years as a student, we would meet for breakfast or coffee from time to time, as friends. I fantasized about more. My roommates made fun of me, saying the crush was all in my head.

One day when I was 21, we had one of our special meals and realized that we were both heading home that evening: me to New Jersey and Garrett to Manhattan. He had been planning on taking the train, and when I excitedly offered a ride, he gratefully accepted.

Our two-hour car ride was filled with exuberant conversation, and when we arrived in Manhattan, he invited me up for wine and Chinese food. I couldn't believe it. He rushed around singing while pouring wine and shaking the take-out onto plates. Then, he sat by my side on the sofa, inched towards me, and ... put his hand on my thigh! *Garrett was coming on to me!* My heart raced. His bed loomed; I could see it from where I was sitting. *Would we have sex?* I felt scared. After years of dreaming, at the threshold of intimacy, I ran. I said "I need to go." He asked to walk me to my car, and there, on the bustling New York City sidewalk, he took me in his arms, dipped me backwards, and planted the most romantic, old-fashioned kiss on my lips. That was the one and only time we were physical. We have stayed connected and continue to flirt, even to this day.

∽

With Jamari, I worried that making the fantasy real might change things for him. I felt sensitive that my age might suddenly seem not sexy, or even repulsive. A few days later when we were texting, I asked how he felt about my being so much older after being physical. He said, "You are like fine wine." That worked for me!

Our second time together was a week later. Sitting together on my bed, I invited him to talk about our boundaries, fears, and desires. I was surprised when he said, "My only boundary is that I don't want to have intercourse."

"That's great!" I responded, "Why?"

"I haven't had sex in four years, since my first girlfriend. After that, I decided I want to wait for the person I'm going to marry. I know I'm weirdly old-fashioned."

"It's very sweet" I said, full of relief. I felt so much fondness for Jamari and was grateful for his boundary. Our physical connection became lighter and easier. Over the next months, he would message late at night to see what I was doing, and I sometimes invited him over. We mostly rolled around, kissed, and talked, and we both loved it when I touched his penis. To teach him how to touch me, I gave him my favorite tip, which I had recently learned from an article written by a man:

> "Touch a woman's genitals with the same fine-tuned sensitivity you would need to feel the individual ridges of your own fingerprints."

Once I taught this to Jamari, combined with going slowly, and paying attention to my signals, he didn't need any more direction. Jamari's fresh, clean smell made our physical connection feel innocent. Our times together usually started by him offering me a massage. I loved his gentle touch, and always said yes.

But I never had an orgasm with him. To his disappointment, I didn't feel comfortable having him go down on me. I enjoyed giving him oral sex, where I felt more in control. When he was getting close to orgasm, he would usually ask me to slow down or stop moving, to delay it. I loved that he savored the experience.

One spring day, he biked past my house while I was in my driveway. When he saw me, he pulled over, dropped his bike, picked me up, and carried me into my bathroom. He placed me in front of the sink and stood behind me, both of us fully clothed. Pressing his erection into me from behind and making eye contact through the mirror, he said, "Why am I so attracted to you?" I felt happy.

Most of our times together were less about my teaching him and more about our sweet, mutual connection. A few months after our exploration began, I started spending much more time with Amir, and Jamari and I transitioned into a forever-warm, flirtatious friendship.

15

THE EXQUISITE ORDER OF THE UNIVERSE

Date #77, Amir Continued: Cuddlingus *Spring-Summer 2019*

In March, Amir returned from a trip to visit his family in California. He called me, feeling down, and asked, "Could you come over? There's a lot I want to talk about." That special day, we lay in bed together for eight hours. He explained that he had been poring over our connection. His fears were about his family: he knew they wouldn't accept me. I was too old to have babies, polyamorous, and not Persian. Despite his anxiety, this conversation created a deep calm in me. *He was considering our relationship, seriously.* I didn't have any solutions but was so happy to be in such an intimate, soothing space with him. Something shifted and he was able to be fully present with me. We held each other all day, whispering and crying.

As we lay in our cocoon, he said that he did want to be my boyfriend. Since he had wavered at my proposal just a month ago, I didn't let myself fully believe him. Yet we started spending four or five nights a week together, though it seemed a bit sudden and slightly forced. He asked for his own drawer in my dresser.

Amir loved cuddling. We would lie down in "power spots." Nestling into his warm sweater was like nothing I had ever experienced before. As soon as we made contact, the whole world went soft, and Amir would often whisper, "This is my medicine." We breathed together naturally, evoking a deep, sensual trance. Sometimes we drifted and napped. As I tapped into the energy between us, many ecstatic kundalini jolts spontaneously shocked through my core. Our cuddling was so good, Amir named it "cuddlingus."

(These body jolts had been happening to me ever since a larger, bubbly woman at Summer Camp West made a big impression on me. I often saw her in extended, euphoric-looking hugs with one of many men. Each time, her body convulsed stochastically from sexual energy. Just from seeing that, the same shocks began to move through me whenever I tuned into my sexuality while I was body to body with Warren, and now, Amir.)

One night, Amir invited me over and asked me to sit down. He was moving around bouncily with his hands behind his back. Clearly excited, he said "Close your eyes and hold out your hands," and put something small in my hands. "OK, you can open your eyes." My favorite lip balm! Then we did it again: a charcoal face mask! The gift game continued, with a fancy bar of chocolate, expensive wine, and massage oil. I felt so happy, being showered with gifts. Then Amir's whole face expanded as he said, "I want to have a girls' night with you!" He had cued up a cheesy romantic comedy for us to watch: *Love, Actually*. Amir was a keeper.

As we indulged, an old structure inside me started shifting. In my serial monogamy relationships, I never fully attached to my partners. Once a relationship stopped thriving, I followed my one-foot-out-the-door and moved on. Polyamory ironically challenged me to bond and commit to working through issues when they arose. The gift of polyamory was that a relationship never trapped or owned me.

In my years-long "menifestation" quest, I was hoping to find both a lover and a partner. Amir and I enjoyed spending time together, and we had special chemistry. *Could I truly bond with Amir? Was he the partner I was waiting for?* I felt inspired but afraid as I spelunked towards the unjaded part of me.

Amir's Perspective

When Amy and I had been dating for about eight months, and had started to spend more time together, I went home to visit my family and celebrate the Persian New Year which starts the first day of spring. I felt stressed about the whole thing. I knew they wouldn't accept her: she wasn't from our culture, and she was older than me. My parents have always been on my case to marry and have babies with a young Persian princess, even though that was never what I wanted. Since my divorce five years ago, I spoke with my parents on the phone nearly every day and they always asked about my love life. My family had never truly accepted any of my American girlfriends in the past, including my ex-wife. Most of my exes had been hurt in some way by them, and I didn't want the same thing to happen to Amy.

After a long weekend with my family, I arrived back to Eugene in crisis. I couldn't help having big feelings for Amy as we spent more time together. I realized that my familial socialization was holding me back. I could tell Amy was getting hurt from the block I had constructed. So I decided to build a relationship with her that was completely separate from my family. I was OK with them knowing about each other but didn't want them to meet.

By the time summer came, Amy and I were getting closer, but we still had rocky patches. There was sensitivity around our sexual relationship in general. I couldn't always understand what she wanted. But we also experimented and went into fun, new territory. One time, we tried to go to a big sex party out of town. We got all dressed up, with lots of nervous, excited anticipation. But the event was like the Walmart of sex parties: not a single sexy feeling in that whole brightly fluorescent-lit dungeon. It was awful, but kind of hilarious and relieving in the end that it was so un-sexy.

The first time Amy and I got together for a drink with Warren, she was completely in heaven, bursting with happiness. Warren is a good guy; I really like him, but I have to admit I was glad to be the one that got to go home with her at the end of the date.

In the summer, Amy wanted me to come with her to a day-long pelvic massage workshop, and I had a lot of anxiety around it. I kept imagining how I would feel being naked in a room full of other naked people. The whole week before the workshop, I lay awake at night obsessing about it. I wanted to go, but the idea of it also freaked me out. In the end, I went, both for myself and because it was important to Amy. Even though there were great things about it, I got confused and hurt by the end of the workshop. I was struggling to just be present, and Amy took it personally, feeling like I wasn't able to connect with her. I felt terrible.

Pretty soon after that, Amy went to Europe and when she was gone, I shut down and we almost broke up. Maybe I was still questioning if it was really right between us.

... to be continued ...

Date #82: A Tantric Dream *November 2019*

I met Noah one day when he unexpectedly stopped by Samantha's house while she and I were having tea. When he walked in, a great calm came over the room. He had rich dark skin, was dressed like a monk, and wore Tibetan prayer beads. Noah smelled familiar, and sexual, with hints of amber resin. He sat down with us and told soulful stories. I imagined he had been traveling the world immersing himself in esoteric experiences.

When he started to leave, I reclined and dramatically leaned my head on the sofa's arm. Batting my eyes, I begged in my most flirtatious voice, "Don't go!" He smiled. Once he left, Samantha noted my swoony interest. She told me that Noah was an herbalist, an acupuncturist, and a scholar of Taoist occult sexuality. Later, I sent him a message on Facebook:

> **Amy:** Hey, Noah! It was great to meet you. Samantha told me that you are a Taoist priest? Is that true? I'm curious!
>
> **Noah:** I don't generally use labels, but I have studied and practiced the authentic tantric arts for over twenty years.
>
> **Amy:** I would love to know more about that!

He messaged a few days later, saying that he had some herbs for Samantha, and asked if I could deliver them. I invited him to drop them off at my house later that day, where I would be breaking down my annual holiday pottery sale. When he walked in, his bright consciousness permeated the space—and *me*. The room filled with dreamlike twinkles. We hugged warmly inside the effervescent cloud and talked while I continued packing pottery away into boxes.

Noah was handling some of the pots that were still on the shelves as I packed. I liked seeing little pieces of myself in his hands. He considered each of them carefully. At times, we would pause and make eye contact. When I told him to pick something for himself, he chose a small teacup. He also bought a beautiful serving bowl for his mother. I wrapped it up and handed it to him, and had an incredibly full feeling as we hugged goodbye. He turned to leave without paying; I didn't say anything, conniving for us to connect again. Noah floated off. Smiling, I returned to packing the pottery.

About fifteen minutes later, he knocked at the door. I tilted my head, faking surprise. He exclaimed joyfully, "I forgot to pay you!" We were both happy to see each other again. As he was leaving for the second time, he said, "Let's have tea sometime."

I nodded, "I would love that."

The next day, I messaged to invite him over. It was a cold, wet, November evening, and I made us golden milk lattes to share. Sitting cross-legged on cushions, we faced each other and had sticky eye contact as we talked and laughed. His big, dreamy eyes were hypnotic. I felt overwhelmed to be taking him in so deeply. The time flew by. *Ah, chemistry!*

When our cups were empty, we wrapped up our tea date, agreeing to get together again. As we were hugging goodbye, I suggested that it would be great for him to meet Amir. He was enthusiastic about the concept.

Amir and I had been going through cycles of getting closer, and then having crises. He pulled away at times, but I chose to stay open and vulnerable. Each time we reconnected, we felt even more in love, as though these little tests were tempering our underlying desire to be together. When I mentioned wanting to organize a date with Noah, Amir's head dropped. I asked about it, and he responded, "I really want to be open, but I can get very jealous."

"I think you guys are going to love each other. But we don't have to do it."

"Let's go. I want to try. He must be a special guy for you to be interested in him."

Noah suggested a new Asian fusion restaurant. He and I arrived first, which felt awkward. We didn't know whether to wait for Amir, or order. I felt excited and nervous being alone with Noah. I was so stimulated in his field and felt guilty about my reaction. Sweaty and scrambled, I tried to navigate the nonlinear Asian (con)fusion menu. Specials were displayed in colorful, angular handwriting on the countertop, on a sandwich board, up on the wall, and in my hand-held menu. Even simple menus under normal circumstances are difficult for me; I prefer asking customers what they are eating. I was already ungrounded from being on a date with a captivating man, with my boyfriend on the way. *Should I pay for Noah?* He solved that issue by stepping up to the register and ordering for himself. I somehow chose the chicken curry plate and a poke bowl for Amir and me. *Paid, done, phew.*

Noah and I sat down at a table. Our words and smiles were slow and spacious as we waited in our special, sparkly consciousness cloud, the energy tangible between us. When Amir finally arrived, ten minutes late, I felt so happy to hold his hand, nuzzle into him, and be loving and affectionate in front of Noah. I settled more deeply into myself and my expanding universe.

They seemed to get along well. When Noah asked about our relationship, Amir said, with a mixture of levity and palpable sensitivity, "Being with Amy is like being on a ride. She is polyamorous. Has she told you about Warren, her 'side bitch'? And now, she wants to start hanging out with *another* guy." Amir's body and voice seemed stiff as he spoke. *Was he jealous?* I had never before experienced him as possessive. It was endearing. I hadn't revealed anything to Noah yet. *Did Noah understand Amir's implications?*

Noah asked Amir, "So, what about you? Do you have a ..." he looked at me with big comic eyes, " ...'side bitch'?" As Amir spoke about the girl he'd recently met on Tinder, he seemed a little looser.

I asked Noah, "How about you? What does your relationship life like?" He told us that he had always been ethically polyamorous, but had recently tried a monogamous relationship, which had just ended. He said that he was giving monogamy a try, but it didn't feel true to his nature.

By the end of our dinner, I sensed greater ease among the three of us. Hugging Noah goodbye, Amir suggested that we meet again, and I volunteered to coordinate. But as he and I walked away, Amir said under his breath that although he did like Noah, he wouldn't want to do that again for a while. When Noah asked me about it the next day, I said I hoped we could schedule something soon.

A week later, I went to Noah's house to pick up some immune-boosting herbs that Noah wanted to give to Amir. When I arrived, Noah had an elaborate tea ceremony set up. We sat together and spoke frankly, for the first time, about our feelings for each other. I said that I was very drawn to him, but also protective of my relationship with Amir, and that I would need to be slow and careful moving forward. Noah was warm as he reflected the same feelings, and the same care for my relationship with Amir. I left our tea date in a high-vibration state, the familiar way I felt with Noah. A twinge of fear was mixed in with my excitement. *What would happen if we fell in love? How would it affect my relationship with Amir?* I wanted to proceed with caution.

The morning after our tea ceremony, Noah texted me: "We met in the astral plane last night and made beautiful love. Do you remember?" I didn't, but had accidentally spilled an entire glass of water on the bed in the middle of the night.

I told him about it and joked: "That must have been the orgasm!" A few days later, he texted again:

> **Noah:** It recently came to my consciousness that you are definitely a dakini embodiment emanation in this world. There is so much synchronicity between us. I have a strong sense that you've been sent by the dakinis and dakas in the other realms to put things into motion and to inspire and ignite a fulfillment and destiny of some kind.
>
> **Amy:** Oh my gosh. Yesterday, I started writing a chapter about you for my dating book. All I wrote was a title idea, "A Daka at My Door." I feel touched that you would call me a dakini: that is the aspect of myself that I want to develop. Thank you for seeing that in me. I know that I would grow so much in a sexual connection with you.

Over the next few weeks, Noah and I continued to message, but Amir felt unsettled, so I slowed down our in-person contact. We went for a swim at a river one day but didn't have any physical contact until we shared a warm and sensual, gyrating, full-body hug goodbye. Noah's hand drifted down and squeezed my ass. Our contact felt inspired and amazing. He said, "This feels too good," and I knew he wanted more.

I felt hopeful that if I went slowly, trust would build, at least between me and Amir, if not between him and Noah. Something beautiful and oceanic matter-of-factly existed between Noah and me; I imagined that sacred, spiritual love and sex could be in our future, but I didn't need to act on those feelings. Noah wished we could connect more often, but I chose boundaries to support Amir, and trusted that would support us all.

I hoped that by deepening my relationship with Amir, feeding it my life blood, it would be stable enough to sustain other loves. I want to always support the same in him. And in everyone. Because that is my sincere wish for all humans: for *everyone* to have the most love possible.

∼

A year after I met Noah, I was texting with Samantha. She and I remained close after we broke up. We are family: we still get together for holidays, and text almost daily. I hadn't seen Noah in a few months; we had exchanged a few friendly texts and video messages, just to say hi. I felt good about where we had settled.

> **Samantha:** Can we check in about the nature of your connection with Noah?
>
> **Amy:** We have always had energy with each other, and started to explore it, but it didn't feel right for Amir, so I didn't pursue it as a romantic connection.
>
> **Samantha:** I thought it was something like that. He and I have decided to move forward into a sacred sexual exploration of love and spiritual union.
>
> **Amy:** That is amazing! I am thrilled for you!

In my heart, I felt a great expansion. Not an ounce of competition, not an ounce of jealousy. Only pure joy in imagining the two of them connecting.

Date #18, Jonah Continued: A Bird and a Leaf *2021 - Forever?*

Jonah and I are like a bird and a leaf, flowing in and out of connection. On a deeper level, we are a mountain and an ocean, solid and strong, beyond human time.

In March of 2019, he got in touch to say that he had been having lots of dreams about me and that he longed to connect. Suddenly, he was actively pursuing me: texting daily, asking to talk on the phone, and even sending me video messages. I was surprised to feel a bit less open to him because of my growing bond with Amir, but we made a plan to go for a hike in Eugene.

He was on time, and there were no glitches. No emergencies, no last-minute fever, no car problems, no childcare falling through. Jonah swept me up from my house and we went to the Ridgeline trail in the southern outskirts of Eugene. On the path, we held hands, strolling lazily and speaking pensively about love, nature, and life. A few times, he stopped, pulled me in close, looked deeply into my eyes, and kissed me soulfully. It felt like we were bathing in the ongoing hilarity and depth of our crazy saga. Sinking into the moment with him, I appreciated everything about Jonah. He lives from a specific locus of consciousness. I experience him as sensitive, aware, and lost.

Afterwards, we stopped at my favorite neighborhood cafe, Party on Friendly's, and savored a decadent mountain of avocado toast. Sipping kombucha together (I chose the flavor called "Love") was a sweet, ebullient ending to our extraordinarily beautiful, simple day together. And then it was over, again. Separating, watching him drive away, became easier every time. I learned to not need anything from Jonah, to be grateful for our chapters as they were. There was always a next time; it had become as predictable as his silence.

Over the years, we have settled into a rhythm: one of us reaches out after a period of distance, and a flurry of excited messaging follows. Sometimes we meet. Each interaction feels epic and synchronistic.

We have never been partner material, due to his chronic financial distress and ethereal style of drifting through life and the world. Jonah settled into a love pocket, a sweet place close to my heart. We don't need to meet in person to feel our connection. Just a text, a simple emoji, reactivates the dream between us.

Each time we connect is a surprise and a blessing, like an unforeseen encounter with wildlife or a visit from a mythological creature. And I'll take it, forever, even if it is just once every thousand years.

Date #60, Warren Continued: Making Love Eternal
2021 - Forever?

Over three years later, things are near-idyllic in my relationship with Warren. Bi-weekly dives into our cosmic, twin-soul connection are enduringly divine. When we are sexual, everything inside and outside us seems to change. We enter another dimension where we feel innocent, sexually undamaged. Our faces come close and we breathe each other's breath. My body and spirit have experienced so much healing from his deep, authentic attraction. Warren helped me feel beautiful, and I am still often moved to tears when we make love. We both want the relationship to last for the rest of our lives.

Over the last two years, Warren, Karen, and I have rarely been in the same place. Keeping our distance felt pragmatic to me, but I could see how the stress of being in the uncomfortable middle affected Warren. I'm sure every polyamorist's ideal is compersion, and I feel hopeful that our situation can change. Increasingly, I am letting go of my blocks to Karen. Though she has done many beautiful and generous things for me over time, I have stayed protected against the intense anger I perceived in her years ago. I want to soften and appreciate her instead of hide.

Karen's Comment:

I prefer not to share much about my own experience. This is what I can say. When we step into love relationships, our hearts are vulnerable. Whether we like it or not, all of us had and have our hands on each other's hearts. Feelings were hurt and trust was not built. Maybe someday we will be ready to do the work it would take to have more ease and care for each other. Then maybe we can begin to truly practice polyamory. For now, we all do the best we can.

There have been changes afoot. When Warren and I couldn't meet at my house for a few months, Karen offered to sleep elsewhere —several times—so he and I could have our overnight dates! Moving cautiously through their house, I appreciated her artistic touches everywhere, including the innovative way she hung her earrings in their little bathroom. *So colorful and funky.* Being among their things, their style, and invited into their home in this special way, I felt cozy, welcome, and embarrassed about the strong walls I kept erected against Karen.

Karen contacted me recently to covertly plan a romantic getaway for me and Warren, as a surprise for him. She paid for our lodging and sent us off with a gift basket. Sitting together on our AirBnb bed, Warren and I unpacked the gifts one by one: chocolate, massage oil, a bottle of wine, and a card. Holding each other, our heads leaning together, we read the card silently. She thanked us, saying our relationship had been a gift that helped her and Warren deepen in unexpected ways. Warren and I looked at each other, then hugged hard, tears spilling from our eyes as we held our eternal embrace.

Date #77, Amir Continued: Persian Mensch *2021-Forever?*

On a sunny day in May 2018, back when I had (temporarily) broken up with Warren, I decided to clean my bedroom. I was moving in a flowy, inspired whirlwind: with the great freedom that comes from finally making a difficult choice. I cleared off my old, dusty bedroom altar, wanting to shift the energy. With more movement than thought, I danced around a box of special-to-me things, intuitively choosing objects and arranging them on the freshly cleaned corner shelf. When I was done, it was covered in hearts. I had created a love altar!

Then, a very strange and dreamlike thing happened. I got a whiff: a cartoon stream of smoke passed right under my nose. I turned towards the smell, to the southeast. In my mind, I saw an image of a beautiful, dark-skinned, linen-cloaked man on a camel, cresting a large dune and turning towards me. I knew that this was the first whisper of our mutual soul recognition, that our relationship's conception had just occurred. I knew it was finally time to do my love spell ritual.

The object that had been sitting in the very center of my deconstructed altar, building energy, was a special love potion. The year I met Warren, I won a "love spell ritual" at the Summer Camp fundraiser auction. The priestess and I did the first part of the ritual, and I came up with my mantra. I wrote it on a piece of paper:

> *"I choose my supremely compatible, home-beautifying, humanity inspiring, sexually reverent life of love."*

She gave me a vial of potion to take, whenever I felt ready to do the second part of the ritual. I was to set aside four hours, drink the potion, say my mantra, and do an art project to call in my beloved. At the time, I feared that a new love might compromise my relationship with Warren, so I set the potion on my altar, on top of the folded-up paper with the mantra. It had been charging up for nine months. I felt ready.

On that May afternoon, my relationship with Warren seemed to be over, and my altar was refreshed. It was time. I messaged the priestess to let her know that I was ready to do the second part of the ritual. She thought the potion's magic would work quickly, and gave me specific instructions. I took a shower, gathered art supplies, lit candles, and settled into a pool of late afternoon sunlight that poured onto my bed. After saying a prayer for the ritual to be effective, I drank the mysterious love potion. Soon, I was amidst wonderful, swirling, emotions. Everything was liquid and color. I laughed and cried and danced, calling out to my beloved. With the generative forces of the universe churning in and all around me, I created this collage from images that were in my altar box of special things:

Each time I glued a piece on, I repeated my mantra out loud. I felt ecstatic, glorious, and filled with hope.

Within a month, I had my first date with Amir.

All through these dating years, while I liked the *idea* of polyamory, I wasn't sure I would be able to love and be sexual with more than one person at a time. With Warren and Amir, everything flowed so beautifully. Amir wasn't jealous of Warren. Warren was affectionate with Amir, and I could sense their genuine affinity for each other.

The first time we all had dinner together, we met for a drink in the Whit, at Sam Bond's Garage, a converted garage turned organic pub. As I was returning to our table, I witnessed them looking into each other's eyes, Warren warmly touching Amir's arm. A rush of warmth ran through my body: the physical sensation of love.

Afterwards, we walked over to Vanilla Jill's ice cream shop to see a friend play music in the courtyard. While the crowd swayed and sang lyrics of ecstatic community love, I straddled a bench between my two loves. Warren spooned into me from behind and I spooned Amir. They were both caressing me. I was completely awash in a sea of love, and could have floated away and died right there.

Later, as we all parted, Warren kissed Amir on the cheek. That first meeting was a best-case scenario for the three of us, and I felt absolutely incredulous. But there weren't many more trio occasions, because of the impact on Karen. Whenever I have a chance to be with both of my loves, I am lifted to a higher dimension, experiencing what is truly possible when humans take the risk to love freely.

In Amir and Warren, I found my perfect partner and my perfect lover.

∽

On a recent sleepless night, I was casually swiping on Bumble at 3 a.m. I changed my settings to women only, to possibly meet someone Amir and I might both like. When I realized I no longer wanted to date, I made my profile write-up vague, admitting that I wasn't sure what I was looking for. Most of my profile photos were of Amir and me together. Sometimes, late at night in bed, I swiped just for fun.

Amir kept his Tinder account active and went through phases of sometimes swiping. We both had lighthearted attitudes about it, though at times I became jealous. Swiping for him, I felt more in control and more excited. I liked the idea that I might be the one to find someone for him—*or us?*—for a romantic flirtation of some kind. Amir's confidence goes up when women are attracted to him, bringing him a special joy.

That night, I unexpectedly matched with Zee, an amazingly beautiful woman who had near-identical interests to me. I looked through her pictures, imagined it must be a fake profile, and didn't think much of it. In the morning, I awoke to a "Well, hello there" text from her. That sounded like a pick-up line from a man. Even more convinced it wasn't real, I sent back a message, just to see. I like to bust people who are misusing the apps when I can. I wrangled the stranger over to Marco Polo to video message, and it turned out that she really was that gorgeous, super talented, artistic ... and *really* into me. We spent a day messaging back and forth, getting to know each other a little. The second day, we decided to have a live video call. We really liked each other, but what could we be? Flirty friends? She lived two hours away.

We messaged for a few days. I couldn't help noticing her new hairdos and disappearing layers of clothes in each new short video. She was trying to seduce me, and I couldn't deny that she was beautiful. It was flattering. I quickly attempted to include Amir, so it could be our thing instead of mine. She played along at first, but after a few days, she said "He's cute; he reminds me of some of the men I dated in my twenties. But to be honest, you're the one who caught my eye." I asked what she envisioned. Hesitantly, she answered, "I could see myself living next door and being your second partner. I really think this is a fated connection. I felt it from the first time I saw your picture." She reminded me of myself in the early Jonah days when I could barely restrain myself from sending him pictures, videos, and songs I'd written about him.

Amir's feelings were bruised from her focused attention on me, and her dismissal of him. What she was dreaming of wasn't at all what I wanted. I felt sensitive about hurting her, yet she was clearly getting more attached and hopeful.

It felt like Zee wasn't hearing my reservations. When I video called her to say, "I don't have space for another relationship," it didn't land well. Her face contorted and she moved uncomfortably as I spoke. Zee had a hard time accepting that I wouldn't make room for her. She wanted to move to Eugene, to help me, to serve me, like a personal assistant. The more she pressed, the more space I needed. After she sent lengthy email declarations of love mixed with criticisms of me, I told her I needed to pause our communications, and that I hoped we could try for a friendship sometime in the future.

Amir and I thrived through the COVID-19 pandemic together. We spent a year-long sitcom of love and deepening communication, mostly in his kitchen. Every day, we danced, kissed, laughed, and sang, blessed for the time together—for having everything we needed, both materially and emotionally. We feel happily "monogamish," open to entertaining flirts, together, but mostly content to cuddle up, just the two of us.

Supremely compatible, we beautify our homes together. We inspire each other to do good work in the world. And we continually recommit to become more sexually connected and reverent. Every day, we celebrate our life of love together.

Amir's Perspective

Amy is the female version of me. We share an attitude of wanting to be good people, but to not suffer. We have so much fun together, all the time.

I have learned a lot about sex. Sometimes when we were sexual, Amy would be in tears. She wanted to connect, and I was having such a good time, but then I would notice that she was crying. It was devastating for me to not understand what she needed; I was trying to be a good lover, but I finally learned that it's about doing LESS. What worked yesterday might not work today. I learned to just touch, listen, and slow the fuck down. I'm a better lover now.

Amy helped me learn to be kinder to myself and to others. I used to be more punishing with my students; I'm more helpful and present now.

I'm excited to do pottery with her. She is a master craftsperson, and I am a master chemist, so we're going up a mega notch to the next level: new colors, new textures, new durability, new types of pots to make. I would love to be in that artist's lifestyle with her.

It's a special feeling when Amy and I drive past Jamari's house and we all wave and smile. It's like we're all jovial passengers on Amy's relationship tapestry ride. I think it's great that he had Amy as a part of his formative sexual life.

I'm happy about Amy's special connection with Warren. When she spends the night or goes on a short trip with him, it helps me remember all the things I love about her. That doesn't mean it's easy, and I usually don't sleep well when she is away, but when she returns the next day and crawls back into bed with me, it gives me that giddy feeling of falling in love.

I was so afraid about introducing Amy to my family, but when I finally did, all of that fear flew away. I could never have imagined the amount of love that they have for each other. Everyone feels safe with her. She's on everyone's side. The fact that my family and my partner love each other is mind-blowingly big. I think bringing her home to them is the biggest gift I've ever given them.

I never thought I would find this kind of love.

Amir is a "mensch," a Yiddish word that means *someone to admire and emulate, someone of noble character*. Everything about him is so pure and good. We talk about everything; we laugh and cry together at the beautiful and difficult things in life. We have the potential for "forever," and I think I might even want to marry him. When we have dessert at night—cookies, or any special treat—we call it "wedding cake." Sometimes we look into each other's eyes and have a spontaneous "wedding" in our kitchen. I say, "Let's get married," and he grabs and kisses me and we say, "OK, we're married!" It might be fun to have a party and rings and everything. *We'll see.*

The great part is that we talk about these things—about everything—all the time. Honesty, my focus since the beginning of my dating journey, has always been the baseline between Amir and me. Being open and direct about sensitive, difficult topics is the norm for the first time in my life. I can't hide with Amir; he knows me too well.

Throughout the night, each time we stir or change positions, Amir whispers how much he loves me. Even in an unconscious state, he pours a steady stream of affection into me. We often sleep holding hands. Almost every night, at some point, Amir spoons me from behind, massages my shoulders, and kisses my neck.

It took a long time for our relationship to fully blossom, but now Amir and I are flooded daily with gratitude and wonder as we sink in, ever deeper, with each other.

In the end, the Universe went above and beyond my longings. I feel ecstatic in my relationships. I never believed in fairy tales before, especially not for myself, until life handed me my very own Persian prince.

As for radical honesty? I have come a long way, but I plan to remain a lifelong student in the dojo of direct communication. And who knows, maybe someday, someone will even call me "Sensei."

Acknowledgments

One summer evening, I was waiting to meet a date in an outdoor plaza. A gorgeous, vivacious woman with a huge flower in her hair walked right up to me, said she had been reading my dating blog, and blurted out "I have a fantasy of being in an erotica writers' group with you." I had known and admired Sara Zolbrod from afar for many years. I had no idea she was an editor, but soon, she became mine. Sara was the single most influential person on this book and has been patiently at my side for over a year. I can't thank her enough.

I pour daily gratitude into my best friend, my pillow-rock, Jess Donohue. She was just an ear away through every date and had astute observations in the editing process. Together, over the years, Jess and I have learned about ourselves in a way that I couldn't have imagined.

Many amazingly generous people made valuable editorial contributions. David Goldstein's love, deep care, soul-searching, and smarty-pants samurai attention was absolutely invaluable. Lauren Welsch and Keith Sheldon both went above and beyond. I send enormous gratitude to my beta readers: Ginny, Jess, and Jesse Donohue, Irina Feygina, Zanne Miller, John Arnold, Bethanne Turnamian-Toci, Heidi Schultz, Katie McConnell, David Mitchell, Neal Conner, Madeleine Brunken, Marlena Victoria, Angela Foster, and Michael Richardson.

Carine Montbertrand, my talented actor-cousin, and Beau Eastlund of the Golden Lab Studio were irreplaceable allies in the audiobook recording project. I am very grateful to everyone who participated in the production of the audiobook.

No reference in the book is made lightly. My mentors, teachers and guides were: Joyce Garvin, the greatest high school teacher ever; Johanna Mitchell (RIP), astrological emissary extraordinaire; and Joanne Williams, my hilarious and spot-on psychic energy intuitive (joanneandyoga@gmail.com). Jan Dworkin and Suzette Payne, my gifted Processwork therapists, helped me harvest the wisdom of my challenges; Katarzyna Bequillard, my incredible Processwork coach, told me I had to write a book; the Eugene Lunch Bunch Toastmasters were enthusiastic supporters; and the Geese—especially Saradee and Emily—gave me so much encouragement and feedback. Stefan Szo was longingly open and helpful. Much gratitude to Arny and Amy Mindell, for their love and for Processwork; the NFNC facilitators and campers; Lawrence and Shoshannah for your unique roles in my life; Catherine, for your part in my story; Sheya Jordan, for the love spell; Kim Spiro, for your wisdom; and Janis Thompson, for being a badass goddess communicator—you're my hero. Words cannot touch the depth of life experience I was blessed to receive in my eternal connection with Sarah Frances Gregory. Thank you, Sarah, forever, for your deep love in our ongoing healing process.

I am so grateful to the encouraging readers of my original dating blog. Thank you to my family and all of my many sweet, close friends in the near background: your patience and love makes me who I am. I feel incomparable gratitude to Nima for his incredible support in every step of this book, and to his whole family for their special love.

Tacovore, Hideaway Bakery, and the Bier Stein in Eugene, and Prasad in Portland were the perfect settings for many of my dates; I am also thankful to OkCupid, Bumble and Tinder; and Marco Polo, my favorite app to test chemistry before meeting.

Last but not least, I send a deep bow of communication dojo gratitude to everyone I interacted with on my dating journey, from the shortest "no thanks" to the deepest connections. Each of you helped me to learn, to grow, and to love.

About the Author

Instead of going to medical school, I became a potter. Luckily for me, in college, I discovered the key to a fulfilled life when Joseph Campbell taught me in three words to Follow My Bliss.

Ever since then, I've invested in whatever thrilled me. First, I had a thriving pottery career, then became a Nia teacher (think: spiritual aerobics/dance/martial arts), and then got my master's degree and became a Processwork therapist (think: radical self-love wizardry and deep, unconditional support).

My life is amazing. Dating was amazing. Writing is amazing.

I got my bachelors in Religious Studies from Wesleyan University, and my masters in Process-Oriented Psychology from the Process Work Institute in Portland.

Now, I circulate between Eugene, Oregon, and La Selva Beach, California with Amir, Numair the cat/wizard, and Delilah the dog/human.

My upcoming book, *Dating Empowered,* is a guidebook that highlights the theories, games, and practices I found and developed over the course of this memoir.

Let's stay connected! www.amypalatnick.com

www.ingramcontent.com/pod-product-compliance
Lightning Source LLC
Chambersburg PA
CBHW071427070526

4457BCB00001B/22